The gift of Lord Franks

THE CITY IN THE WORLD ECONOMY

The City in the World Economy

W. M. CLARKE

Published by

THE INSTITUTE OF ECONOMIC AFFAIRS
EATON HOUSE : 66A EATON SQUARE : LONDON S.W.1.

FIRST PUBLISHED IN GREAT BRITAIN 1965 BY
THE INSTITUTE OF ECONOMIC AFFAIRS
EATON HOUSE, 66A EATON SQUARE, LONDON, SWI

PRINTED IN GREAT BRITAIN BY
SEVERN RIVER PRINTING COMPANY LIMITED, WORCESTER

CONTENTS

PART II

ANALYSIS AND APPRAISAL

LIST OF TABLES

ERRATA

Page 32, line 22: for '1852' read '1862'.

Page 69, Table III: in column 1 the years 1921 and 1924 refer to the USSR and Costa Rica respectively.

Page 90, line 18: for 'Table VIII' read 'Table VII'.

Page 102: for 'Table III' read 'Table VII'.

Page 147, line 26: for 'Treasury' read 'Cabinet'.

Pages 173 and 175, footnotes 3 and 2 respectively: for 'Appendix I' read 'Appendix A'.

PREFACE

WHAT IS the 'City'? In the public imagination it may range from a national asset unrivalled anywhere else in the world to a sinister conclave of the high priests of finance.

When, some years ago, the City was being dismissed by some economists and economic journalists as of little importance and indeed subjected to some denigration, the Institute invited Mr. W. M. Clarke, a distinguished Financial Editor in Fleet Street, to analyse the City's invisible earnings in order to assess the accuracy of judgement of the criticisms. He produced, in 1958, a little book[1] of 100 pages in which he briefly reviewed the City's markets and estimated its earnings at around £150 million in 1956.

Since 1958 British economic policy has undergone many changes, which have left their mark on the City. It was thought timely therefore to ask Mr. Clarke to write a full-length study of the City and its role in the international economy. The present book is the result.

Part I consists of a description and analysis of the main markets in the City, their origins, history and present structure. Students and teachers of economics and business men whose commodities or services are bought and sold in the City's markets will find this part of special interest. In Part II Mr. Clarke summarises his estimates of the City's invisible earnings and reaches a figure for 1963 of £185 million, equivalent, for example, to half the government's overseas spending. Unless his estimates are challenged it would seem that criticism of the City will need to be better informed than it has been in the past.

Mr. Clarke also discusses the changing role of the City in the structure of international monetary relationships, the role of sterling in international trade and the City's significance for economic growth in Britain. And his general conclusion is that, even if sterling's role as a reserve currency is diminished

[1] *The City's Invisible Earnings*, IEA, 1958.

(he thinks it should be), the City has a growing if changing part to play. But he is not unaware of its weaknesses. At several points in his analysis he directs attention to the need for the City's institutions to adapt themselves to change and he criticises its failure to change quickly. Mr. Clarke's analysis seems to lend some support to the criticism that the institutions of the City are based on traditional practices and old-established firms trading on social and even educational links and identities that do not welcome newcomers especially if their methods seem to disturb accepted rules and rites.

Furthermore, he discusses practices in the banks, the issuing houses, the discount market, the bill market, and elsewhere which must, in general, be described as restrictive, and in most cases does not find the reasons usually given for them by City apologists convincing. Hitherto post-war legislation on monopolies and restrictive practices have excluded services, but since the Labour Government intends to include professions and services in the legislation,[1] the City would be wise to reconsider its institutions and its practices before it is impelled to do so by the pressure of public opinion, the law or political prejudice.

We are grateful to Professor E. Victor Morgan of the University College of Swansea, author of *The Stock Exchange* and other works on money and banking, and to Mr. Norman Macrae of the *Economist*, author of *The English Capital Market*, for reading early drafts of the manuscript and offering comments and criticisms. Like them the Institute and the members of the Advisory Council do not necessarily share Mr. Clarke's analysis and conclusions, but his book is offered as an authoritative, independent and scholarly study that should furnish a standard text on the working of the City and its value to Britain and the international economy.

April 1965   ARTHUR SELDON

[1] Monopolies and Mergers Bill, 1965.

THE AUTHOR

WILLIAM M. CLARKE was born in 1922 and graduated in Economics at the University of Manchester in 1948. From 1941-46 he served in the Royal Air Force, first as a flying instructor but from 1944 as RAF lecturer in Law and Administration. From 1948 to 1955 he was on the editorial staff of the then *Manchester Guardian*, joining *The Times* in 1955 as Assistant City Editor and becoming City Editor in 1957. Since 1962 he has been Financial and Industrial Editor.

Mr. Clarke lives in Hampstead with his wife and two children. His publications include *The City's Invisible Earnings* (IEA, 1958) and his main non-professional interests are opera, tennis and the theatre.

INTRODUCTION

IN 1958 a keen controversy was raging about the role of the
City of London. The pound had come under severe pressure
in 1957 and it was seriously questioned whether the City of
London was worth running as the centre of international finance
if, as a result, currency crises could suddenly appear even when
there was a surplus on the balance of payments with other
countries. The lively debate that followed made it clear that
information about the City's foreign earnings were hard to
come by in any convenient form. *The City's Invisible Earnings*
tried in a short space to fill the gap by explaining briefly what
foreign services the City provided and estimating how much
foreign income each section of the City earned.

Since then several powerful new elements have appeared on
the scene. The pound has become convertible; the balance of
monetary power has shifted from North America to Europe;
Britain has grown economically closer to the Continent, without
joining the inner Six; and Britain has continued to have her
regular currency crises which, with full convertibility and greater
exchange freedom, have grown enormously in extent. The last,
at the end of 1964, was the biggest of all. It took a 7 per cent
Bank rate, deflationary measures, $1,000 million borrowing
from the International Monetary Fund and an overnight rescue
operation of $3,000 million from the world's central banks to
ward off an immediate, forced devaluation of the pound in the
fourth week of November. As I complete this book (April
1965) the danger has not passed. A Labour Government is grappling with a financial crisis which it partly inherited and partly
brought on by its own mistakes and which has not been helped
by the clear disunity in financial thought and purpose between
Europe and North America, more specifically between France
and the United States. In these circumstances the role of the
City is again under a critical spotlight. The present book
therefore, while keeping some of the original material and
bringing the City's 'invisible' earnings up to date, attempts not

only to give a much fuller picture of the City's foreign activities but to examine them closely in the light of recent developments.

It has, therefore, a larger aim. It is an attempt to bring some balance into an argument that, even before the sterling crisis of November 1964, was tending to become sterile. Money and the way it is used can be relied on to heighten emotions. The City is no exception. The 'bankers' ramp' of 30 years ago can easily be brought out of its locker and emotional feeling quickly take the place of reasoned argument. The worst recent example of this was probably the period during the Bank rate tribunal of 1957-58 and the parliamentary debate that followed. The City was shocked to find that few people knew what it did or cared. The British Aluminium take-over tussle, during which the City's manners and for a time its senses momentarily left it, hardly helped matters. Many were confirmed in their prejudices; others formed new ones. The City was as much to blame as anyone. It is not the most articulate of places. And it has had a natural tendency, particularly since it lost its close link with Westminster, to dwell overmuch on its illustrious past. It is in no-one's interest to exaggerate the role it plays or the conditions in which it ought to flourish. Yet, in spite of its failings, an industry that (as we shall see) earns £185 million a year in foreign exchange cannot be shrugged aside too easily. It is more than time to take stock. That is the prime purpose of this book. If one question predominates it is this: can London maintain its position as an international financial centre, when Britain is no longer the top industrial nation and no longer commands vast economic resources? More important, should it?

I am indebted to numerous individuals and institutions in the City of London, both for checking many statistical details and for making helpful suggestions. I also have to thank the editors of *The Spectator* and of the *National Provincial Bank Review* for permission to use material in Chapters 2 and 12 which previously appeared in their journals.

April 1965 **W.M.C.**

PART I

THE CITY'S ORIGINS AND SERVICES

CHAPTER 1

THE CITY TODAY AND YESTERDAY

'The City has a great part to play—in its unique contribution to invisible exports, which we shall help and foster, and in the provision of services to industry. I stress service to industry—and the role of finance must be as a servant, never as a master—because all of us would wish to stress the constructive role the City and its wide variety of institutions can play in facilitating and channelling investment.'— HAROLD WILSON, 16 November, 1964.

'I want to see more foreign business attracted to our markets so that we can earn more foreign money. The time has now come when the City once again might well provide an international capital market where the foreigner can not only borrow long-term capital, but where, equally important, he will once again wish to place his long-term investment capital. This entrepôt business in capital, if I may so describe it, would not only serve this country well but would fill a vital and vacant role in Europe in mobilising foreign capital for world economic development.'—LORD CROMER, Governor of the Bank of England, 3 October, 1962.

THESE contrasting reactions to the twin challenge of industrial growth at home and the new world of currency convertibility abroad speak for themselves. Both recognise the need for change in the City—in two directions. What concerns us in this book is whether the City of London, still regarded by many as the world's leading financial centre, can play as useful and profitable an overseas role in the future as it has over the past 150 years, without undermining economic expansion at home. Is the City simply another anachronism left over from Britain's age of power or can it still serve a useful purpose? And even if it can, is the effort worthwhile? This book is written in the belief that the City can continue to act as an international financial centre, while still serving British industry, but that it will do neither unless it realises the true measure of the changes before it. The time for self-congratulation has gone.

Before we begin to look closely at the changing face of the City and to discover where further changes are needed, we should be clear what role it plays today. It is not inconsiderable. For our purposes the City is made up of the square mile of financial and commercial buildings and offices between St. Paul's Cathedral and the Tower of London and between the Thames and the traces of the Old Roman Wall. If it is a question of the amount of money flowing through these banks, brokers' offices, commodity markets and other exchanges every day of the week, New York could probably claim more business because of the vast size of the American economy. But if it is *international* finance—money to finance goods that do not touch British shores, insurance against risks anywhere, foreign transactions in gold, arbitrage in foreign securities, the chartering of ships or aircraft from and to any spot in the world—then London will still have the lion's share of the world's business.

The international City

Here in this financial City within a city (where half a million people work, but only 5,000 live) are the largest gold market, the largest *international* insurance market, the world's main shipping and air chartering exchange, several of the world's leading commodity exchanges, the biggest concentration of foreign banks, and the centre of the largest network of overseas bank branches in the world.

This international flavour is readily apparent to any visitor. Walk up Lombard Street from the Bank of England and look at some of the bank signs on the way. There within a few yards are banks from Canada, France, Spain, America and South Africa. Along Bishopsgate are outposts from Belgium, Portugal, France, Czechoslovakia and India. Nearby are the Moscow Narodny Bank and the Bank of China—both extremely active. Nearly 100 foreign branches can be found in this small area—far more than in New York or Paris, the only comparable centres. And if London has more foreign banks in its midst than any other centre, it is also operating far more branches abroad than any other. While New York can boast of nearly 200 overseas, London-based banks now have over 4,000.[1]

These are the outward signs of London's links with the world. More solid evidence can be found within a few minutes' walk

[1] For further details see Chapter 2, p. 12.

of the Bank of England. In a quiet backwater not a hundred yards away—at New Court—Rothschilds will soon[1] be presiding again every morning over the bullion market that handles as much as three-quarters of the world's dealings in gold. Customers range from the central banks of the world to private hoarders in the Middle East and Far East. The Russians, who have sold gold regularly in the West to meet their payments deficits, have invariably done most of their bullion deals in London. Gold bars with the hammer and sickle insignia are a familiar sight in the vaults below some of the City streets.

Not all the City markets are as compact as the bullion market. Every year the London insurance market takes on risks worth millions of dollars all round the world. Lloyd's of London is well enough known, with its new building only ten minutes away from the Bank of England. But the 5,000 under-writers of Lloyd's are only one part (and the smallest) of the whole international insurance market in London. The rest of the business is taken on by the large insurance companies whose offices are to be seen in all the streets radiating from the Royal Exchange. Between them, Lloyd's and the insurance companies will take on literally anything—at a price. They provided insurance on Mr. Khrushchev's life during his visit to the United States. They are said to have provided cover to Australian shopkeepers against damage by the eventual fall of the first Russian sputnik. They have taken the lead in providing cover against atomic plants. About a half of the London insurance market's income comes from foreign business.[2]

Far more difficult to locate than the insurance market is the foreign exchange market, for all dealings are done in separate offices by telephone, telex or cable. About 130 of the banks within this small area are not only linked with one another but also with the financial centres of the world. As for London's international shipping and commodity sections, both are centred around Leadenhall Street and Fenchurch Street, close to the Baltic Exchange (home of the shipping world)—and both again within a short walk of the Bank of England. The Baltic Mercantile and Shipping Exchange—to give it its full title—has a naturally international flavour. Whether furs have to be shipped from Vladivostock to the United States or a vessel is lying empty in Singapore harbour, this is where a ship can be found for the

---

[1] Rothschilds (and thus the daily gold market) are temporarily housed in Finsbury Square until New Court is rebuilt.
[2] See Chapter 5.

job or a cargo for a ship. And not much more than a few hundred yards away—hardly by chance—are several markets which daily value and auction raw materials from all parts of the globe.

The physical evidence of the City's foreign business is beyond dispute by anyone who takes the trouble to look around. But it does not explain why London has attracted this business and managed to keep it, why Russia normally keeps a fair-sized part of her foreign currency in the form of sterling in London, why the Ruler of Kuwait reputedly keeps over £100 million of his investments here, why Communist China at one stage had some £100 million in the City, and why other foreign countries continue to do the same. Why, in short, did London emerge as an international centre and why has it continued? The reasons are complex, depending on the pattern of world trade, on the role of the United Kingdom in history, on tradition and the like. They are important in our attempt to see where the future lies.

Economic origins

Many of the City's institutions can trace their roots back to the 17th century. A stock market of sorts probably started somewhere around the 1670s; Lloyd's usually talk of their origin in the coffee house of Edward Lloyd in 1687-8; and the Bank of England was formed in 1694. At that time, London was an active trading, merchanting and shipping centre. But it was by no means the leading centre of European commerce. That role was still being hotly contested by Antwerp, Bruges and Lyons, with Genoa and Venice still flourishing in commercial activities and Florence still prominent in finance. The centre of the world's commercial gravity, however, had already begun to move northwards and westwards—from Venice, Florence and Genoa towards Bruges and Antwerp and finally in the 18th century to Amsterdam. The westward movement was slow at first, but by the middle of the 18th century Amsterdam was finally established not only as a centre of shipping and of trade finance but as a source of capital. This provision of long-term capital on a large international scale was the factor that was to distinguish both Amsterdam and (later) London from all their previous rivals. It was a reflection of the age. Trade and industry were developing rapidly. New industrial processes were emerging. Savings were beginning to accumulate in commercial hands. Joint stock companies were starting to develop. The Dutch East India Company, established in 1602, is believed to have been the first joint stock company in the world and the Amsterdam stock exchange traces its origins back to at least 1613.

It is still a matter of debate whether London had overtaken Amsterdam as the leading financial centre before the end of the 18th century. Certainly London was providing three separate services at that time: it was acting as a commercial and shipping centre; as a source of capital; and—a role that was soon to grow and flourish in the 19th century—as the centre of a unique system of settling international payments. London had been a centre of shipping well before it grew to prominence in settling payments and in providing long-term capital. But not until it was doing all three on a significant scale did it really begin to overshadow Amsterdam.

The final blow to Amsterdam was struck by the Napoleonic wars, which played a notable part in London's swift rise to pre-eminence. But even before the overthrow of the Dutch republic by Napoleon, the end of the monopoly of the Dutch East India Co. in 1798, and the failure of the Bank of Amsterdam at the end of 1819, London was supplying growing amounts of foreign capital to Europe. As industrialisation developed up and down the country and as overseas trade began to expand, London not only became the hub of the merchanting and shipping world, but also took on much more of the burden of financing foreign trade. The private banking firms and merchant banks were prominent in this development. Longer-term capital for the development of overseas territories went hand-in-hand with short-term finance for trade. As one commentator has put it: [1]

'Twenty years of war had concentrated the world's trade in the British Empire and had made Britain the one country in the world where capital might be invested with the maximum of contemporary safety.'

Although Amsterdam revived later, increasing its investments in other parts of Europe and even venturing into South America in the 1850s and into the United States in the 1860s, never again did it rival London as the world's leading financial centre.

London as a capital market

The provision of long-term capital in London reached its peak in the 50 years before the 1914-18 war. The large surpluses of

[1] E. T. Powell, *Evolution of the Money Market, 1385-1915*, Financial News, 1915.

British savings available to the London market were quickly put to work in Europe and in most other parts of the globe. But any picture of a steady stream of money leaving these shores year in and year out is highly misleading. The process went in fits and starts. In the five years from 1870 onwards, something like £55 million a year was being invested overseas. Then, with the foreign loan collapse of 1875, the flow virtually dried up, only to burst forth again in the late 1880s. A further arid period followed from 1898 until 1904, when another strong revival set in, continuing almost uninterrupted right up to the outbreak of war in 1914. In those later years, a rate of some £200 million a year was reached and by 1913 British investments abroad, which had amounted to some £500 million in 1850, were put at no less than £3,700 million. Although the loss of £500 million of these investments caused by the 1914-18 war had been made good in monetary terms by 1929, the real volume of Britain's private overseas investments probably never again touched the peak reached in 1914. Most of this vast sum had gone to finance railways, mines, plantations, harbour works and public utilities. Of £3,763 million outstanding in 1913, £1,780 million was invested in the Empire (including Canada and other Commonwealth countries), £754 million in the United States, £756 million in Latin America, and £218 million in Europe (including £110 million in Russia).

Finance for international trade

Equally important has been London's role in providing finance for the movement of goods. By the 19th century, Britain had become an exporter on a growing scale and London was finding the short-term money to finance these exports as well as providing a system for settling international payments. Bills of exchange were already well-established as a means of financing domestic trade in the 18th century (they had been made legal in 1697). But it was not until after the middle of the 19th century and later that the 'Bill on London' began to play such a prominent part in international trade. What is known as the accepting and discounting of bills of exchange enabled the exporter (the seller) to obtain his money as soon as he shipped his goods and the importer (the buyer) to get credit until he received them. Merchant banks (or acceptance houses) 'accepted' bills of exchange drawn on them by clients needing credit.[1] They could

---

[1] This meant they guaranteed that the bill, really a promise to pay a stated sum by a given date, would be paid. Bills accepted in this way became known as bank bills.

then be discounted at once at the lowest rate in the discount market. Thus, the foreign exporter could get his money immediately, change the pounds into gold and take it out of the country in that form. London provided both the short-term credit (through the services of the accepting houses and the discount market) and the means of settlement (by being on the gold standard).

At first, a good deal of this trade credit (as well as capital for overseas development) was provided by the merchant banks and private banking firms, but in the second half of the 19th century the growth of the Eastern exchange banks and the overseas banks, most with their headquarters in London, considerably widened the banking structure. By the turn of the century, London was financing the bulk of the world's trade. The shipment of manufactures to the British overseas territories and to other developing countries and of raw materials and foodstuffs in return accounted for a good deal of London's activity; but London merchants and bankers were also called on to deal with and finance shipments between third countries not touching these shores. No other centre was equipped for the financing of foreign trade to the same extent as London; right up to the 1914 war, most of America's foreign trade was financed in sterling by London banks.

The City today

This was the basis on which the City as we know it today was built. London provided the financial and commercial machinery by which Britain was able to support an expanding trade with the rest of the world. It also provided a currency which every nation could use and trust, a capital market where they could raise loans, commodity markets on which they could sell their materials or by which they could value them, vessels by which they could transport their goods and a network of banks and insurance companies by which they could finance and insure them. That same network of financial institutions is virtually intact today. But it would be idle to pretend that everything remains unchanged. The City is operating in vastly different circumstances. How different?

London is still providing, by the world-wide use of sterling, a system of international payments; the machinery for both *settling* and *financing* foreign payments is still intact. It is still providing finance for foreign trade. And Britain continues to provide large sums of capital for investment abroad. But it is well to be clear how the City's role has changed, especially in the provision of capital. In recent years the outflow of capital overseas has risen sharply, reaching close on £450 million in 1960. Yet the share of this capital raised in the City has been remarkably small. Of the £450 million nearly £150 million was provided by the state and of the £300 million provided privately, only £55 million was raised on the London market. Most of the private capital was either sent abroad by industrial companies or ploughed back abroad by their subsidiaries. And most of the City's overseas issues have been for the Commonwealth. Until the end of 1962, when, as we shall see, a new effort to revive foreign issues was started, only a handful of foreign loans had been floated in London since 1945—for Norway, for Iceland and for the International Bank. Whereas foreign governments once raised funds on the London market and spent the proceeds on British goods, the post-war practice has been for British exporters to extend credit direct to their overseas customers. This has been a useful service to British industry. But whether an international financial centre can survive as such without the ability to provide capital for foreign borrowers has become increasingly doubtful. If London is to regard itself as the potential financial centre of the new Europe—whether Britain is in the Common Market or not—it must clearly have the ability not only to finance and settle international payments, but also to provide long-term loans. The Governor of the Bank of England believes so too. Whether the City can revert to a role which it has hardly fulfilled for well over a quarter of a century without losing sight of the services still required by British industry will be examined in some detail in the chapters that follow. In the next seven chapters we shall trace the changes in City markets since the war and then discuss the City's foreign financial activities as a whole.

CHAPTER 2

THE WORLD'S BANKER

THIS AND following chapters describe the several parts of the City, the role they play in London's foreign business, how they have been affected by the return to convertibility and how they are likely to meet the continuing challenge of Europe. The banking structure is the basis of the City's foreign operations without which few other services could function.

We have already seen that London's capital market is no longer operating as it used to do. This makes it all the more remarkable that no centre has replaced London in its ability to finance trade and to provide means of payment anywhere in the world. As the head of the Research Department of the Federal Reserve Bank of New York said in 1956, after nearly half a dozen post-war crises: London

'remains the primary centre of foreign trade financing. The continuing predominance of the British banks in the financing of world trade is significantly reflected in the much more extensive network of foreign branches maintained by British banks as compared with their American counterparts . . .'

The decidedly secondary role still played by New York in the field of foreign trade financing is attributable to a variety of factors among which the seller's market enjoyed by American exports during part of the post-war period is perhaps the most important. Whatever the reason (the dollar shortage may also have had its effect in the early post-war years), it was estimated in 1955 that, while British banks operate as many as 500 foreign branches, United States banks maintain no more than 112. Even this estimate excludes more than 1,500 branches in South Africa and South-West Africa of the British-owned Standard Bank and Barclays DCO, as well as almost 1,400 branches in Australia and New Zealand of three British-owned Australian and New Zealand banks. If full allowance is made for these branches London's dominant position becomes clearer. My own estimates, based on details provided in *The Bankers' Almanac and Year Book, 1963-4*,[1] show that London-based banks, i.e. with their headquarters in London, have some 4,300 branches of representative offices abroad. The bulk, about 2,300, are in Africa. Australia and New Zealand have about 1,400 and the Middle and Far East between 200 and 300. Although many of these branches are concerned mainly with domestic deposit banking, they are also available for any foreign trade business arising in London. New York, by contrast, has 182 bank branches abroad. Over half of the total is accounted for by the First National City Bank of New York which, with the Bank of America (based in California) and Chase Manhattan Bank, dominates American foreign banking business.

London's network of foreign branches comprises mainly what are known as the overseas banks and the Eastern exchange banks. But this is only part of the story. It omits the highly individual work of the merchant houses—the banks with such well known names as Hambros, Lazards, Rothschilds, Baring, etc.—and the large volume of foreign business undertaken by the big clearing banks. London's predominance is also reflected in the number of branches which foreign banks have decided to establish here. London still has the largest concentration of foreign-owned banks, with New York second and Paris third. According to the annual *European Banking Gazeteer*[2] there are now around 160 international banking offices in London. But if allowance is made for the numerous Commonwealth banks and the head offices of British banks, the true *foreign* branch total amounts to some 98.[3]

This is still well above any other financial centre. On the same basis New York has 63, Paris 48, Frankfurt 25, Zurich 17, Brussels 16, Milan 9, and Amsterdam 6.

London thus possesses both the largest network of its own branches abroad and the largest number of foreign-owned banks in its midst.

This complex banking structure, the merchant banks, overseas banks, Eastern exchange banks and the clearing banks, as well as the foreign banking community in London, has ensured that British banking practices have penetrated to all parts of the world. The lifeline of all these branches with the City of London has had a double influence: they have tended to remit

---

[1] Thomas Skinner and Co. (Publishers) Ltd.
[2] Manufacturers Hanover Trust Company, 1964.
[3] Estimates based on *Bankers' Almanac and Year Book, 1963-64, op. cit.*

surplus funds to the London money market for investment and they could rely on getting strong financial support from London should the need arise. In other words, surplus funds could be switched from one side of the sterling Commonwealth to the other with little trouble.

Perhaps even more important, this assorted array of banks has enabled payments to be made from London to virtually every corner of the globe with ease. Even where sterling is no longer the most acceptable currency, it is still possible for these branches to maintain holdings of foreign currency balances to facilitate payments.

It is unsafe, however, to generalise too much. Each sector has developed and thrived differently, and each is operating differently today. They must be looked at more closely.

A. THE MERCHANT BANKS

THE merchant banks are important and highly individual. Possibly around 60 City firms could carry the name, though members of the exclusive Accepting Houses Committee[1] are limited to 17:

Sir Edward J. Reid, Chairman,
  Baring Brothers.
Angus Mackinnon, Deputy
  Chairman, Brown Shipley.
Rt. Hon. Lord Aldenham,
  Antony Gibbs.
Rt. Hon Viscount Bearsted,
  M. Samuel.
Kenneth Keith,
  Philip Hill, Higginson, Erlangers.
Louis Franck,
  Samuel Montagu.
C. E. A. Hambro,
  Hambros Bank.
H. S. H. Guinness,
  Guinness, Mahon.

R. A. Harari,
  Charterhouse Japhet.
Ernest G. Kleinwort,
  Kleinwort, Benson.
Hon. R. H. Kindersley,
  Lazard Brothers.
Rt. Hon. Viscount Harcourt,
  Morgan Grenfell.
Edmund L. de Rothschild,
  N. M. Rothschild.
H. W. B. Schroder.
  J. Henry Schroder.
Geoffrey C. Seligman,
  S. G. Warburg.
Walter A. Brandt,
  Wm. Brandt's.
S. R. Alsopp,
  Arbuthnot Latham.

[1] Membership is controlled by the Committee itself. There are three factors influencing choice of new members: their size, diversification and business reputation. A restrictive feature of the the Committee's activities is its agreed minimum rate of commission on acceptances; its main privilege the fact that its chairman has direct access to the Governor of the Bank of England. Non-members are not discriminated against by the Bank of England, since it buys bills of exchange from other merchant banks as well as from members of the Committee.

Their names often provide a clue to their origin. Several were foreign merchants or banks, or both, who opened offices in London or switched their business here. Many were refugees after the Napoleonic wars, and it was in the 19th century that most of them began to flourish. Merchanting was predominant at first. Barings were in wool, Morgans in cotton, Schroders in wheat, coffee, etc. Success in trade led to pure financing. Money earned in merchanting gave them the ability to back others. Often their name was enough to ensure success. This merchanting soon developed into banking and the transition from commodity trading, through foreign exchange and accepting bills of exchange to issuing business, was gradual but persistent. As wealth increased, reputations were enhanced. Before long these embryo merchant banks were undertaking a growing volume of acceptance business in which for a commission they lent their name to bills of exchange, thus backing transactions with their name but potentially with their money. By the second half of the century the heads of the leading firms met twice a week on the Royal Exchange and decided exchange rates between the pound and other currencies. 'At this time', one writer puts it,[1] 'the foreign exchange business was practically a monopoly, in the hands of great private banking houses like the Rothschilds, Barings, Ambroses, Huths, Duxats, Bates, Salomons, Curries, Wilsons and Raphaels.' Many of these names have vanished from the City, but this closed shop led to the obvious, and later important, business of undertaking foreign capital issues in London for foreign governments as well as private firms. Schroders' first issue, for example, a railway loan to Cuba, was made in 1853. In 1870 they issued the first Japanese loan in London to finance the first railway line in Japan. And there followed a long list of European, South American and domestic issues. Other houses did the same. Hambros were linked with Scandinavia, Brown Shipley with the United States, Lazards with France, Barings with South America. By the outbreak of the First World War the merchant banks were supreme in the City's foreign business. Two sets of figures illustrate the point. It is estimated that out of some £3,600 million lent by Britain to overseas countries between 1870 and 1914, about 40 per cent was provided through the merchant banks. Secondly, out of the £350 million of acceptance bills in circulation in 1914 it is estimated that some £200 million

1 E. T. Powell, *op. cit.*

were provided by the merchant banks and only £30 million or so by the clearing banks.

Repercussions of the Depression

The supremacy did not last. The City's foreign business and the merchant banks' dominance had developed in line with Britain's role in the world. The decline in Britain's power naturally had its repercussions on the City's affairs. The remarkable thing is that the side-effects, instead of delivering a knock-out blow to the merchant banks, enabled them to demonstrate a marked resilience and flexibility. This was first shown throughout the 1920s and 1930s. In the 'twenties the underlying changes were largely marked by the continuing emphasis on foreign trade and by the efforts (now seen to be disastrous) to recreate the pre-war conditions of the gold standard. Even as late as 1930 foreign business remained the main work of the merchant banks. According to the Macmillan Report[1] issued in 1931, acceptance on foreign account between 1927 and 1930 represented 88 per cent of the total engagements of the merchant banks; foreign deposits held by them accounted for between 70 and 80 per cent of their total deposits; and no less than 50 per cent of total new issues between 1921 and 1931 were for foreign borrowers—a large part undertaken by the merchant banks. And, the Report added significantly, the City of London was 'more highly organised to provide capital to foreign countries than to British industry'. Much the same could have been said of Paris, Brussels, Zurich or Amsterdam. Yet, even as the Macmillan Report was being printed, these international capital markets were closing their doors one by one to foreign loans. They did not re-open for close on 30 years.

The foreign emphasis of the merchant banks in London changed rapidly with the devaluations of the early 1930s and the many foreign failures. Domestic business, already enlarged in the 1920s through industrial amalgamations, grew further in the difficult trading conditions of the 1930s with its forced re-organisation schemes affecting major industries. Failures abroad and financial difficulties at home were the twin influences affecting the merchant banks in the 'thirties. Even by 1931 the total of overseas issues had dropped to £50 million, compared with over £150 million in both 1927 and 1928. The

---

[1] *Report of the Committee on Finance and Industry*, Cmd. 3897, 1931.

average from 1932 to 1937 fell further to £34 million. From making up a half of all issues on the London market in the late 1920s, foreign issues formed no more than 19 per cent by the middle 'thirties. Foreign defaults were the major cause; but the restrictions imposed on foreign loans generally by the British government in 1932, and extended in 1936, put a strait-jacket on some of the foreign activities of the merchant banks. This continued during the war and throughout the early post-war years.

This early background of the merchant banks has been dwelt on at some length to show that their post-war emphasis on domestic affairs has been a relatively brief episode—in tune perhaps with the 'thirties and 'forties but not with their past. It has also been presented in this way to show their continuing flexibility and to suggest that if big changes could be accomplished in the past they might equally be contemplated, if the need arose, in the future.

Competition from abroad

Since the war the merchant banks have gone through two phases: an early period until the mid-fifties when their foreign business was still curtailed by exchange control, by the remaining restrictions on world trade and when domestic finance was similarly controlled from Whitehall. This period was followed in the second half of the 1950s by growing financial freedom at home, with take-over battles absorbing much of their energy, and by currency freedom abroad as convertibility led to the massive movement of funds across frontiers once more. As a result the foreign challenge is being heard again. Are the merchant banks prepared to accept it? Are they prepared to modify their newly-established domestic business—especially in advising industry (in mundane amalgamations as well as the headline-catching take-over tussles) and in the management of funds?

What business are most merchant banks now undertaking and what specific form will the foreign challenge take? So far we have herded these banks together as a recognisable species. In practice they are far from it. Even members of the Accepting Houses Committee undertake a variety of financial tasks. All 17 do accepting business. Many act as issuing houses. Some are bullion brokers; some do foreign exchange business; a few still undertake merchanting. And to the extent that they receive deposits they are a minor outpost of domestic banking.

While some have continued to specialise, others have managed to straddle several activities at once. What can be said in general, however, is that as a group they are active in four special areas:

  a) They manage individual funds—for private individuals, firms or charitable trusts—on a scale that must now run into hundreds of millions of pounds.
  b) They finance foreign trade, both in acceptance business and in the post-war practice of arranging medium-term export credits.
  c) They advise growing numbers of industrial companies not only on how and when to raise capital but in their financial affairs generally (between 1946 and 1956 they handled 58 per cent of all capital issues by public companies). As the Radcliffe Report[1] summed it up, 'The market is far better organised to meet the needs of British industry'.
  d) To an increasing extent they engage in foreign security business, placing American shares in Europe and vice-versa; running European investment trusts; concerning themselves with the revival of foreign loan business.

They have many other side-lines. One has a refinery. Another has insurance companies as subsidiaries. But the above are their four main activities today. It is here, therefore, that the merchant banks will be put to the test in coping with the problems of the 'sixties. As we shall see more fully in Chapters 10 and 11, the challenge is likely to come from abroad. Europe's strong economic recovery since 1957-58 has brought a new world of opportunity. It has led to more confidence in certain currencies and to an accompanying reduction of exchange barriers. Money can flow more freely across frontiers than at any time over the past 20 or 30 years. Prosperity in Europe has produced a corresponding increase in investible funds wanting to move across these frontiers. As a result investment advice is being called for on an international scale. Industrial companies too are keener to venture abroad not only to sell but to set up subsidiary plants. They also are in need of financial 'know-how'. The merchant banks have already shown what they can do in supplying it. They will be expected to do more for, whether Britain joins the Common Market in the foreseeable future or not, British firms will be relying on their advice as

[1] *Committee on the Working of the Monetary System*, Cmnd. 827, 1959.

Continental Europe tends to shrink in size economically (because of the increased size of industrial groupings) and as a Transatlantic Community—linking Europe more closely with North America—becomes an economic (if not a political) reality.

The merchant banks were already receiving growing requests for help from industrial firms in the months of Britain's negotiations to join the Six. Was the looser relationship between British banks and British industry in any way superior to the tighter links in some European countries? While British clearing banks had done little more than provide short-term working capital and, in recent years, medium-term credit for exports and the merchant banks had arranged for the raising of fresh capital and given advice generally, their Continental counterparts (often bigger and offering combined services) had held long-term investments in industry and been far more closely involved. Which was the better way of giving support to industry? A few of the more far-seeing (and active) merchant banks have been wondering for some time.

It has been assumed far too readily that the Continental type of link with industry—often, as in Germany, forced on industry during periods of severe adversity—has more drawbacks than it is worth. The risk to the banks in providing long-term equity capital for industrial firms has always been emphasised in London. What has to be faced now is whether the advantage to industry may not outweigh the added risk to the banker— whether clearing or merchant. It remains doubtful. One important difference between Britain and the Continent is that, because of the smooth workings of the London capital market, British industry has rarely been able to complain of any significant lack of money for expansion (apart from a possible gap among the smaller firms). Since the merchant banks have gone out of their way to provide both advice and capital to industrial firms since the war, it can be claimed, probably with some justice, that British industry is at no significant disadvantage vis-à-vis the Continent. This is not the end of the problem, of course, for capital reorganisation schemes as well as outright take-over bids and mergers also have to be reckoned with. Does the Continental system provide a better answer? It remains debatable. For the top-grade British firms, many of which have a partner of their merchant bank on their board as finance director (in some outstanding cases the firm will have a merchant banker as chairman), there is no real problem.

The difficulty often arises in the medium-sized firms where the personal contact is neither so direct nor so continuous.

Merchant banks and the smaller firm

Several of the merchant banks are, however, showing an aggressive reaction to criticisms that they spend more time giving advice to foreign firms than to British industry. They are no longer content to sit in London waiting for industrialists to turn up on their doorstep or to be introduced to them by others. More and more of them are setting up subsidiaries or offices in the main industrial centres in the provinces. That Rothschilds, once the supporter of a string of foreign governments, should set up an office in Manchester was one of the more significant events of recent years. Singer and Friedlander, S. Japhet, Lazard's and others all have their provincial connections. And all have gone after industrial business. No longer are they confining themselves to the large corporation: now they are interested in the small, active firms. They want their deposits; they keep an eye open for firms needing financial help and a guiding hand through the London capital market; and export finance is one of their major concerns. On the face of it, therefore, the post-war concentration of the merchant banks on domestic affairs should provide a solid foundation both for them and for British industry in meeting foreign competition.

The increased freedom for investment abroad will call on the resourcefulness of the merchant banks in their traditional activities too: in the investment of funds abroad, arbitrage in foreign securities, meeting changes in the financing of foreign trade, and in arranging loans for foreign borrowers. It is here above all that the nature and experience of these banks becomes important. This is an area of risks and of new opportunities where quick decisions, snap judgements and personal flair are needed in high degree. And these the merchant banks can provide.[1]

Change can be accomplished by mergers as well as the introduction of new blood. Both have been undertaken by the leading merchant banks. Rothschilds, for example, have recently introduced new partners from outside the Rothschild family

[1] The Partners' room in any of the leading merchant banks is very much a combination of half a dozen individualists, each expert in his own particular field, but all 'pooling' their experience. They work together as equals. The chairman of one of the largest of these banks once described himself simply as 'the first among equals'. The blend is as important as the individuals.

for the first time since they settled in London. And the following mergers have brought together firms specialising in different financial spheres, investment expertise often joining forces with a knowledge of foreign trade financing: S. G. Warburg acquired Seligman Brothers; Philip Hill, Higginson first merged with Erlangers and later with M. Samuel; Charterhouse Group acquired S. Japhet & Co.; Schroder merged with Helbert, Wagg & Co.; Lazard Bros. acquired Edward de Stein & Co. These amalgamations were also a recognition that financial resources often need strengthening, not as is so often assumed to cope with death duties, but rather as a response to changed business conditions. This is equally true of the transition of many firms from private companies or partnerships to public companies in recent years. Now nine of the 17 members of the Accepting Houses Committee are public limited companies. Even with the addition of financial resources and the enlargement of individual firms, their strength will ultimately depend on their flexibility and on whether the closeness with which the partners work together, physically as well as mentally, can produce an attitude towards a changing international financial scene that will grasp opportunities as they emerge. They no longer wield the financial resources they once did; as the late Lord Brand of Lazards once said, while the clearing banks 'live on their deposits, we (the merchant banks) have to live on our wits'. They have already shown how clearing bank money and merchant bank expertise can be combined in working out schemes for financing the building of oil tankers (in which the needs of shipbuilders, shipowners and charterers are married with the financial services of the banks and insurance companies) and in developing consortia for the financing of capital projects abroad as well as in organising the more routine medium-term credits for exports.

New opportunities

The freedom of exchanges and the increased movement of funds from one country to another in the past six or seven years have opened up other opportunities. Take the following examples over the past few years. In this period Argentina has borrowed money from New York and European banks; big oil companies have switched their funds from one country to another; Belgium has raised capital in Amsterdam; Italian banks have lent money to the World Bank; American shares have been placed in European centres by British banks; British firms have raised money in Zurich; Japan has borrowed funds in New York; an Italian dollar loan and a Belgian dollar loan have been floated in London. And while American firms have invested millions of dollars in new plant in Britain and Europe, British firms have been investing millions of pounds in Europe and North America.

The question is whether and how many banks in London and elsewhere are capable of taking on these kinds of transactions. In most cases in the British market merchant banks have been involved, as well as in the placing of American shares in Europe. They have the connections abroad and they have the expertise. But in saying this we are really narrowing the field down to no more than ten of the merchant banks in London. It would perhaps be invidious to name them. But anyone who has worked in the City could quickly tick off those members of the Accepting Houses Committee falling into this important category. Ten may not seem many. But it becomes numerous when the same question is asked of foreign centres. New York could probably muster the same number; but Paris and Amsterdam have probably no more than four and Brussels perhaps three. In Italy, Germany and Switzerland the big commercial banks dominate the financial field.

It is in this type of comparison that London emerges in such an apparently strong position. But it is significant that the ten active merchant banks able to cope with truly international investment business in London do *not* include several long-established banks still members of the exclusive Accepting Houses Committee; and one of its number hardly existed before the war. Survival will depend neither on longevity nor on an established reputation. It rests solely on individual initiative and technical expertise in a world yearly becoming smaller and more competitive. London built up its merchant banking expertise because Britain was on the trade routes of the world and was the first industrial country. Initially, geography provided the international connections. Today these personal connections have to be maintained and renewed constantly. Without them London could wither overnight. The lifting of financial restrictions at home and abroad has already in a matter of six or seven years marked off those merchant banks that intend to revitalise and re-equip themselves by the introduction of new blood, the adoption of new methods and the merging of complementary interests, from those that, once lulled into a false security by comforting restrictions, are now settling back into a respectable but insecure backwater. For up to the middle 1950s exchange controls at home damped down initiative; margins on foreign exchange were fixed, and exchange allocations closely controlled. Opportunities to explore new avenues were therefore limited because in so many fields business and trade were based on the *status quo*. But those days are now gone.

B. THE CLEARING BANKS

THE merchant banks originated in the finance of foreign trade; the clearing banks came into it at a much later stage. In the words of the late Lord Brand, merchant banks live on their wits, clearing banks on their deposits. The extent to which the clearing banks have begun to dominate the City's foreign financial activities by the volume of monetary resources at their disposal provides the key to their post-war development. Money for export was needed on a growing scale; only they could provide it. Fifty years ago the clearing banks had only just begun to dabble at all seriously in foreign trade; now they tower above all others.

In effect the familiar banks on the street corner have become as dominant in foreign trade as at home. Eleven clearing banks carry on domestic business up and down England and Wales. They include the so-called 'Big Five' (Midland, Barclays, Lloyds, Westminster and National Provincial) accounting for almost 90 per cent of the total deposits. Their combined deposits are just below £9,000 million and they maintain a network of around 12,000 offices, of which something like 10,000 belong to the Big Five. In the main it was this large domestic network that kept the clearing banks out of foreign business for so long. As we shall see in the next section on overseas banks, the clearing banks felt it was their role to let depositors' money earn its keep at home. This was still the general attitude at the turn of the century, though it was being undermined here and there. Before the 1914-18 war the merchant banks, overseas banks and London offices of foreign banks received a large share of the foreign business going to the clearing banks; it was regarded as natural to pass it on to institutions with more stake and expertise in foreign trade.

Growth of foreign business

Nevertheless the first moves towards foreign business were being made by the clearing banks. Fifty people, for example, were working in what was known as the Foreign Banks Department at the London City and Midland Bank (later the Midland) at the beginning of the century. By 1902 a separate section had had to be established to deal with the growing volume of bills of exchange on foreign and Commonwealth countries. Three years later came a separate Foreign Branch Office. Other clearing banks were following the same pattern. The London and County Bank, which amalgamated with the Westminster in 1909, had opened its foreign branch office in 1908 after acquiring the firm of Burt and Co., foreign exchange dealers, in 1907. But it was not until after the First World War and the bank amalgamations that followed that they began to build up a network of banking correspondents abroad on a significant scale. Thus between the two wars most of the large commercial banks established what are called 'overseas' or 'foreign' branches in the City. They were branches in London through which each clearing bank directed the whole of its foreign work. Some banks also established foreign or overseas branches in the provinces. In general, therefore, these banks passed what business they had abroad through their foreign branches in London or the provinces to one or other of their banking correspondents in other countries. These correspondents were normally foreign banks. The same system exists today. Its advantage, it is claimed, is that the clearing banks do not compete with foreign banks on their own ground and that the foreign banks in return pass what business they have in this country back to them.

This system has been (and is being) used in some degree by all the clearing banks, but especially by the Midland Bank which, until quite recently, continued to have no foreign branches abroad. As we shall see later in this section, this policy is now being changed. The other Big Five banks have supplemented their correspondent system by branches overseas. Lloyds Bank has Lloyds Bank Europe with eight branches in Europe and, until they were transferred to National and Grindlays Bank in exchange for a shareholding, it also ran an eastern department with 19 branches in India, Pakistan and Burma. Westminster has Westminster Foreign Bank with seven branches in Europe. And Barclays Bank has Barclays Bank (France) with 12 branches overseas.

Links have also been forged between some of the clearing banks and some of the overseas banks. The obvious one is Barclays Bank's majority stake in Barclays Bank DCO. Three of the clearing banks (Westminster, Lloyds and National Provincial) and Standard Bank have a similar majority holding in the Bank of West Africa.[1] Lloyds also has an interest in the National Bank of New Zealand and in the Bank of London and South America. The latter, in turn, owns half the capital of the recently formed Bank of London and Montreal. Yet in spite of these inter-connections, all the clearing banks continue to rely extensively on the correspondents system described earlier. The size of these informal networks is roughly as follows: the Midland has approximately 1,200 correspondents abroad, the Westminster 800, Barclays 650, Lloyds 500, and National Provincial 450.[2]

Services for exporters

Thus, although the clearing banks entered foreign business at a later stage and have persistently confined themselves to facilitating payments and providing, so far as possible, only short-term finance (rather than capital for development), their foreign business is now larger than that of any other banking sector in the City. Their contribution to the City's foreign mechanism is twofold. They provide a variety of services from credit to travel and theatre reservations. And they offer a machinery without which no other section of the City could go about its foreign business. This machinery is at the service of domestic customers wanting to undertake foreign business as well as foreign customers undertaking transactions here or in third countries. The clearing banks will collect export bills, open credits to buy commodities in Malaya, collect a legacy left in the United States, look after securities held abroad, and provide tourists with currencies. They will make payments, with or without credit, and will switch one currency into any other. In short they will undertake a thousand and one separate transactions. But it is in the provision of credit and of a method of payment for foreign trade that the bulk of their overseas activities lie.

One of the major changes since the war has been in the provision of growing quantities of credit for exporters by the

[1] See the merger of the Standard Bank and the Bank of West Africa mentioned at the end of this section and in the next section on Overseas and Eastern Exchange Banks.

[2] Estimated from *The Bankers' Almanac and Year Book, op. cit.*

clearing banks. Several developments have led to this remarkable expansion. The basic one has been the closing down of
the European capital markets to foreign borrowers. Whereas
before the war (certainly in the 'twenties, partly in the 'thirties)
it was customary for foreign customers, either governments or
corporations, to raise capital by bond issues in the London and
other financial markets and to use the proceeds to pay for
imports, the closing down of these markets during the currency
upheavals of the 'thirties forced customers to search for other
ways of financing their necessary imports. The pressure naturally
fell on their suppliers and the world's exporters were increasingly
called on to finance shipments to overseas customers.

Second, the proportion of capital goods sent to foreign
markets was increasing all the time. Thus the short-term finance
needed to cover consumer goods (and normally freely available
from the clearing banks) was having to be replaced by longer-
term finance for the shipment of capital goods. In 1913, for
example, only 2 per cent of Britain's exports were made up
of capital goods. Now the percentage is around 25 per cent.
Since Britain's clearing banks, in contrast to many of their
counterparts in Europe, have tried to stick rigidly to the rule
of supplying mainly short-term credit, to back up the export
of capital equipment has forced them to re-assess their whole
attitude to export finance, particularly since the war.

Third, because of the circumstances of the 19th century,
Britain's export pattern was orientated towards the under-
developed countries of the Commonwealth. This meant that
the increasing demands of these countries since the war for
development finance have added to the pressures on the clearing
banks for finance for capital exports, though the demand has
come as much from South America as from the Commonwealth. Increasing competition in these markets naturally led
to corresponding competition on the lengths of credit offered
by exporting countries. Hence the need for lengthier export
credits and, in turn, for flexible export credit insurance.

Exports, government and the clearing banks

Thus the Export Credits Guarantee Department which supplies
these insurance guarantees has played an increasingly important
role since the war. This government-run agency now insures
over a fifth of all British exports, and has supplied the essential
basis for the remarkable switch in clearing bank export finance

since the end of the war. As the Bank of England summed up the position: [1]

> 'The provision of finance for exports has come to rest to a much greater extent than in the past on the joint stock (clearing) banks. A large part of the banks' contributions to export financing still takes the form of overdrafts to provide working capital for their customers, whether at short or medium term. In addition the banks provide finance for specific export transactions, normally at medium term, though they are usually unwilling to do this for a period of more than five years from the date of shipment.'

A variety of techniques has gradually been built up to meet demands from exporters. The basic arrangement for semi-capital goods like agricultural machinery, trucks, buses, diesel engines, etc., is for the ECGD to provide insurance guarantees and, as a result, for the banks to provide the credit against promissory notes or bills of exchange. For larger amounts and longer periods special syndicates have been formed by clearing banks and merchant banks. While the merchant banks have undertaken to do a good deal of the work in tying up a package deal, the clearing banks have usually supplied the credit. In some cases, for a steel plant in Bengal, or a hydro-electric project in Peru, consortia have had to be formed. Other techniques, such as factoring, the provision of what is technically called 'undisclosed non-recourse finance'[2] and the international arrangements of the instalment credit firms, have been developed side by side with this broadening of the clearing banks' role.

At the same time government backing has been seen in various ways. During every credit squeeze, either the Chancellor of the Exchequer or the Governor of the Bank of England has made it clear to the banks that export finance should have first priority. Whatever restrictions were to be imposed, they were not to impede the provision of credit for exports. Even the workings of the banking mechanism have been amended to help the export drive. In February 1961, it was made clear by the Bank of England, for example, that it would be ready to re-finance certain parts of an export finance arrangement

---

[1] *Bank of England Quarterly Bulletin,* June 1961.

[2] A type of financial arrangement under which the foreign importer will not know that his supplier (i.e. the exporter in Britain) is obtaining finance from a factoring house. In addition, 'non-recourse' finance implies that the borrower will not be called upon to make good any losses arising from the credit he is receiving.

undertaken by a clearing bank. In effect this undertaking meant that the banks could regard a part, roughly 30 per cent, of such credits as liquid reserves and therefore the requirements of their liquidity ratios no longer acted as a restraint upon the provision of medium-term export finance. Two months later the government agreed to guarantee certain large projects (not less than £2 million each) for periods beyond five years. The purpose was to help to finance power stations, steel mills, harbours, dams and railway projects abroad. The use of these guarantees was to be strictly selective. Then in January 1962, the clearing banks extended their services still further—to provide credit for the export of heavy capital equipment for between three and five years after the date of shipment at a fixed rate of interest. Here the purpose was to protect exporters against wide fluctuations in lending rates arising from rapid changes in Bank rate. The rate of interest was $5\frac{1}{2}$ per cent. This was combined with the provision of £100 million by the insurance companies to help cover periods exceeding five years at a fixed rate of interest of $6\frac{1}{2}$ per cent. Thus exporters could take advantage of both schemes together in order to get terms beyond five years and at fixed rates of interest. The Insurance Export Finance Company was formed in 1962 by 68 insurance companies to administer their part of the scheme. The demands were so large that the total committed by the insurance companies was eventually raised to £150 million. Subsequently, in January 1965, the banks took over the whole burden of this financing at $5\frac{1}{2}$ per cent, thus allowing the insurance companies to get out of the arrangements. The banks in return were given the right to re-finance part of such credits at the Bank of England. The result has been a steady increase in the volume of export credit facilities offered by the clearing banks. It is virtually impossible to know the total being supplied largely because overdrafts may be used to finance either stocks at home or exports. The bank is often not aware what share of its facilities is backing the export drive. But a general impression of the expansion and of the volume of credit involved can be derived from the figures of ECGD financing shown in Table I.

TABLE I
EXPORTS INSURED BY ECGD
(£ million)

	Short-term[1]	Extended term[2]	Specific[3]	Financial guarantees[4]
1958-59	438	17	115	—
1959-60	549	36	109	—
1960-61	593	36	114	—
1961-62	675	61	109	39
1962-63	746	101	129	39

[1] Up to 6 months.
[2] In theory up to 5 years but averaging about 3 years.
[3] From 6 months to 5 years or more in theory but averaging 4-5 years in practice.
[4] Over 7 years.
Source: *Overseas Trade Policy*, FBI, February 1963.

Shift from merchant to clearing banks

Beyond these exports backed up by the ECGD are the shipments for which bank credit is given without recourse to credit insurance. And on top of all this are the thousand and one services behind the country's trade in general. Arbitrage, documentary credits, bills for sale, loans and overdrafts, clean payments—whatever the technical jargon—all lead to payments and transactions passing through the banks' clearing mechanism. With national trade reaching around £10,000 million a year, the total transactions passing through the clearing machinery in the City are bound to be high. Not all trade concerns the London clearing banks, of course. Some payments made here are offset against payments made to people or firms abroad before the banking mechanism is brought into play. This offsetting reduces the total needing to pass through the banks. There is also a significant share of trade that is naturally channelled through the London offices of the American, Commonwealth and overseas banks, rather than the London banks. And many large firms make sterling payments for customers abroad direct to other firms in Britain. These payments on 'open account' naturally reduce the banks' foreign commissions and earnings. Nevertheless the total foreign business undertaken by the London clearing banks and passing through the clearing machinery might as a guess reach between £5,000 million and £6,000 million annually.

In spite of all the skills of the merchant banks, their flexibility, their intimate knowledge both of markets and people, and their

long tradition of foreign operations, the money now lies elsewhere. The day has long gone when Rothschilds financed
governments or sustained many during war crises, or when the
clearing banks were confined to domestic affairs. The merchant
banks have kept their flair. They are still extremely active in
furthering export finance and in drawing up specialised
schemes. But the money power has now moved to the clearing
banks. At the end of June, 1964, the net deposits of the 11
clearing banks totalled no less than £7,800 million, whereas
those of the 17 accepting houses (the leading merchant banks)
amounted to £925 million. More and more of the clearing
banks have been drawn into foreign business. If the merchant
banks were drawing up plans and the clearing banks finding
the money, it was not unexpected if the clearing banks wondered
whether they should not go further and do more of the arranging themselves. There is, of course, no easy dividing line here.
Each case will be different from others. But it is plain that the
encroachment of the clearing banks into the foreign trade
business of other parts of the City is bound to continue.

Yet it is equally clear that the clearing banks may not be
able to take full advantage of their world-wide opportunities if
they maintain their present structure. Each bank is resolving
the dilemma in its own way. The advantages of having branches
abroad are increasing. Not only can they be used flexibly in
conjunction with other banks but they can operate differently
from banks based in Britain alone. The growth of the Euro-
dollar market[1] and the use of non-resident foreign currencies
to finance trade and development have increased the usefulness
of banking subsidiaries abroad. Banking subsidiaries need not,
of course, be *abroad* to be effective in the Euro-dollar market
and for taking up additional deposits by offering higher rates.
For the former they merely need to be free from the 30 per
cent liquidity requirement, and for the latter from the Committee of London Clearing Bankers' agreement on deposit
rates. At the same time the onset of convertibility, the closer
co-operation in international monetary affairs and the growing
size of overseas commitments have all persuaded banks in
different countries to re-appraise their present structure.

The Midland's new overseas system
The decision of the Midland Bank, after years of dependence
on the correspondents' system rather than on branches abroad,

[1] See Chapter 3, p. 53.

to branch out in three different directions in a matter of 12 months indicated developments in the clearing bank world. First it set up the Midland and International Banks Ltd. in London in association with the Commercial Bank of Australia, the Standard Bank and the Toronto-Dominion Bank. Its aim is to promote joint operations with member-banks in all parts of the world and to become a convenient channel for large-scale international financial operations. Secondly, the Midland Bank reached an agreement with three European banks (Amsterdamsche Bank, Deutsche Bank and Banque de la Société Générale de Belgique) 'to enlarge and deepen co-operation in special fields'. Thirdly, it opened an agency office in New York. The aim, in short, is to set up a network abroad or in conjunction with banks abroad that will be able to undertake business that the Midland Bank cannot do at present.

Similar links have been forged or given a new lease of life by the other clearing banks. During 1964 the Westminster participated, with other banks in London, New York and the Continent, in the Banco des Financiacion Industrial, an investment bank in Spain.

Having reached a state of dominance in the foreign field, largely on the basis of domestic deposits and domestic business, these banks are now looking further afield not only for deposits but also for business. The first might be tapped without encroaching too much on the domestic business of foreign banks, by special arrangements either in the formation of new institutions with joint shareholdings or in looser agreements. Whether the way ahead in the foreign field includes the further linking of clearing banks, overseas banks and merchant banks, as suggested in the next section, remains to be seen.[1] Sustained growth across frontiers plainly lies in that direction.

C. OVERSEAS AND EASTERN EXCHANGE BANKS

HISTORICALLY both the overseas banks and the Eastern exchange banks followed the merchant banks in financing Britain's foreign trade. Though all but one of those remaining (the Hong Kong and Shanghai Banking Corporation) have their head offices in London, the bulk of their business is still con-

[1] An interesting development early in 1965 was the support given by National Provincial, Westminster and Midland to the new organisation to be formed by the merger of the Standard Bank and the Bank of West Africa. This is referred to in the next section on the Overseas and Eastern Exchange Banks.

ducted in territories abroad. Most have their roots in the middle of last century, when British banking practices were introduced into overseas territories to finance both local development and trade with Britain. India, Africa, Australia, China, Argentina—wherever development was taking place British traders were prominent and British bankers not far behind. It was the period when Britain's Empire was being built up to support industrial expansion at home. Money was needed to trade with these developing areas, to finance the supply of raw materials and food for Britain and the sale of British manufactured goods abroad. Local developments needed help—in farms, plantations and mines. And local British traders needed deposit banks. In some areas deposit banking lagged far behind the financing of trade and development. In others (such as India) it followed within a year or two. The link with London was soon found to be vital. It was not only a source of finance for development; it was also a place where surplus funds could be invested at extremely short notice.

It might have been expected that the joint stock banks—the 19th century forerunners of the Big Five today—would have been in the forefront of overseas business. They had developed deposit banking quite rapidly at home and the use of the 'Bill on London' was growing all the time. Yet they were content to let foreign business be taken up by others. As one prominent joint stock banker[1] told the Select Committee on Banks of Issue in 1875:

'Our credit and our funds should be available here and not made use of, as it were, by granting a double credit in foreign and colonial countries either in India, Australia or America or wherever it may be; we hold that the depositors have a right to look for the proceeds of their property entrusted to us as being on the spot and not used abroad.'

It was, as we saw in the last section, a view held by the joint stock banks right up to the beginning of this century. But where the joint stock banks would not venture, others would and did.

Types of business: early examples

The type of business these early overseas banks undertook was a direct reflection of what was going on in the under-developed world of over a century ago. Take the following

[1] Quoted in *National and Grindlays Review,* January 1963.

three examples from Africa, India and South America. In the two colonies and two republics in what is now South Africa the Standard Bank began to support agriculture but was soon involved in gold, diamonds and a thousand other commodities. As one commentator[1] put it, the bank

'nourished the wool industry of the Eastern Cape; it was the first on the diamond fields; first at the alluvial gold finds at Barberton and came with the pioneers to the great gold-mining industry on the Rand. For half a century and more it was both diamond and gold broker—buying and selling the stones of Kimberley, the gold of Barberton, of Lyden-burg, and of the Rand. Most early businesses of commerce and manufacturing in the colonies of the Cape and Natal and the Republic of the Transvaal were financed by it.'

Soon it was releasing £40,000 to President Kruger to help him to meet some of his Government's bills; then it was advancing £20,000 to De Beers for Cecil Rhodes to pay for fitting out his pioneer column on its march into Rhodesia; and eventually lending £75,000 for the rebels of 1914 to prevent their farms from being sequestered in order to pay fines.

About ten years before John Paterson set up the Standard Bank in 1852 to finance the wool trade in Port Elizabeth, the prospectus for the Chartered Bank of India, Australia and China was painting a similar picture thousands of miles to the East. 'In 1851', Sir Compton Mackenzie tells us in *Realms of Silver*,[2]

'the discovery of gold in Australia two years after the California gold rush had opened new vistas for trade, but even before this, as the Bank's prospectus noted, a considerable trade had already developed between the Australian colonies and India, China, Singapore and the East Indies. Tea was shipped from China; coffee and rum from Java, Ceylon and India; tobacco, and spices and other products from Manila and the islands of the Eastern Archipelago . . . Moreover, the East had always been the greatest market for the precious metals, large quantities of which were shipped from the west coast of South America as well as from Great Britain. The directors believed that the greater part of the gold produced in Australia would find its way direct to India and other Eastern countries as the nearest market.'

[1] *Financial Mail, Johannesburg,* 12 October 1962.
[2] Routledge and Kegan Paul, 1954.

Less than a month before the Standard Bank's memorandum of association was signed in southern Africa, a notice appeared in the *Banker's Magazine*[1] in London concerning South America:

'An enterprise to be called the London, Buenos Ayres and River Plate Bank (Limited) with a capital of £500,000 in 5,000 shares of £100 each, and a power to increase has been announced . . . The concentration of banking energy in this direction would under careful management be productive of large results.'

A century later, the present-day Bank of London and South America had emerged with 56 branches in South America, Europe and the United States and (with the Bank of Montreal) a further 26 agencies in Central and South America, the West Indies and the Bahamas. Looking back, the bank was able to write: [2]

'the opening up of the pampas and the transformation of Argentina into one of the granaries of the world was the work of many military expeditions and of the railways, the banks, and the immigrants who followed them . . . and the year 1862, in which both the London, Buenos Ayres and River Plate Bank and the Buenos Ayres Great Southern Railway were founded, may be said to mark the beginning of this great period of Anglo-Argentine co-operation.'

Similar stories abound in the histories of the forerunners of the overseas and Eastern exchange banks that remain in the Square Mile today. The survivors listed in Table II have had more than their share of risk and disaster to contend with. Within a year or two of the opening of the Calcutta City Banking Corporation, the forerunner of the National and Grindlays Bank, the end of the American Civil War led to a remarkable crash in cotton prices and a high toll among Indian domestic banks. Within a further twelve months, the new bank was facing the repercussions of the Overend, Gurney

---

[1] September 1862.
[2] *A Short History*, Bank of London and South America, September 1962.

TABLE II

LONDON'S OVERSEAS BANKS

(Overseas Banks and Eastern Exchange Banks with Head Offices in London)

£ million, to nearest £100,000

	Capital		Published reserves including Profit & Loss £	Total Assets £	Date of Balance Sheet	Comments
	Authorised £	Issued £				
A. Eastern Exchange Banks						
Hongkong & Shanghai Banking Corporation[1]	6.3	4.9	15.3	369.4	31.12.63	Group Consolidated
	6.3	**4.9**	**15.3**	**639.7**	**31.12.63**	Balance Sheet
Mercantile Bank[2]	4	2.9	2.4	107.9	31.12.63	
British Bank of the Middle East[2]	2.5	2.5	3.1	145.9	31.12.63	
Chartered Bank	10	6.6	8.4	481.7	31.12.63	Consolidated Balance
	10	**6.6**	**9.7**	**579.7**	**31.12.63**	Sheet
Eastern Bank[3]	2	1	1.9	104	31.12.63	
National & Grindlays Bank	9	5.7	5.7	356.8	31.12.63	
B. Overseas Banks						
Bank of London & South America	20	13.7	8.3	454	31.12.63	
Ottoman Bank	10[4]	5	1.3	105.5	31.12.63	
Barclays Bank	25	24	20.5	1,088.7	30. 9.64	Consolidated Balance
DCO	**25**	**24**	**22**	**1,094.3**	**30. 9.64**	Sheet
Standard Bank	17	11.7	13.6	509.2	31. 3.64	
Bank of West Africa	6	4	4.2	97.2	31. 3.64	
Australia & New Zealand Bank	22.5	14.0	12.9[5]	513.9	31. 3.64	Consolidated Balance
	22.5	**14.0**	**14.2**	**628.8**	**30. 9.64**	Sheet
National Bank of New Zealand	6	3.5	3	86.6	31. 3.64	
English, Scottish & Australian Bank	7	7	5.1	202.2	30. 6.64	Consolidated Balance
	7	**7**	**7.2**	**262.2**	**30. 6.64**	Sheet

[1] Head Office in Hongkong.
[2] Owned by Hongkong & Shanghai Banking Corporation
[3] Owned by Chartered Bank
[4] £5 million uncalled
[5] Includes £4,335,000 share premiums.

crisis.[1] Although three major Anglo-Eastern banks failed, both the National Bank of India and the Chartered Bank survived. The opening of the Suez Canal in 1869 and the extension of the telegraph to Bombay in the following year eventually stimulated their activities. But the fluctuations in the exchange rates of Asian countries on a silver standard (when silver was depreciating) provided conditions in which only the fittest would survive. By the 1880s the Standard Bank was grappling with troubles of its own in Southern Africa—and surviving. And in 1891 the London and River Plate Bank was riding out similar financial storms in Buenos Ayres at a time when both the official banks and several others were unable to cope with the repercussions of the July Revolution of the previous year. These overseas and Eastern exchange banks were thus steeled in the hard commercial world of the 19th century. Their successors today may not face such sharp shocks, but if they are to survive and, more important, to expand in line with overseas developments they too will have to be prepared to take similar risks.

Nationalism and competition

The post-war climate has not been as comforting as many of them would have liked. In Australia the three London-based banks[2] (the so-called 'Anglos') have had to contend with stringent banking regulations, with the stubborn truth that nationalistic feelings cannot be shrugged aside even within the older Commonwealth, and with intense competition for business. In Asia the Eastern exchange banks have been grappling with rising nationalism,[3] with partition and its aftermath in the Indian sub-continent, with the rise of communism in China and with the re-emergence of Japan in the commercial world. In Africa there have been the political troubles of the Union, the

---

[1] The failure of Overend, Gurney & Co. in 1866 led to a financial crisis in the City. As Bagehot wrote in *Lombard Street* (1873): 'Ten years ago that house stood next to the Bank of England in the City of London; it was better known abroad than any similar firm—known, perhaps better than any purely English firm. The partners had great estates, which had mostly been made in the business. They still derived an immense income from it. Yet in six years they lost all their own wealth, sold the business to the company and then lost a large part of the company's capital. And these losses were made in a manner so reckless and so foolish that one would think a child who had lent money in the City of London would have lent it better.'

[2] Australia and New Zealand Bank; National Bank of New Zealand; English, Scottish and Australia Bank.

[3] This has sometimes taken the form of outright nationalisation (e.g. the Burma Nationalisation of Banks Decree, 23 February, 1963); sometimes only the insistence on proportions of local officers.

new sovereign states farther north and the severing of previous ties with many former colonies. And in South America the Bank of London and South America has struggled single-handed with political instability, irregular devaluations and rampant inflation, as well as increasing competition from United States and domestic banks alike.

In all these territories British-based banks have had to contend with the growing needs of the under-developed and with the replacement of private with public finance. In Africa and Asia (not so much in South America) they have also had to concern themselves with the problems of the newly-independent nations. In countries where this new sovereignty has replaced previous membership of the British colonial Empire, the London overseas banks have faced the possibility of losing many of the old connections and business without at the same time acquiring new areas of activity with the same rapidity. Some of these banks have reacted swiftly and flexibly to the potential threat. Others have clung to old habits. Enough time has now passed to show what the new conditions may imply and what needs to be done about it.

As in so many other cases, the transfer of political power on such a large scale within the Commonwealth was bound to have deep economic implications. Even now the full significance of what has happened (and is happening) has not sunk in completely in Whitehall. The City and industry are increasingly becoming aware of what has taken place. Britain has continued to congratulate herself on one of the most generous transfers of political power in history. The Congo fiasco has added to the stream of praise. Whether British influence and the British way of life will continue to dominate the former overseas territories is still being debated comfortably in London and elsewhere. What is not so often discussed is the full economic cost of this shift in political power. Only now is it becoming clear that the automatic channelling of money, orders and business to London has ended at a time when further aid, both economic and military, is needed. These broader effects need not detain us. But their impact on the British banks operating in these territories should. Just as British Overseas Airways Corporation quickly found that landing and other rights in these former British territories were ended or modified overnight, following independence, so the British banks operating from London found their situation completely transformed. The outlook of the newly-formed governments was naturally different from that of the previous Colonial administrations. They have continued to rely on the established London-based banks for many services. But both domestic banks and foreign banks are likely to be given far more scope than in the past. Just as many of the newly-independent governments want to have their own prestige airline, they may eventually want to have their own nationally-controlled banks. New central banks have also had to be set up, and their activities may have direct repercussions on London-based banks. In short the demands made on British banks in these Commonwealth countries may increase at a time when the new governments have changed or undermined many of the banking arrangements the banks had once relied upon for part of their prosperity.

Let us be more specific. In Africa, for example, the Standard Bank and Barclays DCO may well face increasing competition from newcomers in many of the newer African territories. At the same time the gradual establishment of new African central banks to replace local currency boards, based on sterling, will probably bring potential currency risks to the London-based banks that previously could be ignored. If these banks found themselves with an excess of local currency and short of sterling in earlier colonial periods, they rarely felt the need to take defensive action. The exchange risk was eliminated in their mind (or at least put on a par with that of the pound itself) because of the tight links between the colonial territory and London. Now that these links have been severed, the risks are correspondingly higher and the banks operating from London have to take them into account in all their operations. In addition, not only is it becoming more difficult to carry out full direction from London but the advantage of switching resources from one territory to another are being whittled down by local restrictions on the movement of funds.

Outside Africa, the change has not been the same. Until 1939 the Eastern exchange banks always had to cope with moving exchanges as the Asian currencies were based on silver, but since the war some of them have been linked to sterling— notably India and Pakistan. The Bank of London and South America has continued to have the worst time of all, trying to cope with the unstable currencies of Latin America.

The post-war dilemma

The encroachment of other banks, restrictions on banking habits, the increased competition and the bigger risks, combine to face the London-based banks with an acute dilemma. Should they continue to operate in these areas in much the same way as in the past, keeping a direct stake in the prosperity of the territory by the continuation of deposit banking (not in itself immediately profitable) and, more important, by helping development directly? Or should they opt out of these risk-taking areas and go after the cream of the business that some of the newer banks are largely concerned with? To their credit—and possibly eventual profit—the London banks are continuing to take the first way out, though some of them have still to realise the size of the risks they are thereby taking. It is one thing to operate a network of deposit banks in a territory when outside competition in other banking business is naturally limited. It is quite another to bear the burden of the overheads of a network of deposit banks and deliberately try to develop a new banking spirit (as well as habits) among the prosperous Africans, when others may come in at a later stage to pick up the best parts of the business. Moreover these changes are taking place when the developing nations need increasing amounts of capital. At one time banks in these territories were able to tap private investors both inside and outside them. Now this natural source of private funds is drying up; and, although public funds are increasingly taking the place of private capital, the role of the local banks is less than it was.

This is as true of Asia as Africa. The Eastern exchange banks have found themselves meeting much the same problems in India, Pakistan, Ceylon and Malaya as have their counterparts in the new Africa. Finance for trade is still their predominant activity, and, as in Africa, these banks have looked to their exchange business for a large part of their profits. But increasingly they have to find money for investment in manufacturing industry and for the development of new sources of raw material and foods. Thus the Eastern exchange banks have found themselves coming into closer competitive contact with the domestic Asian banks in all these activities. They have also felt obliged to make contributions to the development corporations sponsored by the new governments in their territories. Thus they have been asked to find additional funds for investment, directly and indirectly, in industry at a time when government funds that used to be placed with them (often for use in financing trade) are now naturally placed with the new central banks. The only basic difference between the London overseas banks operating in Africa and the Eastern

exchange banks is that the latter have been facing these
problems far longer.

The City's role in overseas investment

If the City of London is to play a prominent role in the world's
finances, it must remain flexible and abreast of developments.
So must its constituent banks, particularly those operating
abroad. We have already seen what this implies. Primarily it
means that the Eastern exchange banks and the overseas
banks operating from London must deliberately decide to
take risks. They need not seek them out. If they are to maintain their influence and the banking business in the territories
they are concerned with, however, they must be prepared to
ride the political tides and to take on the new business that will
be needed. What seems to be increasingly clear is that any
decision to do none of these things is, sooner or later, going to
turn out to be a decision to stagnate, losing business and
influence just as surely as accepting the wrong risks. But facing
the future in this way should not be a blind move. Most of
these banks are aware of the problems they already face. If
they are to stay and operate in the new conditions, with all the
restrictions that may continue to go with them, they will have
to fashion themselves accordingly. It is time to see how.

The risks in these areas are bound to be bigger than in
the past, for all the reasons we have already outlined. This
implies the need for more flexibility and bigger resources. In
some cases development capital will be wanted on a growing
scale; the more primitive the local banking system, the larger
the development needs. The banks will be providing longer-
term capital, directly or indirectly, in order to prime the
economic pump and in the hope that, as development proceeds throughout the territory, prosperity will flourish and the
banking habit spread. Prosperity would provide increasing
banking business within the country and enable the banks to
channel increasing business back to London. But, apart from
the need for larger long-term funds, the London-based banks
have a growing desire for greater liquidity. The combination
of possible political instability and economic difficulties (often
arising out of over-ambitious industrialisation or of unstable
commodity prices or both) may lead to a sudden demand for
sterling at a time when official funds are no longer channelled
through these London-based banks. The restrictions on switching funds from one territory to another have much the same

effect, stressing the need for more liquidity locally as well as in London.

Mergers and co-operation

This combination of bigger risks and larger financial needs has underlined the desirability of further banking mergers. Several have already taken place. The Eastern exchange banks have now reduced themselves to three from seven immediately after the war. The Bank of London and South America has followed up its creation of the Bank of London and Montreal (with the co-operation of the Bank of Montreal) for the development of the Caribbean area, with the acquisition of the merchant banking firm of Balfour, Williamson and Company. Both Barclays DCO and the Standard Bank have continued to open branches throughout Africa, more than doubling them in the past 15 years. But, as the world grows smaller and communications develop, the need for bigger units and fewer banks increases too. National and Grindlays already have a foothold in Africa; the Standard Bank has offices in Paris and Milan and has recently opened an office in Tokyo; and the Bank of London and South America has been concentrating some of its energies on the Continent of Europe and claims that over 50 per cent of its business comes from countries outside South America. The question is whether this widening of interests should not be extended by deliberate steps to merge more of the London-based banks. This would at once provide larger resources, more flexibility and an easier shouldering of risks. The liquidity problem too would be eased considerably.

Sir George Bolton, chairman of the Bank of London and South America, has already spoken of the waste of resources in American and British banks competing for business in so many parts of the world. At least the time has come when competition among British overseas banks could be reduced with advantage. This is not an argument for a banking monopoly. Anyone who knows the fierce competition for business in the developing territories of Asia, Africa and South America would be unlikely to assume that these are areas of easy profit. It *is* rather an argument for enlarging the scale of operations of British banks in some of these areas and for gaining additional flexibility from operations in several parts of the world. There is now a clear need for two or three large overseas banks operating from London, with the whole world for their activities and not simply one part of it. It is a need that is already recognised in more than one influential banking quarter. And some ideas have already moved ahead to the further possibility of international banking co-operation in some of the developing territories. The innovation of the Midland Bank in starting the Midland and International Banks Ltd. in co-operation with three Commonwealth banks[1] is a move in the right direction. So is the merger of the Standard Bank and the Bank of West Africa supported by three clearing banks[2]. The big clearing banks, as we saw in the last section, have much experience to offer in overseas business. But it is the merchant banks and above all the overseas banks that should now take up the running again. They will have to move away perhaps from deposit banking in some areas (or at least give this less attention than development) and take on the role of banques d'affaires. The merchant banks could help. Where the clearing banks now have the resources, the merchant banks could provide the techniques, the contacts, the people, above all the ideas. All that may be holding back the establishment of a holding company, the umbrella under which two or three overseas banks could be brought together and which could also shelter contributions from one or two of the merchant banks, is the will and the right blend of personalities. The second may turn out to be the bigger stumbling block.

D. LONDON'S FOREIGN BANKS

LONDON has built up connections over the years with all parts of the world. This has not, however, been a one-way business. Foreign banks have staked their claim in London too; and there are few countries in the world that have not established a bank branch or banking representative in the Square Mile. It is not unusual for international centres of finance to have

[1] The Commercial Bank of Australia, the Standard Bank and the Toronto-Dominion Bank.

[2] Proposals for the merger of the Standard Bank and the Bank of West Africa 'for the purpose of forming the basis of a new overseas banking organisation centred in London' were announced in March 1965. The new organisation was to be supported by further investments from the National Provincial Bank, Westminster Bank and Midland Bank. In addition the Chase Manhattan Bank intended to acquire a shareholding, subject to the approval of the US banking authorities. Thus British and American banking interests were being brought together (with possibilities of later European participation) to launch an international banking organisation with connections in Africa.

foreign banks in their midst; it is equally true of Zurich, Milan, Paris, Brussels or New York. What marks London out from the others is the number of foreign banks established there. In all close on a hundred foreign bank branches or representative offices are contained in the City. What has brought them there? What do they do?

It is natural for bankers and financiers to follow trade. From the beginning of the 19th century, as the centre of the world's financial activities moved strongly from Amsterdam to London, many rich Continental merchants found their way to the City. Some came of necessity—like so many other political refugees before and since. Others came because business brought them. While a number of the City's merchant banks can push their origins back two or three centuries, it is surprising how many of them date from the first half of the 19th century. But by the end of it these immigrants were part of the London scene. They were no longer strictly foreign bankers. Some maintained, as they still do, close connections with their countries of origin. But for all political purposes they had been absorbed into the City's scheme of things. This, in a sense, was the first influx of foreign bankers and merchants—at least since London's rise to pre-eminence about a century and a half ago. The second influx at the turn of the century took quite a different form. By this time foreign banks were beginning to establish branches in the Square Mile. By 1900 there were still little more than a dozen. Yet within another eleven years the number had jumped to 26. Over much the same period their combined capital doubled from £50 million to £100 million and their combined deposits rose no less than seven times.

Influx from Europe

Possibly the first of the new type of influx was the Comptoir d'Escompte de Paris, later to be known as the Comptoir National d'Escompte de Paris, which opened offices in Leadenhall Street in 1867, to be followed four years later by the Credit Lyonnais and the Société Générale. The Swiss Bank Corporation opened a London office in 1898. By the outbreak of war in 1914 the so-called German 'D' banks (the Deutsche Bank, the Dresdner Bank and the Discontogesellschaft), the Italians (the Banca Commerciale Italiana and the Credito Italiano) and the Russians (Russian Bank for Foreign Trade, Russian Commercial and Industrial Bank and the Russo-Asiatic Bank) were all firmly established. The Banque Belge, soon to become one of the most active, and the Swiss Bank Corporation, one of the largest of the foreign banks in London, had appeared in 1909.

It is not hard to see why they came. (The question is rather why so many of them did not come earlier). By 1900 London was financing the major share of the world's trade; it was finding growing amounts of long-term capital for the rest of the world; and the merchants and banks in London were shipping and financing goods and materials round the globe. Commonwealth, European and American trade was largely financed in sterling by banks in London. Since sterling was used to such a growing extent in trade, and since it was useful for foreign traders to maintain their currency balances in London in the form of sterling, it was not long before several foreign banks began to open offices in the City to undertake some of the business formerly done almost exclusively by British banks. It was a profitable business. There were no restrictions to keep them out and before long they were undertaking business in bills of exchange and entering the foreign exchange market. As a writer in the *Journal of the Institute of Bankers* put it in 1911:

'It has been said that our pre-eminent position as the financial centre of the world was the main factor in drawing the foreign banker to London; but there is another reason of far-reaching importance not only to the foreign bank, but to our gold market. We refer to bills of exchange. The foreigner looks upon the buying and selling of bills as the main part of banking, and as these bills are the recognised media for settling international transactions, they are a source of great profit to the foreign banker. He is well aware that merchants all the world over know that a bill of exchange on London is readily negotiable, and in connection with his financial assistance to foreign trade it is of vital importance for the foreign banker to have a branch in London where he can deal first-hand with the bills.'

This brought added competition for the City's banks and before the First World War the question of the influx of these foreign branch offices was often a sore point to the established banks. Yet as the years went by their numbers increased. By the 1930s they had exceeded 80, without catastrophic effect on the business of the domestic banks. There was plainly room for all. Now there are even more foreign banks than before the war. Although the German branches have not been re-opened, many others have taken their place. In fact something like 30 foreign branch or representative offices are entirely post-war establishments. New faces have appeared; old ones have changed their character. The Italian banks, which before the last war had full branch offices, undertaking all kinds of banking services (including branches in the Italian quarter in Soho), now confine themselves to representative offices. There are seven of them. The newcomers include the Banco de Santander, Bangkok Bank, Bank of Baroda, Fuji Bank, Rafidain Bank and the First National Bank of Boston. The Japanese are in London in probably the largest numbers, with six representative offices and six branch offices. Under a dynamic manager, the Moscow Narodny[1] has shown the biggest expansion, undertaking most of the transactions of a merchant bank—trade credits, including acceptance credits, investments in local authorities and British Government securities for its short-term surplus funds, etc. Its assets rose from £8.6 million at the end of 1958 to no less than £208 million at the end of June 1964. It has naturally been prominent in financing East-West trade. As a group, however, the American banks, consisting of seven full branch offices and three representative offices, probably do most business. Several have full establishments in the West End as well as in the City. Their importance can be judged from the last figures of their combined London assets—£122 million, compared with the £184 million of the other foreign banks and £748 million for the British overseas banks.

The work of the foreign banks

Not all foreign banks in the City work in the same way. There are in effect two distinct types—those that carry out full banking services, including the acceptance of deposits, and those that are merely representative offices, maintaining contact but not competing directly with London banks. The decision to have one or the other depends on several factors. The main ones are the size of the local colony of nationals in London and whether they are residents or tourists; the demands from their own nationals for full banking services; the distance from their head office; and whether they consider it wiser to get British banks to act as local agents in the hope that reciprocal business will be done on the British banks' behalf in their home territory. The Japanese have both representative offices

---

[1] For an outline of its operations by its managing director, see *The Times*, 28 October, 1964.

and full branches. The leading American banks have full offices in London. The Italians, on the other hand, contrary to their pre-war practice, now rely on representative offices, maintaining reciprocal arrangements with London banks.

Most of those with full banking offices are doing what their governments came to do no more than half a century ago. They are now primarily concerned with three types of business as the Radcliffe Report[1] summed up:

'1. They operate as exchange dealers;
2. They grant credits to finance the movement of goods between the United Kingdom and the other countries in which they operate (and, exceptionally, trade which does not touch the United Kingdom at all): these credits include acceptance credits giving rise to bills of exchange which can be negotiated in the discount market; and
3. They employ in London funds arising from their general business.'

All three activities hang together; though transactions in their own right, directly or indirectly they are concerned with the financing or settling of foreign trade. Since at least a third of the world's trade is still done in sterling, most countries still find it useful to maintain working balances in pounds in London. The foreign banks facilitate these operations. While their main activity is in the provision of credits for trade, other kinds of business accrue also. Foreign currency balances are held in London in the form of pounds to meet the seasonal needs of trade. These funds vary in size for other reasons too. The fortunes of individual currencies have a bearing on them, as the various sterling crises have shown. But even through the worst of these attacks on the pound, minimum balances were maintained by the foreign banks in London. Moreover, since most European currencies (including the pound) became fully convertible at the end of 1958, these balances (especially European) have increased further. The need to keep working balances in London to facilitate trade and other financial transactions partly explains why, after a sterling crisis, money usually flows back to London fairly rapidly.

Although these funds are primarily attracted to London to help trade, they also flow in on a short-term basis because of the London money market (where money can earn a rate of interest overnight) and, increasingly in the past four or five years,

[1] *Committee on the Working of the Monetary System, op. cit.,* p. 71.

because of the growing Euro-dollar market established by London dealers.[1] The fluctuations in these deposits, partly the result of changes in trade, partly arising from changes in the fortunes of different currencies, usually persuade the foreign banks to maintain a fairly high level of liquidity in London. This they invariably do by putting a significant proportion of their funds in the money market, in British Treasury bills, in short-dated Government securities and, again at short-term, with local authorities.

In recent years the foreign banks have also begun to move back into the business of foreign security transactions and into foreign transactions relating to industrial firms. The American banks in London have been prominent in the heavy influx of American companies to Britain and Europe as have European banks in the growing links between British and Continental firms. Arrangements for the quotation of British firms on Continental bourses and, more particularly, for the quotation of foreign firms on the London Stock Exchange, have also engaged their energies. This has revived an investment interest that was one of their earliest activities, for many of them are still paying agents for their own country's sterling loans and still remain a useful source of information on foreign securities. Their security departments have become increasingly active since the development of the Common Market and the growing interest in European shares and investment trusts.

Foreign banks and the City's future

It can be argued, as it was close on half a century ago, that there are now too many foreign banks sharing the business that should belong to London banks alone. The competition in the City is fiercer now than it was when convertibility was established at the end of 1958. Turnover in virtually all areas in which the foreign banks are involved is appreciably higher than it was; profit margins are invariably narrower. This could lead, but so far has not, to a demand for restrictions to be placed on foreign banking activity in London. It would be an understandable reaction. To do so, however, would strike directly at London's international status. It is because foreign bankers can operate so freely from London and because transactions in pounds can be undertaken with the least difficulty from London that both foreign business, and hence foreign banks, have been drawn to the City. The removal of one (the

[1] See Chapter 3, p. 53.

banks) could easily lead to the diminution of the other (international business). Even relative restrictions can hamstring the true functionings of an international centre, as both New York and Paris, in their different ways, have discovered since the war. New York has, until recently, kept out foreign bank branches capable of receiving deposits by specific banking restrictions. Paris has done much the same by its continuous financial restrictions on the movement of capital. This partly explains why London, in spite of a series of sterling crises, has managed to maintain its role as an international centre. Whether this role is really worthwhile to Britain is more fully explored from Chapter 10 onwards. If it *is*, the activities of the foreign banks are an integral part of it.

CHAPTER 3

FOREIGN EXCHANGE

THE FOREIGN EXCHANGE MARKET is one of the most baffling of
the City's markets. It manages to be both intimately concerned with virtually every overseas transaction and yet somehow
remarkably aloof from most other City operations. Its job is
simple; its methods highly complex. An investment in
Argentina, the payment for a shipload of Australian wool, the
receipt of dividends from a shareholding in Malaya, the
currency wanted by British holidaymakers—all these and many
other transactions lead to the switching of pounds into other
countries' currencies, and *vice-versa*. A simple operation, it
might seem. But since the exchange rate between one currency
and another fluctuates from minute to minute (usually between
margins agreed with the International Monetary Fund), since
interest rates also vary in different centres and since both (i.e.
exchange rates and interest rates) have a marked influence on
forward exchange rates, switching a few pounds into any other
currency is not the easy, automatic transaction it might appear
to be.

The functions of the dealers

Mr. Harold Wincott once described a foreign exchange
dealer's office during a busy spell as 'the nearest thing to
Bedlam I have struck'. Others have been equally baffled by the
jargon and by the tempestuous activity. Although almost every
sort of bank is involved with foreign exchange, it remains
probably the only London market with no central meeting
place. The foreign exchange rooms of the hundred and thirty
or so major banks and large firms authorised to deal are linked
by telephone and telex to nine broking firms (five more than
in 1951 when the market re-opened), as well as to other foreign
centres all round the world. This makes for flexibility and
opportunity. It also leads to a complex network of rates and
orders for currencies and to a frantic attempt to marry one

48

transaction against another. A dealer in London wanting to buy dollars for a client in Liverpool may find the rate temporarily cheaper in one centre than another, but equally discovers that the amounts involved do not tally. He is pushed into other calls to tidy up the first. Meanwhile rates are still on the move. If he wastes time his client will suffer; if he clinches a deal too soon he may regret it. Time is money in a foreign exchange dealer's room as nowhere else in the City. Some of the flavour of such a room and of the dilemmas faced there are brought out in the following description by a foreign exchange dealer:[1]

'Calls from customers, calls from foreign banks overseas, calls from the brokers. Some merely seeking information, some seeking rates on which to base their day's work. There will be calls from Paris, Amsterdam, Copenhagen, Brussels, Hamburg and many other financial centres. Some with genuine propositions, some hoping for an advantageous quotation somewhere in the list . . . The babel rises a few decibels as the linguists join the chorus. Rates are being quoted in French, Italian and probably German. Each operator will be dealing with the requirements of his own particular caller, whilst keeping his ear cocked to any possible changes in rates by his colleagues as they effect their deals and look for a covering operation elsewhere . . . The textbooks discourse widely and wisely on spot rates and forward rates. They delve deeply into the mysteries of arbitrage. Unfortunately, especially when dealing with exchange for a forward delivery, it rarely works that way. When one wants to buy dollars for, say, three months' delivery, one finds the broker offers in lieu some two months or some six months, or he cannot offer the outright date, but can offer the swap. What shall one do! Will one of the propositions fit the book? Many questions flit through the dealer's mind. Try another broker? But the first will already have scented blood and be out scouring the market for a chance to close up a deal. To put someone else in will accentuate the effect. Take him off? He might see the opportunity to deal and go elsewhere. Try Paris? They will read a change in the market and be nipping back on another line and clobber the market under one's nose. Try Germany? Might work against marks. Can the mark dealer help? Has he something on his books which will help the arbitrage price. Questions and answers are flitting through the dealer's brain and he alone must find the answer.

[1] Jack R. Higgins in a symposium, *A Day in the Life of a Banker*, published by the Institute of Bankers, 1963.

Meanwhile he is probably dealing with a fractious importer who is demanding last night's closing price as shown in *The Times* for $27.53 drawn on Milwaukee, Wis.'

It was not always so. Only since the 1914-18 war, when it left the Royal Exchange, has the foreign exchange market been made up of brokers and authorised dealers linked together by telephone. Before the turn of the century it was the custom for the heads of the larger firms of merchant banks to meet on the Royal Exchange twice a week to decide among themselves 'the rates which ruled exchange and credit between the the various monetary centres'.[1] This top-hatted meeting continued up to the First World War, but by the Edwardian period the influx of foreign banks and the switching of merchant banking interest to foreign government issues and bigger things had already attracted a growing part of the foreign colony in the City into this exchange business. After the war the improvement in communications, the need to cover transactions in the forward market because of the political (and economic) uncertainty, led to a natural expansion in the work of the foreign exchange market. Its work broadened and deepened, bringing into its orbit most of the banks that had hitherto held aloof. By the end of the 1930s, in spite of (or perhaps even because of) the successive devaluations and currency disturbances, there were over 140 banks and large firms authorised to deal in foreign exchange and 30 brokers acting in the customary role as intermediaries.

Post-war restrictions

During and for some time after the Second World War dealings were restricted. *Every* foreign exchange transaction had to be covered with the Bank of England at the official rates of exchange and a commission charged to the customer. The first post-war change came when banks were allowed to carry their day's dealings and buy or sell the balance with the Bank of England at the end of the day. Finally, in December 1951, a limited market was re-opened. The margins between which foreign currencies could be exchanged were widened, and forward dealings were also freed from control. Business in the American and Canadian dollars and in the main European currencies began to increase. But the main step forward was made on 18 May, 1953, when arbitrage dealings within the

[1] M. T. Powell, *op. cit.*

European Payments Union were introduced. From that date it was possible to buy, say, Dutch guilders in Paris or Belgian francs in Amsterdam. In short, European currencies could be bought in the cheapest market. The following year the gold market was re-opened and the transferable sterling account system was broadened considerably. This was a further move towards the wider use of sterling. If France, for example, sold goods in the sterling area, she received transferable sterling in return which she could spend anywhere in the transferable account area. By this time the area covered most of the non-dollar world. And it was not long before the Bank of England was forced to intervene in the main centres where this brand of sterling was quoted and dealt in abroad—mainly Zurich and New York. Because of these overseas markets it was possible to convert transferable sterling into dollars (still a hard currency at that time)—at a price. At times the price (i.e. the discount on transferable sterling in exchange for dollars) was extremely high. But from the spring of 1955, the Bank of England stopped the rate from falling too far. This was to prevent so-called 'commodity shunting' operations. Thus holders of these types of pounds were assured of convertibility into dollars at a rate only slightly below the official dollar-sterling rate in London. As a result the turnover in transferable pounds in Zurich, New York and other centres expanded considerably. In some quarters an annual turnover of at least £1,000 million was estimated to be taking place outside the London market.

Convertibility restored

This situation hardly suited anyone. The foreign holder of transferable pounds still did not have the full assurance that convertibility would give. The monetary authorities in London had the difficult job of keeping the sterling rate in these financial centres not too far removed from the official rate. And the City of London could see foreign dealers taking business that could otherwise be dealt with in London. The pressure on sterling at the time of the Suez crisis and the continuing weakness of the pound in the following autumn delayed further official moves. But by the end of 1958, the authorities were prepared for the next step forward; this time an extremely large stride into the world of convertibility. Taking courage from the Gaullist election successes and the growing determination in Paris to set France's economic and financial house in order, Britain approached France and Germany with a positive plan to extend full external convertibility to all the leading European currencies at the end of the year. As a result of close consultation with other members of the Organisation for European Economic Co-operation, the final plan was announced just after the Christmas holiday. From 9 a.m. on 29 December, 1958, sterling held by people outside the sterling area became freely convertible into gold or any other currency, including the dollar. Similar moves were made by France, Germany, Belgium, Luxembourg, Holland, Italy, Denmark and Sweden.

The wider results of all this need not concern us at this stage. But these moves had immediate and direct implications for the City's foreign exchange market. Technically the so-called transferable account sterling and American account sterling were merged into one type of external sterling. This meant that holders of transferable sterling were henceforth able to switch it into dollars (or any other currency) at the official rate *and in London*. Thus at one throw the business previously done in foreign markets was transferred back to the City. It had other side effects in the gold market. Previously some gold transactions had been attracted to Zurich because of the better sterling rate in the transferable sterling market. Once it disappeared, some of the bullion deals moved back to London too. These technical changes were quickly reflected in the London market. Almost overnight the dollar-sterling exchange rate became the main hinge of the foreign exchange markets of the world and, as a result, transactions between the dollar and several European currencies, which had previously been passed to Continental centres, were channelled through London. And the larger the volume of transactions switched to London, the deeper the whole market became and the smaller the fluctuations. This development in turn attracted still more business.

The onset of full external convertibility for the leading currencies of Europe, which thus joined forces with the dollar for the first time since the war, was a major turning point. Only now is it possible to see just how big. Although investors, traders and business men had been able to switch money freely (and reasonably safely) round the world before, the added protection of official convertibility (coupled with the full economic revival of Europe which had made it possible) led to a fresh upsurge in financial transactions across frontiers. Industrial corporations were given more confidence in switching money from one country to another. The European capital market, which had closed its doors in the setbacks of the early 1930s, gradually began to re-open them. The start of the Common Market within a matter of three days of the announcement of convertibility also brought more incentive to move capital towards Europe. Money began to flow more freely again. Industrial corporations, relieved of the old anxieties of devaluations, began to work out how to use their foreign exchange holdings to best advantage. Where was the best place to invest? Where was the cheapest place to borrow? Some leading American firms opened up their own exchange departments. The oil companies became as well informed about currency problems as about the sources of new oil. It paid them to do so. The result was a massive increase in the movement of short-term money across frontiers, with interest rates acting as larger magnets than currency fears. For the authorities, as we shall see in Chapter 11, this led to the need to build up new and stronger defences round the major currencies. For the London foreign exchange market it meant far more business. London soon moved into the lead as the biggest foreign exchange market in the world and, according to some American estimates, New York replaced Zurich in second place.

The Euro-dollar market

The continued dominance of London has been admirably illustrated by the remarkable development of the so-called Euro-dollar market. This phenomenon, in which foreign currency deposits are put to use in countries other than their country of origin,[1] has mainly appeared on the scene since the return to convertibility in 1958. But there were signs of it a year or two earlier. It is, of course, a misnomer. The currencies concerned are neither confined to Europe nor confined to dollars. In effect an international money market has grown up, mainly centred on London, and parallel to the domestic money markets still under the strict control of the individual monetary authorities. Encouraged by the growing faith in currencies and by the increased freedom from exchange regulations, London banks began to accept foreign, mainly dollar, deposits in order to provide dollar loans to finance overseas

---

[1] E.g., a Frenchman, who has earned dollars from selling goods to the United States, may decide to deposit them in London. He may want dollars for future transactions in a few months time and, in the meanwhile, gets a good rate of interest from a London bank. The banks in London are enabled to offer good rates of interest because of their ability to invest money quickly.

trade following the ban on sterling finance late in 1957. Soon, given a remarkable new impetus by the onset of convertibility, London banks were restoring the business of re-lending foreign deposits which had been active in the late 1920s and had come to an end in 1931. But the two factors that led to the real upsurge in the Euro-dollar market were the stultifying effects of American banking legislation (primarily Regulation Q) and the continuing deficit in the United States balance of payments from 1958 onwards.

Regulation Q limited the rate of interest that American banks could pay on deposit (no interest on deposits for less than 30 days; no more than 1 per cent on time deposits of between 30 and 90 days; and, until the summer of 1963, a maximum rate on time deposits of between 90 days and six months of $2\frac{1}{2}$ per cent). Since, at the same time, American lending rates were maintained at a high level, this wide margin provided London banks with ample scope for attracting business. As the Bank of England put it:[1]

'Banks in London have been able to attract large sums in dollars by quoting better rates for deposits, including interest on money at call and short notice—categories which earn nothing at all with New York banks—and have employed them at less than the US lending rate and still made a worthwhile turn. They are able to operate on a fairly small profit margin because the additional overhead expenses of conducting their Euro-dollar activities are minimal.'

Since surplus dollars were being supplied by the continuing deficit in the American balance of payments, the market was able to grow rapidly. The Bank for International Settlements puts the whole Euro-currency market at about $7,000 million, of which some $5,000 million are in dollars. Squaring this with the Bank of England's own estimates of London's role in the market—£1,300 million equivalent to $3,600 million —suggests that London banks account for just over one-half of the market. Because of the double counting almost inevitable in working out these deposit figures, it is almost impossible to be accurate, but it is unlikely that the orders of magnitude are far out. What is remarkable is how fast and steeply the foreign deposits of the London banks have risen in recent years. Between 1955 and 1957 foreign currency deposits rose from

[1] *Quarterly Bulletin*, June 1964.

£55 million ($154 million) to only £70 million ($196 million). By March 1964 they had jumped to no less than £1,300 million ($3,600 million). Of this £1,100 million ($3,080 million) was in dollars. The balance of £200 million ($560 million) was made up mainly of Swiss francs and Deutschemarks, no doubt reflecting the policy of both Switzerland and Western Germany in deliberately discouraging an inflow of foreign funds by paying no interest to foreigners. Only a small part of these vast currency deposits with the London banks has been switched into sterling and lent to hire purchase finance firms and local authorities. The bulk has been re-lent abroad. Thus dollars accepted on deposit by London acceptance houses and overseas banks have either been re-lent as dollars to gain a margin on interest differentials or switched into some other currency on a 'swap' basis still yielding a useful margin. As the Bank of England once remarked:[1]

'London banks especially the accepting houses and overseas banks with their wide overseas connections and long experience of international business, are well equipped to play an active part in this market.'

It added that the number of banks involved was in the region of 130 (virtually the whole of the foreign exchange market), though the bulk of the business was in the hands of about 40 of them.

The real post-war turning point for the foreign exchange market came in 1958 with convertibility. It brought more freedom and confidence. Even the problems that these changes brought for the authorities—the need to offset big movements of short-term funds—produced solutions that in turn added still further to confidence. The growing signs of central banking co-operation, which we shall examine in more detail in Chapter 11 gradually took some of the bad elements out of the exchange market. Just as the central banks have managed to remove most of the speculative fever from the bullion market, they have considerably reduced that in the exchange markets. The more uniform changes in interest rates, coupled with the improved means of communication, have also reduced the margins for arbitrage. Yet the increasing soundness of the market has encouraged a remarkable expansion in exchange business in general. As turnover has increased, competition between centres

[1] *Quarterly Bulletin*, June 1964.

and certainly between dealers has also increased, cutting down profit margins still more. London, with its expertise, its reliance on sterling, its ability to make use of short-term deposits overnight, and (an important influence in exchange markets working round the world and round the clock) with the time factor in its favour (New York is active when most of its clients in Europe are asleep), has more than maintained its pre-eminence. The main obstacles to the further development of the London exchange market largely remain what they always were: exchange control in all its forms; any weakening of the dollar and the pound; and any loss of confidence in currencies generally.

CHAPTER 4

. . . AND GOLD

THE RE-OPENING of the gold market at 10.30 a.m. on Monday, 22 March, 1954 marked the first step in the attempt to re-establish London as the world's leading bullion centre. When the representatives of six bullion houses met at Rothschild's in New Court that morning, after an interval of fifteen years, it was expected that the revival of London as a gold centre would be a long process. Sterling was still not freely convertible into dollars or gold, and a sizeable proportion of Commonwealth production was being sold on other free gold markets throughout the world. Yet within eighteen months the Bank of England's chief aim had been achieved. In its first full calendar year of operation, 1955, no less than 85 per cent of all the fresh supplies of gold coming on to the free markets of the world had been handled in London. Recently the Bank of England said simply: 'London is the largest and most important gold market in the world.'[1]

London's rivals come in all sizes, from the exotic to the industrious—from Macao and Hong Kong to Zurich and Paris. Some are little more than black markets (like Bombay), some feeding the appetites of Far and Middle Eastern investors (Beirut, Kuwait, Bahrain, Cairo, Saigon, Bangkok), some simply domestic markets (Paris). All of them provided an outlet for surplus gold supplies and a focal point for hoarding demand while the London market remained closed between 1939 and 1954. None of them could keep the level of turnover they had formerly had once London dealers appeared on the scene. Many of these markets had fed on the continuing urge of many people after the war to hedge against the declining value of currencies, to switch money from one area to another, and to avoid currency controls. The physical movement of gold was often the prime transaction in these operations, most of

[1] *Quarterly Bulletin*, March 1964.

them, when not through London, being channelled through Zurich, Beirut, Tangier or Hong Kong. Once London re-opened, these centres (apart from Tangier which eventually changed its international status) lost much of their business, but continued to act as feeding agents, tending to pass on local demand for gold to the London market.

The demand for gold

Although gold currency has not been in general circulation since 1914, gold coins and small gold bars are still in demand in many parts of the world by private buyers, largely for hoarding but also as a way of keeping liquid resources. This, of course, covers a variety of purposes and raises the perennial question of why people buy gold at all. Is it due to a fear of currency devaluation, a foolproof way of saving—or simply pure avarice brought to a head by the yellow metal? In the East gold is a normal method of saving as well as a generally accepted token of wealth, both in clothing and ornaments. But one need not go so far afield to see gold being hoarded on a large scale as a normal method of saving. Just across the Channel the French peasant has long been used to putting his gold coins or small bars beneath his bed; and the Paris gold market openly caters for this demand.

Apart from the industrial demand for gold from jewellers, the other main buying strength derives from central banks. Gold is still one of the main media of settling international debts as well as being one of the chief ways in which a government keeps its monetary reserve. Thus a central bank will sometimes want to exchange gold for foreign exchange, or vice-versa. Central banks, acting on behalf of their governments, at one time dealt in gold with the Federal Reserve authorities in New York, or with the International Monetary Fund in Washington or the Bank for International Settlements in Basle. After 1954 these transactions were invariably on the London market. Because of its broad turnover and world-wide contacts, London quickly brought a stability to gold prices not seen on other centres—another reason why central banks found it convenient to do business in the City, quite apart from the avoidance of costs. In the past three years yet another shift in central bank business has taken place.[1]

[1] See Chapter 11.

. . . And the supply

A market, however, involves a two-way traffic. Supplies are needed as well as a regular demand. And it was here that London scored, for it was the natural centre for the sales of fresh gold from the Commonwealth countries, as they all were then. The Bank of England, for example, acts as agent for the South African Reserve Bank, the central bank of the world's largest producer of gold. Australian, West African and Canadian supplies also find their way to the London market, as do the periodic sales of the Soviet Union, the world's second largest gold producer. The Republic of South Africa and the British Commonwealth account for 88 per cent of the world's new gold supplies, excluding the USSR. And Russian sales in recent years have been remarkably high. The Soviet Union has for years deliberately sold gold in order to balance her payments deficit with the West. Her 1963-64 wheat crisis forced her to sell even larger quantities on Western gold markets. The annual average of Russian gold sales over the last eight years is estimated[1] at £90 million. In 1963 alone the figure is estimated at £180 million. At one period, after selling the bulk of their gold in London, the Russians made an attempt to sell in a variety of Continental centres, such as Paris and Zurich. But they finally returned to London when it was realised that most of the gold eventually found its way to the London market.

London's dominance and the goldsmiths

The London market can be said to depend on the regular supplies flowing to its dealers. Yet this was not the reason for its original dominance well over a century and a half ago. The goldsmiths were the forerunners of the modern banking system and it was natural for any financial centre to have a market in gold. Appropriately one of the present member-firms of the market was established even before the Bank of England. Mocatta and Goldsmid was founded in 1684, a full decade before the Bank of England was given its Royal Charter. Yet, as in many other parts of the City, it was not until after the Napoleonic wars that London began to lead in the provision of a market for gold as well as credit. The gold discoveries of the later 19th century, which can be said to have oiled the wheels of the industrial revolution at a crucial point as well as the large expansions in international trade which followed it,

[1] *Annual Bullion Review,* Samuel Montagu & Co., 1963.

enhanced London's dominance. This was particularly true of the South African and Australian discoveries, which found their natural outlet on the London market.

The biggest blow came in 1939, when the market closed its doors for fifteen years. The dealing firms themselves were not entirely inactive, in spite of the complete closure of the market, for they were authorised to deal elsewhere. By 1952, for example, those specified had been given permission to act as agents to sell Commonwealth gold for dollars outside the sterling area. Although they could not act as principals in these markets, the arrangements enabled them to keep in touch with the free gold markets abroad. This experience was invaluable once the London market re-opened a few years later. By that time the feverish heights reached by the free gold price after the Korean war had subsided and sterling itself was regaining its strength.

There were inevitable changes when the market re-opened in 1954, compared with the pre-war arrangements. Then sterling area residents had free access to the market. By the middle 1950s they were severely limited by the exchange controls still protecting the pound. Moreover for the first four years after 1954 non-residents using the gold market had to pay with special sterling called 'registered sterling'. It was a way of keeping the market open and at the same time maintaining a closed circuit of gold and American dollars in order to protect the pound. The non-convertibility of sterling (which disappeared at the end of 1958) was not allowed to hold up the establishment of the London market. When the pound became fully convertible in December 1958 the opportunities for expanding the gold market were considerably increased. Continental currency business which, because of the inconvertibility of the pound, had had to take place in overseas markets such as Zurich and New York, was switched bank to London. Bullion business came with it. The ability of the London bullion dealers helped too. As Mr. Julien-Pierre Koszul, then Directeur-General of the Foreign Services of the Bank of France, explained in a recent article,[1]

'The British banks very quickly and efficiently won back the international gold market from the Swiss when the London market was re-opened in 1954. The British . . . acted straight-forwardly and decisively; whether buying or selling, they

[1] *Opera Mundi Europe*, 21, 1964.

dealt on margins deliberately smaller than those of the Swiss banks and thus recaptured this market by direct competition.'

London's exceptional service takes three main forms. It maintains a relatively stable price, keeping quotations within a fairly narrow range. It can absorb large quantities of gold because of its world-wide contacts. It offers the cheapest commission rates available. Even when gold is offered in other centres it is noticeable that part of the supplies are often resold by dealers to the London market. The narrowness of its rates is quite distinctive. Quotations are fixed in shillings and pence per troy ounce, and even down to farthing fractions. These clearly leave narrow margins to the five firms[1] that now make up the market. Competition has forced others out of business.

For a time after the re-opening in 1954 turnover rose continuously, particularly the business of the major central banks. By 1956, according to Samuel Montagu and Company,[2] activity of central banks accounted for about one-third of the total turnover in London and by 1957 it had reached over one-half. This expansion, especially from European central banks, arose because within the European Payments Union (which provided a monthly clearing of payments among member countries) individual countries had to settle a proportion of their deficits (in later years 75 per cent) in gold valued at $35 an ounce. As soon as the London gold price fell below the $35 level, it paid central banks to acquire in London the gold needed to meet their EPU commitments. Thus countries in deficit in EPU tended to come to the London market and even those running surpluses found it worth while to sell their surplus gold. Even at that time London offered attractive enough rates to persuade central banks wanting to switch part of their reserves from gold to currencies or vice-versa to use the City's

---

[1] *Bank of England Quarterly Bulletin*, March, 1964: 'There are at present five members of the London gold market: Johnson, Matthey and Co., Mocatia and Goldsmid, Samuel Montagu and Co., N. M. Rothschild and Sons, Sharps, Pixley and Co. Two (Montagus and Rothschilds) are merchant banks, one (Mocattas) is wholly owned by a merchant bank, one (Sharps, Pixley) is a pure broker, and the fifth (Johnson, Matthey) is a metallurgical firm of international repute. Two of the members (Johnson, Matthey and Rothschilds) melt, refine, assay and process gold. Rothschilds act as chairman of the market and have done so since the market was constituted in its present form after the First World War and the daily gold price fixing takes place on their premises.'

[2] *Annual Bullion Review*, 1956 and 1957.

facilities. Once the EPU business came to an end, following the onset of convertibility, this other business grew in volume.

Central banks and the gold price

Convertibility, however, also brought its difficulties. We shall be looking more closely at the currency implications in Chapters 10 and 11. But the growing freedom to move money around the world, the parallel strengthening of the European currencies and the weakening of the dollar brought new dangers for central banks to cope with. The dollar came under renewed suspicion throughout 1960, with the United States payments deficit widening and doubts growing as the Presidential election approached in November. Demand for gold began to expand. Suddenly tension increased, pushing the London gold price up from $35 to $35.35 and then finally up to $40 a fine ounce. Strong action was required. The Bank of England, which had always intervened in the London market either on its own account (as manager of the UK Exchange Equalisation Account) or on behalf of others (as selling agent for the South African Reserve Bank or as buying or selling agent for other central banks), moved into the market with large selling orders on behalf of the United States monetary authorities. These official gold sales steadied the market and brought the price down. More important, it was the start of central bank co-operation in controlling the gold market. Soon the central banks realised that it was up to them to order their business in concert, and that, because they could always buy gold from the US Federal Reserve authorities in New York at $35 an ounce plus shipping and handling charges, they need not buy over a certain level in London.[1]

This first intervention was highly successful and the absence of central banks from the London market above a certain price level helped to stabilise the market. But by the autumn of the following year, pressures were building up again, both political and financial. The threat was a double one: either the gold price was bound to be pushed upwards, thus bringing

[1] Since 1935 the US has stood ready to provide gold for dollars to official holders (governments and central banks) at a rate of $35 an ounce. This has been the main link between gold and currencies. But the gold price (in terms of dollars) fluctuates on the free gold markets. Thus central banks used the London market when the price suited them rather than conduct the transaction direct with the US authorities. Equally, if the London price went too high it paid them to go direct to New York even allowing for the extra cost of shipping it abroad.

on yet another wave of speculation, or the pressure would fall on the American gold stocks in New York. As a result, the central banks began to realise that further, combined action would be necessary. In October 1961 the American authorities proposed an informal arrangement to share the burden of official intervention in the London market. It was the start of what was to become known as the gold pool. The central banks of Belgium, France, Italy, the Netherlands, Switzerland, Western Germany and Britain agreed to co-operate with the US Federal Reserve Bank of New York in a sales consortium, to be run by the Bank of England. Quotas were agreed and the Bank of England was enabled to draw supplies of gold from members in order to intervene in the market. The Americans put up half the supplies. To see whether the new machinery would work, the Bank of England used some of the gold to support the market price. Thus the gold pool had an initial trial run and was then kept for further action later.

Soon the problem seemed to be turning upside down. By 1962 the pressure was downward on the gold price and the Americans naturally suggested co-operation among the central banks to buy gold from the market. This they did, through the Bank of England. Their purchases reached $80 million at one point. Yet within a further three months, by the late summer of 1962, the market had reversed itself again, forcing the central banks to use the whole of their accumulated purchases to damp down the price again. By the end of September, they had followed up the $80 million with an additional $50 million of their own. Yet by the end of the year another change of trend had occurred, eventually leaving the central banks all square. The year 1963, however, saw a growing need to absorb gold from the market again and led to a remarkable share-out among the central banks amounting to some $600 million. In short, the gold pool now stands ready to intervene both ways. It is a selling consortium and a buying syndicate combined.

The effects of the gold pool

We shall be considering the stabilising influences of these co-operative efforts on the West's monetary structure in Chapter 11. Here it is important to note how they have affected the operations of the gold market itself. The major change is that central bank buying has virtually vanished from the scene. The European central banks, for example, which used to be extremely active in London, now tend to channel their business through the gold pool. Some of the central banks outside the official gold pool continue to use the market, of course, but some estimates put the fall in central bank business at over 75 per cent. The gold dealers have naturally missed the turnover. Moreover, to the extent that the activities of the gold pool have been successful in damping down speculation in the gold market, total turnover has been depressed too.

Against this has to be set one important item of progress. The establishment of the gold pool has at last given the London market the official approval of the American authorities. This is a major step forward, for the Americans never failed to show their opposition to the existence of the London gold market whenever the value of the dollar in terms of gold shown there was not to their liking. They saw no reason to have a market in gold and were against what was reflected in it. The opposition reached its climax at the annual meeting of the International Monetary Fund in Vienna in September 1961, when the American delegation informally suggested the closing down of the London gold market as one of the ways of defending the dollar. What went on behind closed doors at Vienna has still to be revealed, but the stiff resistance of the Bank of England to these American suggestions proved highly successful. Rumblings continued for some months, occasionally supported by some European central bank governors, but London's gold dealers were soon to be breathing more easily again. Following the success of the gold pool in stamping out gold speculation, this threat to the London market has vanished.

CHAPTER 5

THE INSURANCE MARKET

LONDON still runs the largest international insurance market in the world. New York does a larger volume of business, but the bulk of it is domestic, and a vast volume of re-insurance business is passed every year from New York to London. In 1963 alone American companies re-insured $241 million of their business in the London market, compared with $68 million in all other international markets. This international flavour, the London market's outstanding feature, is illustrated both by the world-wide risks it insures and by the large foreign income.

British companies[1] are estimated, for example, to pay out £1,000 a minute all over the world in fire, accident and marine claims. Hardly a disaster hits anywhere but London becomes involved directly or indirectly. The riots in Georgetown, British Guiana, in 1962, led to insurance payments of some £2.4 million, of which well over half was borne by the British insurance market. Much the same happened when Hurricane 'Flora' inflicted widespread damage on Tobago, Jamaica and Haiti in 1963, about £1 million of the £2½ million insurance claim falling on London. Similarly in 1961, when Hurricane 'Carla' ripped across Texas and Louisiana leaving damage estimated at $100 million, British insurance firms were heavily involved. They also paid out the biggest claims following the fire which swept through a sugar terminal at Townsville, Australia, causing £4.5 million worth of damage.

The framework

To many people the London insurance market is synonymous with Lloyd's; hardly surprising, perhaps, in view of its world-wide reputation. Yet Lloyd's is only one part of the whole

---

[1] The insurance companies are divided into mutual companies run on behalf of policy-holders, and companies controlled and owned by shareholders. The former are non-profit-making organisations.

65

market, which is basically made up of (1) insurance companies, (2) Lloyd's underwriters, and (3) insurance brokers. Of some 300 British insurance companies and 'mutual' organisations, roughly a third take on international business. Although a few have head offices outside London (in Liverpool, Edinburgh, Perth, Norwich, etc.) most of them maintain large offices in London. They do foreign business in two ways. Some have established subsidiaries, branches or agencies in overseas territories. Others simply take on foreign business in London. Lloyd's underwriters do all their business on the spot in London.[1] Another difference between the companies and Lloyd's is their use of insurance brokers. While Lloyd's underwriters accept business solely from Lloyd's brokers and have no direct contact with the general public, the insurance companies do both, though often preferring to deal directly with clients. The following figures help to put the respective capacities of the companies and Lloyd's in perspective. The insurance companies received a premium income of some £2,090 million in 1963, comprising £980 million life business, £326 million fire, £690 million accident and £94 million marine. The total premium income of Lloyd's underwriters in 1961[2] (the latest year for which accounts have been completed) amounted to no more than £346 million. Finally, to complete the picture of the market, London is the home of some 220 branches and subsidiaries of foreign insurance companies.

This is the simple framework of the market. What sort of foreign business does it do? Its total premium income is some £2,400 million a year, taking the companies and Lloyd's together. But the picture becomes a little blurred when this

---

[1] The Corporation of Lloyd's provides simply the premises, shipping intelligence and other facilities for individuals to undertake insurance business on their own behalf. The 5,000 members are formed into some 300 marine, motor, aviation and non-marine syndicates of different sizes. A recent chairman of Lloyd's (Mr. P. W. Milligan in 1962) described the essential characteristics of the underwriters in these terms: 'Lloyd's underwriters are often in the headlines for their willingness to "have a go" at the unusual risks, whether the cover be against holing in one, being hit by a straying satellite, or the drowning of a mechanical whale. This type of risk is, of course, very much of a sideline to the main volume of business, but it is indicative of the individuality of the market and it provides the reason why a great many risks of a much more important nature—burglary insurance and loss of profits from fire to name but two—have been pioneered at Lloyd's before becoming the general practice elsewhere.'
[2] The delay in publishing final figures for Lloyd's is due to the practice of Lloyd's syndicates of waiting three years before closing a year's accounts.

total has to be split between home and overseas. Several proportions have been mentioned from time to time.The chairman of the British Insurance Association has stated that roughly one-half of the insurance companies' total business originates abroad. The share of life business is known accurately year by year (it was 12 per cent in 1963). But the amount of fire, accident and marine business arising overseas is less well known, a figure of 70 per cent usually being assumed. Lloyd's have never given figures of their overseas business, but a similar figure of 70 per cent is unlikely to be far out. The dominance of the insurance stake in the United States has never been questioned. As a recent chairman of the British Insurance Association calculated, it is possible that nearly one-half of Britain's investment interest in the United States is represented by British insurance.[1]

Reasons for success abroad

All this is enough to establish the importance of the insurance market's foreign dominance. It can be seen in other ways: Lloyd's immediately conjures up a vision of 'having a go' and taking on risks that others would hardly dream of considering; when new risks appear on the world scene (such as nuclear plants), it is the London market that provides the basic lead for new contracts and rates. It is essential to understand this readiness to cover new risks and to ask whether it can continue. What in fact is the basis of the London market's growing business? How has it managed to achieve the flexibility on which much of its business depends? Historically, of course, both Lloyd's and the individual insurance companies were ahead of their competitors overseas in so many insurance activities. Given the obvious opportunities that flowed from London's activities as a world trading centre and, equally important, the economic stability that went with them, the London market was fortunately free from many of the legal and financial restrictions that have continued to dog so many of its rivals. Individual incidents, such as the prompt (and large) payments following the San Francisco earthquake and

[1] The late Sir Charles Trustam, in his annual report of the BIA in 1959: 'The US Department of Commerce recently valued British investment interest (in the US) at $1,900 million. Against that total I estimate that the intrinsic worth of British insurance in the US is of the order of $850 million. Policyholders' surplus alone amounts to approximately $600 million and it would not, I think, be over-optimistic to estimate a further $250 million as the value of the equity in reserve.'

fire, consolidated reputations. This domestic freedom naturally enabled London insurers to trim their risks according to their judgement, to invest in ways which suited them best and to spread the risks round the world. Stability at home enabled them to avoid the strict supervision (on investments as well as business) that insurance firms have faced in other countries. As one member of the market once put it,[1] the essential features of the London market are freedom from detailed control and freedom of contract. He went on:

'Not only have the limitations on establishment in this country been reduced to a minimum, but in most classes insurers are free to charge the premium they judge to be appropriate for each risk and to offer cover in terms and subject to conditions which they regard as desirable. The other side to this is, of course, that the proposer is free to accept or reject the policy offered to him, and to seek alternative quotations and conditions in a competitive market . . . By the same token the insurer is free to raise capital and to invest funds and reserves in whatever manner he judges will best promote the security and profit of his policyholders and, in the case of a company, of its shareholders. That his accounts comply with the requirements of the Companies Act has to be certified by Auditors, but there is no detailed governmental supervision . . . These basic freedoms . . . have produced at the same time stability and flexibility, security, and continual development of new forms of insurance to meet new needs.'

Nationalisation and restriction

This description has been quoted at some length to show where the main threat must now be sought: in all the developments abroad that are leading, for one reason or another, to restrictions on the operations and investments of London insurers. They are coming in various forms. Some countries no longer allow their traders to get insurance cover in competitive markets abroad. Some have laid down legal restrictions on the maintenance of guarantee deposits or technical reserves. Others have appropriated foreign insurance business outright. One or two have accomplished the same by setting up state insurance corporations with special privileges.

The outright nationalisation (with or without compensation)

[1] Mr. C. G. W. Whibley in a paper to the Charter Celebration Conference, London, July 1962.

TABLE III
NATIONALISATION OF INSURANCE ABROAD

A. Before 1956:

Year	Country	Class of insurance nationalized	Compensation
1911	USSR	All	—
1921	Costa Rica	All	—
1924	Uruguay	All	A state monopoly of insurance, exercised by the Banco de Seguros del Estado, was introduced in 1911. However, companies irrespective of nationality then operating were allowed to continue to write the class of business they were then writing, fire and marine. This situation has continued with the result that the 'State Bank' has a practically complete monopoly in Accident and possibly life business. In Riot insurance, Riot Material Damage is a monopoly of the State Bank.
	China	All	One state-owned company and two joint state-private companies.
	Bulgaria, Roumania, Poland, Yugoslavia, Hungary, Czechoslovakia	All	All post-war.

B. Since 1956:

Year	Country	Class of insurance nationalized	Compensation
1956	India	Life	By agreement with Indian Government compensation was based on 20 years purchase of the share of the surplus allocated to shareholders, subject to a limit that the shareholders' allocation brought into account should not exceed 5% of the valuation surplus — the surplus being that determined on the results of actuarial valuations carried out by the company prior to the nationalisation.
1956	Egypt	All	By agreement between the Egyptian and British Governments a sum of £27½m was allocated as compensation to British nationals (companies and individuals) who lost property in Egypt. Claims have been met from this sum and we know that insurance companies, claims have included a 'goodwill' element.
1961	Syria	All	British insurers received no compensation.
1956	Ceylon	Life (new business)	
1964	Ceylon	General	The Ceylon Government has indicated that it does not propose to pay compensation to insurers. British insurers maintain they are entitled in respect of general business to receive compensation in respect of such features as loss of goodwill, obligations to staffs, expenses incurred in servicing existing contracts, losses on fixed assets. The matter is under consideration.
1963	Burma	Life	—
1964	Burma	General	—

of foreign insurance business has had the immediate effect of narrowing down the world-wide flexibility on which the London market has been developed. As Table III shows, insurance was in state hands in Costa Rica and Uruguay as well as the Soviet bloc countries well before the more recent round of expropriations began. In the past eight years the process has been extended to India (life insurance, *with* compensation), Egypt, Syria, Ceylon (life first, later extended to all forms, *without* compensation) and Burma (life in 1963, now extended to all forms of insurance).

Although several newly independent nations have been the worst offenders, legal restrictions even in Europe can hardly be regarded favourably by London insurers grown used to the basic freedoms in investment policy. The prospect of becoming a full member of the European Economic Community was unlikely to be relished by many London insurance firms, and throughout 1961 and 1962 much heart-burning went on in the Square Mile at the thought of what legal restrictions might have to be swallowed in the wider cause of joining Europe. The restrictions largely concern the maintenance of guarantee deposits and the establishment of technical reserves. In some cases there are the added complications of discrimination between domestic and foreign insurers. Add to all this the different structures of the individual capital markets and it becomes clear (as it did when Britain's application was still under discussion in Brussels) that any closer links with the Continent are going to be difficult in the extreme. Either Britain would have to consider introducing similar regulations and restrictions of her own or, the more likely and wiser solution, the London market would maintain its customary freedom but assume that the market on its doorstep was unlikely to give it much more scope for expansion. Now that any closer link with Europe is postponed for the moment, the problem of how to resolve the dilemma has receded and London can enjoy its flexibility alone. But the European market, as a source of business for London, remains problematic. As one leading insurance man summed up the position in private:

'The European market doesn't matter to us. There are few profits to be made. The French market has been disappointing for some time. Belgium and Italy have deteriorated. Holland has been good but is now getting worse. Norway and Sweden have always been a little difficult.'

What has happened in Europe is symptomatic of what is deterring the London market more generally elsewhere in the world. The reasons for restrictive, perhaps protective, legislation vary (economic instability, destructive competition among domestic insurance firms, sometimes a misguided determination to protect policyholders, etc.); yet the form of the legislation has tended to follow a simple pattern. Most countries lay down rules compelling insurance companies to set up reserves to cover their liabilities and often stating specifically what sort of investments they should consist of. A few of the smaller colonial territories such as Malta, Gibraltar, etc., and the newly independent British territories such as Ghana and Nigeria have followed the British practice of having no deposit or reserve requirements, relying simply on each company showing that it is solvent. But they are tending to be the exception. Reserve requirements are now widespread. Most insist on an initial fixed deposit either for each separate class of insurance or for all combined. In addition technical reserves[1] usually have to be covered as well. Countries have different combinations. Some such as Australia, Norway, Israel and Sweden only have fixed deposits; others like South Africa, Chile and Morocco insist on technical reserves; others again allow the initial fixed deposit to count towards the technical reserves.

These fixed deposits are very often restricted to cash, government or semi-government stocks, and many countries insist on at least a proportion of the technical reserves being covered in a similar way. Most allow a certain proportion of the reserves to be covered by such things as Ordinary shares, real estate and mortgages, etc., although in one or two territories the percentages allowed are abnormally low. In Germany, for example, London insurance companies cannot invest in Ordinary shares to cover technical reserves, whereas in the United States life companies are restricted to having only 5 per cent of their assets in common stock.

Many of these restrictions may appear marginal. In total they have a marked effect on the operations of the London market, for its ability to take risks depends on its ability to pay quickly and promptly and this, in turn, depends on its ability to switch money round the world as quickly and easily as possible. The compulsory maintenance of deposits or reserves

[1] These are either unexpired risks reserves (often between 40 and 60 per cent of premiums, though there are variations) or outstanding claims reserves.

impedes London insurance companies' freedom to centralise their reserves. The companies would be the first to admit that they would not want to add currency risks to underwriting risks and to recognise the case for matching assets and liabilities in the same currency. Yet they must be prepared to mobilise their reserves to meet exceptional needs following major disasters anywhere in the world. The compulsory retention of funds (or even a part of them) in a growing number of territories reduces this mobility. If the compulsory local investment specifies not only the amount of funds to be retained but also the type of assets to be held this hampers investment policy even more. In some inflation-ridden countries, it would be safer to be invested in equities, but quite often the amount of reserves able to be put into Ordinary shares is restricted by law.

Problems of the American market

In many overseas countries, therefore, the difficulties come in two forms, one usually supporting the other. One is nationalism;[1] the other growing legal requirements. The developing countries tend to have both going hand in hand. There are no simple answers. Nor are there easy alternative markets in richer territories of the world. As we have already seen, Europe is hardly a profitable substitute and in any case is sufficiently tied up with regulations to prove difficult of access. As for the United States and Canada, the low profits or losses of British companies in both countries in recent years have hardly demonstrated that North America is the place in which to expect easy returns. Table IV shows recent experience in the United States. Underwriting losses have been persistent (and heavy) since 1956. Yet in most years the return on investment earnings has been enough to turn underwriting losses into net surpluses. It is a fiercely competitive market, made all the more difficult by the strict control exercised by the State Insurance Commissioners, who for a time held premium rates at unprofitable levels and even now are likely to keep them down longer than justified. London companies operating there have continually tried to resist the idea, prevalent among American companies, that it is unrealistic to expect profits on underwriting business. But the past eight years have hardly proved the

---

[1] Nationalism presents a special problem for Lloyd's because the Insurance Act of 1871 stated that Lloyd's underwriters should only write risks in London and that Lloyd's insurance policies should only be issued in London.

TABLE IV
UK INSURANCE EARNINGS IN USA, 1935-63
(British Insurance Companies and their American Subsidiaries)
FIRE, ACCIDENT AND MARINE

Year	Premiums $m.	Underwriting Profit $m.	%	Investment Earnings $m.	% to P	Remittance & Dividends $m.
1935	239.0	14.6	6.1	17.7	7.4	7.0
1936	247.3	14.7	5.9	17.9	7.2	5.7
1937	260.9	16.2	6.2	19.6	7.5	21.9
1938	246.5	18.0	7.3	17.8	7.2	18.4
1939	244.7	15.6	6.4	17.9	7.3	15.4
1940	265.7	12.6	4.7	18.0	6.8	17.8
1941	301.1	6.8	2.2	18.2	6.0	21.9
1942	347.4	5.2	1.5	17.4	5.0	11.5
1943	303.9	21.6	7.1	19.1	6.3	19.4
1944	329.4	8.6	2.6	19.7	6.0	22.1
1945	345.9	2.6*	0.7*	20.4	5.9	19.8
1946	440.6	37.8*	8.6*	20.5	4.7	15.7
1947	517.5	14.0*	2.7*	22.1	4.3	6.4
1948	523.3	19.4	3.7	24.2	4.6	12.6
1949	525.8	46.0	8.8	26.9	5.1	15.2
1950	538.8	4.9	0.9	29.1	5.4	19.2
1951	586.1	11.4*	1.9*	29.5	5.0	14.7
1952	628.0	14.2	2.3	31.1	5.0	14.9
1953	655.6	22.2	3.4	33.3	5.1	14.8
1954	655.0	17.7	2.7	36.3	5.5	15.0
1955	681.8	7.7	1.1	38.7	5.7	18.3
1956	715.7	33.9*	4.7*	41.3	5.8	17.2
1957	774.9	58.6*	7.6*	43.2	5.6	16.8
1958	768.9	33.3*	4.3*	44.4	5.8	14.5
1959	812.5	8.1*	1.0*	47.0	5.8	23.7
1960	848.5	12.7*	1.5*	50.1	5.9	28.6
1961	853.1	20.4*	2.4*	52.4	6.1	26.0
1962	875.8	10.1*	1.2*	55.1	6.3	16.2
1963	907.6	32.4*	3.6*	57.8	6.4	16.2

* Losses.

contrary—at least in general terms, though some of the leading British companies operating there have managed to keep their underwriting operations in the black.

Thus in some areas—mainly the under-developed world— legal restrictions are allied to emergent nationalism; in others —North America and the older Dominions—restrictions are allied to intense internal competition (and nationalism in a different form). Before assessing the prospects ahead of the London market in its overseas business it is essential to know how these different markets compare in importance. Although the industry publishes a mass of figures annually, statistics of foreign business are not strictly comparable for all markets. We shall be forced, therefore, to work out estimates as we go along, in order to see the relative significance of the North American continent. Readers wishing to miss out the details may move to the conclusion on page 76.

Estimates of overseas earnings

(i) *Insurance companies*

The overseas earnings of the London insurance market have to be built up section by section. First come the companies' earnings abroad. We know their earnings in the United States; we know within certain limits their premium income in Canada; and we also know fairly accurately their total overseas premiums. These details can be taken in turn. Table IV shows their experience in the American market. Underwriting profits (and losses) there have varied violently over the years. But in the period shown the average rate of underwriting profit was roughly one per cent. If allowance is also made for interest earnings on investments (at present running at about $6\frac{1}{2}$ per cent of premiums) and for Federal income tax, we can assume that, on the average, over a period of years the insurance companies will earn some 6 per cent net of Federal income tax on their American premiums. Since the premiums in 1963 amounted to $900 million, average earnings at 6 per cent were around $54 million or £19 million.

Total premiums earned by British and British-owned companies in Canada in 1963 amounted to $270 million. The same percentage of 6 per cent can be used in Canada as in the United States, since the differences between the two markets probably cancel each other out. Interest earnings in Canada will not be so high in relation to premiums as in the United States. For one thing, companies do not have to carry the same amount of surplus assets in Canada as in the United States, and a portion of their liabilities is often covered by sterling securities. On the other hand, underwriting results are often likely to be better than in the United States. Since British companies pay no Canadian income tax (though their subsidiaries there do), 6 per cent is probably conservative. On this basis the total premiums of $270 million produce some $16 million in net earnings, or £5 million.

There remain the earnings from other overseas territories. Since premiums in Canada and the United States together amounted to some $1,170 million or £410 million in 1963 and total foreign premiums were £770 million, the balance of £360 million accounts for the rest of the world. In most of these territories, interest earnings are not likely to be as high in relation to premiums as in the United States, but average underwriting profits are said to be considerably higher. It is believed that the rate of profit and interest in the rest of the world is nearly double that in North America, or close to 12 per cent. A proportion of 8 per cent would certainly be conservative. On premiums of £360 million this would represent earnings of £29 million.

Thus if we add the net income in the United States, Canada and the rest of the world together (i.e. £19 million, £5 million and £29 million), the insurance companies' total foreign income works out at £53 million.

(ii) *Lloyd's underwriters*
We now turn to Lloyd's. Here rather more guesswork creeps in, though the results may still be regarded as reasonably accurate. Since their figures are compiled for three-year periods, the latest accounts are unfortunately for four years ago. Between 1948 (when details were first published) and 1961 the average underwriting profit of Lloyd's underwriters on their world-wide income worked out at $7\frac{1}{2}$ per cent (ranging from 14.8 per cent in 1948 to 6.4 per cent in 1961.) On my assumption (see page 67 above) that Lloyd's undertake some 70 per cent of their business overseas, this proportion of the £346 million of premiums written in 1961 is equivalent to £240 million. The profits earned on this (at $7\frac{1}{2}$ per cent) are £18 million. In the same year, net interest earned on their total investment brought in £2$\frac{1}{2}$ million. It is unlikely that more than £1$\frac{1}{2}$ million of this came from abroad. Thus the £18 million

from underwriting and, say, £1½ million from investments bring Lloyd's total foreign income to £19½ million in 1961.

To the earnings of the insurance companies and of Lloyd's should be added those of the insurance brokers. If they are assumed to be 5 per cent of Lloyd's overseas premiums, the total comes to about £12 million. This figure, however, makes no allowance for the considerable amount of foreign business passed by brokers to the companies in the London market.

(iii) *Total overseas earnings*
Table V assembles these earnings.

TABLE V
OVERSEAS EARNINGS OF
BRITISH INSURANCE MARKET, 1963

Companies					£ million
United States ...	...	...	...	19
Canada ...	...	...	...	...	5
Other overseas ...	...	...	...	29
					—
Total companies	...	...	...	53
Lloyd's ...	...	...	...	...	19*
Brokers ...	...	...	...	...	12
					—
				TOTAL	£84
*1961.					=

As the figures making up this total are themselves fairly rough, a round total of some £85 million seems to be indicated, especially since no real account has been taken of life insurance business transacted abroad. Life business undertaken by Lloyd's is short-term and negligible. The insurance companies, on the other hand, received total premiums of some £760 million on ordinary life business in 1963, of which 12 per cent or £90 million came from abroad. But as a large part of the profits earned go back to policy-holders, especially those holding with-profits policies, the net income from overseas life business is extremely small. It can be regarded as part of the £85 million.

It is not hard to see, therefore, why in spite of intense competition and other operating troubles, the London market has not turned aside from North America to other markets. In total value, the UK insurance stake on that Continent is extremely valuable and increasing yearly. But, as we have just shown, premiums from the United States and Canada account for well over a half of the market's total overseas premiums. Thus, although the return is almost half that elsewhere in the world, net earnings from North America are only slightly below those from the rest of the world (£24 million against £29 million).

To sum up, insurance business is a natural development of a prosperous economy. But to operate efficiently two conditions are necessary: the ability to spread risks round the world and the freedom to invest and to switch money from one country to another. As the United Nations Trade and Development Conference demonstrated so clearly in the early summer of 1964, the underdeveloped countries see insurance in quite a different light. They feel that the premiums paid for insurance should not leave their country; they have strong views on how the premiums should be invested; they want any discrimination operated by their own nationalised insurance bodies to be accepted as part of the aid of the rich nations; and they are attracted by the thought that, by legislation, they can keep the net earnings of the international insurance companies (particularly those in London) in their own territories. It can be argued that these are reasonable attitudes and requests. And it can be further argued that the London market must get used to the idea of premiums being channelled to state-owned corporations and go out after the reinsurance business from these state-owned companies rather than the original business. It is an attractive idea, full of sympathy for the problems of the under-developed. But it tends to overlook one important point. The state-run insurance corporations in many of the under-developed countries allow operating costs to rise to such an extent that the margins offered to the London market are often too narrow to allow normal insurance business to be transacted.

Growth in size of risks

It is hardly surprising, therefore, that many of the leaders of the London insurance market still see their future in those territories that cling to private enterprise in their insurance business, whether they be hamstrung with too much red-tape (Europe) or generating far too much internal competition (North America). Even in these territories one further problem is agitating the London market. The size of individual risks is rising continually. Before the war, for example, it was possible to insure a liner for £4 million. Six years ago the 'Oriana' was insured for £15 million. Now the highest insurance arranged for a liner has jumped to no less than £24 million, for the 'France'. No doubt the new Cunarder will set a further insurance record. The story is the same in aircraft. A jet airliner is now insured for £1 million or £2 million, depending on the type, whereas the supersonic aircraft on the drawing boards are estimated to cost between £4 million and £8 million. A completely new risk has been provided by the nuclear power stations, the value of a Calder Hall type of reactor being estimated at no less than £30 million. Later versions will cost even more. And the growing size and complexity of industrial plants are also pushing up their cost yearly. The largest industrial risks nowadays include factories of up to £50 million or more insured under one roof.

The expansion in the value of individual risks naturally puts pressure on individual companies (and on individual syndicates at Lloyd's) to spread the load. It has been one of the main influences behind the moves towards larger individual units and the mergers of a few years ago. At Lloyd's there has been a tendency for individual syndicates to become large; and many people expect this to go on, with the present dozen or so names in a syndicate expanding, in 20 or 30 years' time, to twice that number. But this expansion in the size of individual risks emphasises even more the need for the London market to spread its risks as widely as possible and to maintain its world-wide flexibility for as long as possible. It has one further, important lesson for the insurance market, especially for its overseas business. The investment of their funds must be as efficient as their underwriting. In North America the return on investment, on average, has offset the losses incurred on underwriting. Some companies, however, have run into difficulties in that market: the return on investments has been too small to offset their losses on underwriting. Some companies delayed merging into larger units, yet recent experience strongly suggests that only insurance companies of a certain size can expect to compete with the large American firms. To linger on too long—making just enough from investments to make up for insurance losses—is a waste of a company's money. It is also a waste of national resources.

CHAPTER 6

COMMODITIES

FEW PARTS of the City have changed so radically as the commodity markets. Yet few have shown such strange powers of survival in an alien world. Even the physical damage to the major markets has now healed from the scars of war. The Commercial Sale Rooms, known far and wide as 'Mincing Lane,' succumbed to enemy bombs as long ago as 1941. Until just before the end of the war, these old-established markets (the Sale Rooms dated back to 1811) virtually camped out with the Rubber Exchange in Plantation House. But after four years of such relations a more solid merger was accomplished and a wider-based London Commodity Exchange emerged early in 1945. Not only have these markets returned to some of their pre-war activities but their earnings have also grown with their enlarged freedom. From 1939 to the early post-war years, bulk-buying of food and raw materials by the government and strict control over exchange spending reduced these earnings to a trickle. But as one market after another re-opened and developed its activities the importance of the merchants and the large merchanting houses to the country's overseas earnings returned to prominence.

Although most of the commodity markets as we now know them were established some time during the 19th century, their roots go back further. London has been one of the world's main trading ports for longer than a leading financial centre. It was a thriving commercial city when Europe's financial centre of gravity was still moving from Northern Italy to Holland. London has been forced to deal in commodities because, as industrialisation spread and the country had to maintain a growing population on the proceeds of its exports, food and raw materials from abroad were essential. In some periods, half of all the country's imports passed through the Port of London. Even before the war, the figure was 40 per cent. Now it is just over a third. Britain's rising standard of living has depended on this constant flow of imports, certainly for the past two centuries.

London's re-export trade

But the merchants of London did more than this. Being well placed on the world's shipping routes between the consuming centres of Europe and the commodity-producing areas of Africa, Asia and America, they quickly established a growing re-export trade through London. This entrepôt trade is still thriving to this day. The re-export figures since the war, for example, show that large quantities of rubber (grown in the Far East) have been re-shipped from London (and Liverpool) to the Soviet Union. In 1956 and 1957 alone, the value of this series of transactions reached some £42 million. The total value of re-exports in 1963 (not all handled in London) was £153 million. This was the measure of the amount of imported goods and materials eventually re-shipped abroad. A high proportion must have been brought into the country through merchants and their organised markets. In addition, London merchants have always been prominent in organising trade between commodity-producing countries and foreign markets.

In the volume of turnover, the metal, rubber, grain, cocoa, and wool markets are perhaps the outstanding examples. But the marketing of coffee, sugar, copra, furs, diamonds, hides and skins, spices, shellac and tea, some of the leading commodities, is equally important in attracting to the City not only merchanting commissions, but freight, banking and insurance earnings as well. Before the war, these markets were financed by sterling. Holders of sterling knew that they could buy any commodity they wished in London and finance, ship and insure it in sterling, irrespective of its origin. In short, the London commodity markets provided full convertibility for sterling holders, since dollar commodities could be bought with no more difficulty than sterling commodities. It was clear when the London markets were gradually re-opened again that, if they were ever to be regarded as truly world markets, something would have to be done about the difficulty of marketing dollar commodities. In the event, the problem was tackled with some courage by the authorities, and even before formal convertibility at the end of 1958, the London commodity markets were providing what was virtually full convertibility to overseas customers.

Commodity market schemes

This service was accomplished by the introduction of special exchange control arrangements, known as Commodity Market Schemes. Table VI shows how the markets were gradually re-opened, especially from 1951 onwards. Schemes were first introduced for coffee, rubber, tin, cocoa, lead, raw sugar and zinc. Then came arrangements for grain, copper, refined sugar, copra and a futures market for wool. Business in copper, copra, lead, rubber, tin and zinc was allowed to be transacted in sterling from the outset, regardless of the location or origin of the commodity; but that in cocoa, coffee, grain and raw sugar was permitted solely on the understanding that when the commodity was bought for dollars it could be sold only for dollars. However, early exceptions were made in the case of cocoa and coffee, and later for raw sugar, which could be sold to countries in Europe for sterling even though originally grown in the dollar area. These exceptions gradually increased, the area in which sterling could be used to buy dollar commodities being extended to the whole transferable account area. Very soon the Bank of England's commodity schemes made it permissible for holders of sterling to buy most, if not all, commodities on the London market whether of dollar origin or otherwise. In short, the conditions under which the markets had flourished before the war were rapidly re-introduced by the authorities, as far as currency conditions permitted. They led to a marked recovery in business.

This account of the post-war drive to re-establish the commodity markets (as well as the recovery in their currency earnings) leaves a strong impression that the pre-war position has been largely restored. It is far from being so. These markets have changed their character to a degree only partly discernible in 1939. Commodity markets in general have three specific roles to play. They provide for the delivery of commodities; they establish free prices; and they include hedging facilities. The first has changed significantly more than the others since the war, though hedging facilities are still in need of further strengthening. The physical movement of commodities through these City markets has been slowly undermined by both political and economic influences over the past 50 years. Even before the First World War, the old-established trade emanating from the East was changing because of the gradual shift in the economic pattern of world trade, the growing up of local consumer markets in the producing countries, developments in other consuming countries (America and Europe) and, above all, the growing size of the producing units. It is surprising that these influences had left so small a mark right up to the end of the 1930s.

TABLE VI

RE-OPENING OF LONDON'S COMMODITY MARKETS

Commodity	Date of Re-opening	Detail
Furs	February 1946	First post-war sales
Raw wool	September 1946	First wool auction
Coffee	May 1946	Merchanting trade
Rubber	November 1946	Rubber Exchange dealings
Tin	November 1949	Cash and futures dealings
Cocoa	January 1951	Merchanting trade and terminal market
Tea	April 1951	First auctions
Lead	October 1952	Cash and futures dealings
Raw sugar	November 1952	Merchanting trade
Zinc	January 1953	Cash and futures dealings
Coffee	January 1953	First post-war auctions
Wool Tops	April 1953	Terminal market
Grain	June 1953	Merchanting trade
Copper	August 1953	Cash and futures dealings
Barley and Maize	January 1954	Terminal market
Refined sugar	July 1954	Merchanting trade
Copra	December 1954	Merchanting trade
Sugar	January 1957	Terminal market
Coffee	July 1958	Terminal market

It is often suggested that the London markets have most to fear from competing markets in other countries, either in the producing countries of the East and of Africa or in the consuming areas of Europe and America. The growth of tea auctions in India and Ceylon, for example, is ofen cited as an example of what is really undermining London's business. The same is said of New York. Yet neither constitutes the real threat to London. Some trade has certainly been attracted from the London market by local markets where the produce is grown. Yet, apart from the Singapore rubber market (a dealers' market in rubber rather than rubber futures), eastern competition has not been significant. This is not quite so surprising as the failure of New York to overtake London's influence, especially during and after the war and post-war period when commodity controls and centralised buying dominated the

London scene. America had become the largest industrial nation; was the world's largest producer and consumer of a wide range of raw materials and foodstuffs; and it seemed the natural place for commodity markets to take permanent root. Yet many factors were against her. In grain and other temperate products, the 'New Deal' era, with its emphasis on government intervention, price supports and the like, was a major obstruction to any natural development of the New York and Chicago grain and produce markets. They were not the only obstacles. In metals, the difficulty arose in private enterprise rather than in the government sector. The growth of large mining units produced a natural desire on their part to fix their prices direct with consumers rather than rely on free markets. This tendency is still strong today, and is beginning to be felt in the London market too. Even when the volume of business in New York has been maintained at a high level, the share of outright speculation has sometimes been enough to undermine confidence and to lead to price fluctuations.

The effect of government controls

For all these reasons, London has continued to throw off foreign competition, even through periods of severe distress. It has mainly suffered from interference in other directions, all of which have affected physical turnover as well as London's general efficiency as a pricing and hedging centre. These have largely arisen from government influence at home or abroad. The war-time controls were naturally the biggest setback, for under the Emergency Powers (Defence) Act of 1939 the government took complete powers to control the production, import, distribution, pricing, stocking, etc., of primary commodities. The Ministry of Supply and the Ministry of Food took over the functions of the commodity markets during and after the war. And the Labour Government, immediately after the war, was loath to change the system. It believed in state trading and feared a slump in commodity prices in the early post-war years. More important, perhaps, it hoped that it might be able to buy large supplies of foodstuffs at favourable prices by delaying its purchases or at least confining them to twelve-month agreements. Most of these hopes (and fears) proved false. The expected slump did not come; and neither did the opportunity for the state to make a killing in the world's food market. Gradually some controls and paper work were abolished. As time went on, it became clearer that the reasons for state trading were not as convincing as had originally appeared, and greater flexibility had to be introduced into the pricing of industrial raw materials if industry was not to be placed at a serious disadvantage abroad. The climate for the re-introduction of private trading was re-emerging. The first advance came with the re-opening of the rubber market in the winter of 1946-47. But it was several years before the last traces of governmental control over commodities disappeared.

Meanwhile, the interference of governments abroad also continued to set a limit to the operations of the London commodity markets. The effects of Roosevelt's New Deal throughout the 'thirties affected London (and Liverpool) markets almost as much as those in New York and Chicago, for any attempt to support such a large sector of the world market in grain was bound to have repercussions on markets everywhere. It was equally true of the large American producers of minerals who tried to fix their prices direct. And the post-war efforts to introduce international commodity schemes and protectionism in some countries have tended to curb the turnover of the commodity markets. The protectionism tends to occur when an industrialised country produces raw materials or foodstuffs —sugar, oil, butter, coal, etc., to take a few examples. Internal prices are fixed to suit domestic producers and the world market tends to receive the brunt of the fluctuation in marginal supplies. This situation cuts down the high turnover that leads to stable markets and deprives the free markets of valuable business. Beyond these protective devices lie commodity schemes themselves, going back in time to the 'twenties and 'thirties, when tin, rubber, sugar and tea schemes were all introduced. Whether these plans have aided the under-developed countries by attempting to stabilise prices is a moot point.[1] Some commodities, such as tin, can be shown to have experienced just as sharp fluctuations by the operation of the agreements as they might have done without them. And it can hardly have been to the full benefit of the commodity markets concerned.

A further important point is now emerging from the recent discussion of world commodity agreements in general and of those including compensatory finance in particular.[2] The pricing yardstick by which these schemes are to be judged must be

---

[1] For a discussion of commodity stabilisation schemes, see Sir Sydney Caine, *Prices for Primary Producers*, Hobart Paper 24, 1EA, 1963.
[2] UN Trade and Development Conference, Geneva, 1964.

provided by some outside agency; few countries show signs of wanting to be saddled with the job of fixing commodity prices or of handling or distributing commodities themselves. If prices are to be controlled between upper and lower limits, according to international agreement, some form of market is needed to allow fluctuations to take place at all. In other words, governments are in the mood to interfere far more than they have ever done before in fixing or controlling market prices; but they are unlikely to want to do without markets in general.

Growth of large suppliers and direct selling

Yet, when all this has been said about past and potential governmental interference with the free workings of world markets, the biggest threat to their operations may well come from private enterprise. The London markets worked best when they brought together thousands of producers and millions of consumers. But gradually producing units have grown larger. The cost of opening up and developing new lands, the cost of exploration and development, the cost of marketing growing quantities have all led to bigger enterprises. Some units have grown so large that they dominate the supply of the commodity; and it is natural, faced with the perplexing fluctuations of the market, that some of them should have tried to fix their prices direct with the main consumers—outside the market. Uneasy relationships have developed as a result. Some of the big producers have regarded market fluctuations as too wide; yet many of them have been loath to go the whole hog and undermine the market completely. This reluctance has been particularly marked with the copper producers over the past few years. The problem remains unresolved even now. Some large units have emerged as the result of economic necessity. Others have been created by governmental decree as official marketing agencies. Both have much the same effect on market operations. They tend to by-pass the market by dealing directly with the consumer. The market is still used as a pricing mechanism, but the price is based on only a proportion of the total turnover.

Other influences have worked in the same direction. There has been a remarkable expansion in world trade in primary products since the war. Rubber and sugar output have probably doubled. Cocoa production has risen sharply and the volume of other materials coming on to the world markets has been well above pre-war levels. The amount of money needed to finance such a large expansion in raw material output was unlikely to be forthcoming from the merchanting houses as in the past; and, in the absence of radical changes in the commodity structure of the City markets, other sources were needed. The absence of finance was not the only facet of the problem. In order to encourage the expansion itself, it was also necessary to have more than a short-term assurance of a ready outlet. The finance needed for exploration, development and marketing of so many of these commodities was so large that longer-term contracts—with some assurance of prices—were required. The financial situation also, therefore, pushed arrangements towards agreements between big producers and big consumers. In some trades the same situation stimulated a drive towards vertical integration. In others the output from one region of the world was tied to consumption in another largely through political relationships. For all these reasons the proportion of world output finding its way on to the free markets was bound to decline.

The outcome is that the turnover of some of the commodity markets has become relatively thinner, their operations less smooth and their efficiency reduced. Although some of the commodity experts in the City still do business as middlemen with government buying or selling agencies, their business through the market is directly impeded. The main result of the thinning is that the markets become far more vulnerable to temporary shifts in supply or demand. If too many consumers are tending to work on insufficient stocks, it is hardly surprising that the slightest jar (either a strike or a political disturbance abroad) tends to lead to bigger price fluctuations than would be produced by the underlying conditions of supply and demand. And these shifts in prices undermine the smooth working of the essential hedging facilities. They make the hedging facilities more necessary but harder to operate.

Economic change and commodity markets

Thus the City's commodity markets have firmly re-established their international reputation. They have no immediate rivals. But the character of their business has changed; and so have the threats to their livelihood. Some parts of the pre-war scene have virtually disappeared. The trade in gums has been heavily hit by the newer plastics and synthetics. And the market in pepper has been reduced in volume, reflecting the change in the consumer trade as well as swifter communications between centres. For the rest, several of the basic markets have maintained their turnover remarkably well. Volume generally is above pre-war, though the share of world output passing through the markets is down. The rubber market, while still leaving occasional hints of a somewhat dated atmosphere, has kept a solid turnover on which to base world prices. The Metal Exchange has maintained business at a high level and, in spite of difficulties with producers and with the international regulation scheme (for tin), still provides the world with its main price indicator. As for wool, cocoa and sugar, all have continued to flourish. Apart from their primary purpose, the provision of a price mechanism, the commodity markets have kept abreast of developments in other directions. They have redeveloped contractual terms for most of the main materials, establishing accepted qualities, adapting changes in qualities to new conditions and providing accepted means of arbitration; in short, they perform all the technical work of a world centre.

The main charge against these markets is that they have not moved fast enough to keep pace with the large changes in world conditions. It is an easy one to level against them. It is harder to conclude that they could have avoided many of the changes resulting from government action and from the structure of the producing industries. Even if they had been far-sighted, had established a means of coping with the prices and marketing of synthetics, had the additional finance to help producers, been more persuasive with individual governments, and developed a more active defence of their own interests, it is far from certain that they could have maintained the position they once had in the commodity trades. They could certainly have done more to educate public opinion in the workings of the markets and in publicising their affairs. Their administration has hardly reflected the air of dynamism shown in other parts of the City. Yet, when all this has been said, it has not been easy to defend a market which, in spite of its earnings, serves foreign customers as much as, if not more than, domestic. Commodity brokers have had to defend themselves against near-monopoly producers both inside and outside the sterling area. They have provided free market prices for individual governments and for international regulation schemes. And free markets are a useful, perhaps essential, yardstick for countries like Britain that depend so much on a high volume of international trade. The users of the market have not been its natural defenders.

Throughout all this, the merchanting houses have kept an admirable sense of balance. They have fully accepted that, in order to get the full expansion in commodity output the world is capable of, most of it cannot pass through the free markets. That would be expecting too much, particularly at a time when the producers are growing bigger and dealing directly with consumers. But, equally, if producers, consumers and governments are to have any true indication of the state of supply and demand, then a reasonable share must continue to pass through these markets. This is the basis on which the London commodity markets are continuing to operate. It has one important implication, relating to other commodity markets in the world. Far from trying to squeeze these other markets out of existence, London is now tending to take the view that there is room for all. It has already given help to new markets starting up in Paris and Tokyo. And it assumes that the operation of the New York market helps London by leading to a growth of business between markets, provided the New York market continues to operate freely and not under restrictive influences. The more markets there are operating in the world, the argument goes, the fewer bilateral deals outside the market will be necessary. It is for this reason that London would welcome any further development in Europe, rather than the opposite. The more numerous the markets and the more the freedom from government and monopoly interference, the larger the turnover expected. This is an attitude of mind plainly generated by the encroachment of non-market influences. It makes sense in the atmosphere of the post-war world. But it assumes, perhaps, too readily, that London will always be able to take the cream of the business. That may depend as much on the future role of the City in general as on the skill, expertise, dynamism and readiness to take risks of the individual merchants and merchanting houses.

CHAPTER 7

SHIPPING

IT IS hardly surprising that a seafaring nation should earn more from shipping than from any other commercial service. Since Britain still has the world's largest merchant fleet, shipping earnings remain high in spite of the long recession in freight rates. But in and around Leadenhall Street, as in many other parts of the City, although new opportunities are opening up, competition is increasing, new habits are being formed and, most important of all, the free movement of goods across the oceans (on which these earnings are based) is slowly being restricted. Here too the new forces in the world need to be recognised. They are formidable.

The conditions in which Britain built up and maintained a remarkable maritime lead in the second half of the 19th century are no longer with us. The combination of the Port of London (the centre of a thriving Empire), the expansion of the City as a provider of credit and capital and the construction of the world's first, and biggest, merchant fleet based on steam inevitably brought prosperity to the shipping firms, already growing roots in or near the City. The Baltic Exchange, on which representatives of these firms as well as of shippers and merchants had built up the world's leading freight market, also thrived. Its proximity to the banks and insurance companies proved invaluable. Not only did British shipowners, merchants and exporters make increasing use of these services, but foreigners found it convenient to make their shipping 'fixtures'[1] in London too. The Baltic was the meeting place for anyone wanting to shift a cargo from one side of the world to the other and equally for a shipowner wanting to find cargoes for his ships to carry.

[1] An agreement on rates fixed between the owner of a ship and the owner of a cargo: usually arranged on their behalf by shipping brokers.

Competition and restriction

It still is. And it can still claim to be the largest shipping market in the world. But rivals have sprung up. The freedom of the seas is being threatened. The under-developed world want merchant fleets of their own. They also want to decide how to direct their trade. The rich countries are not immune from these desires, the US often insisting which of its cargoes should be carried in American ships. The more rigidities of this sort enter into international commerce, the less the need for the City's services and the smaller the role to be played by the Baltic and the hundreds of shipping offices that surround it.

It is often assumed that British shipping dominated the seas well before London became the world's leading financial centre. Shipping naturally played a prime role in the life of an island people; and the Port of London thrived long before the City came into its own in international finance. But the important expansion in Britain's merchant fleet largely took place in the second half of the last century (Table VIII). For it was only then that American rivalry was finally overcome. As Sir Donald Anderson, a recent President of the Chamber of Shipping, described this transformation.

'By the time the industrial revolution was getting under way in the early 19th century, the Americans and the British were the great rivals at sea, with the Americans undoubtedly holding the technical lead. The British were still building ships in very heavy timber and with very little capacity for going to windward. The Americans were using lighter woods, better hull models and gear, and were undeniably the more efficient.

But steam was just beginning to be developed, and although the Americans adopted it for their inland waterways and built extremely fast lake and river craft, they rejected it on the oceans, where they remained wedded to sail, perhaps just because they knew that they held the lead in this technique. Great Britain, on the other hand, took up steam wholeheartedly and in every direction. At a crucial time, in 1850, the Navigation Acts in this country were abolished, much to the disgust of the shipowners, who thought they were going to be ruined by the loss of the protection which they had formerly enjoyed. In fact they benefited enormously from this stimulus to their competence and this freeing of trade . . .

From this time onwards British shipping forged right ahead,

supported by great exports of coal, by rapidly growing industrial development, by increasing imports of grain and other raw material, and in the passenger world by intense emigration to the United States, Australia and elsewhere. Thus, by the 1914 war, Great Britain with 44 per cent of the world's tonnage held a most dominant position in this industry, world wide. By that time, the United States had effectively priced itself out of competitive shipping.

Origins of the Baltic Exchange

While this oceanic expansion was going on, a similar expansion was taking place within the City itself. The merchants and shippers several centuries earlier had taken to meeting together in the Virginia and Maryland Coffee House, later known as the Virginia and Baltic. By the early 19th century in the re-named Baltic Tavern they decided to draw up stricter regulations for their club. It was the Baltic Exchange in embryo. To the original trade in tallow, oils, hemp and flax were soon added grains. Both commodity trade and freight business flourished side by side. The expansion led to the acquisition of new premises. Trade increased further with the introduction of steam and the chartering of tramp ships became one of the basic transactions on the Baltic, as shown by the title of the 'Steam Department' retained still by some of the Baltic's largest member firms.

By the turn of the century it was necessary to come to terms with a new shipping exchange opened specifically to cope with the new liner trade. The old Baltic and the new exchange (the Shipping Exchange) decided to join forces and by 1905 a new joint exchange building had been completed. It still stands in St. Mary Axe today.

A market for shipowner and trader

During some 60 years the Exchange has expanded further. Membership is nearly three times what it was at the turn of the century. Although the pattern of the world's merchant fleets has changed and new tasks have been added to old, the Exchange is basically doing the same job. Tramp ships, which still account for a significant share of the tonnage of the oceans, are organised on voyage charters. Unlike liners or vessels on long-term hire, they are ready to take almost any cargo to and from any port. But their increasing flexibility (to the orthodox types have been added bulk carriers ranging from 15,000 to

35,000 tons and over) means that they need to be used economically and to have their voyages fixed as efficiently as possible. It means indeed that both ship owners and traders should be brought together as regularly as possible. A daily meeting place, or market, is necessary.

This is what the Baltic has always provided: a market in which the shipowner can offer the services of his vessels and where the trader can find the right ship at the right time. Agents of both shipowners and traders from all parts of the world meet on the Baltic Exchange daily. With a total membership of some 2,700, the Exchange can normally boast of at least 1,000 of them attending at one or another of the two markets each day. They appear in one of two guises: as shipbrokers trying to find suitable cargoes for vessels or as charterers' agents wanting ships. The result is the fixing of cargoes for tramp ships from one side of the globe to another. Whether it is grain to be moved from the Pacific or the River Plate or coal from the East coast of the United States, the Baltic Mercantile and Shipping Exchange (its full title) is where cargoes and shipping space are married together.

It is not its only business. Ships that need to be built, sold or scrapped are also traded or negotiated on the Baltic. Several firms specialise in the sale and purchase of ships, supported by many other brokers who run departments devoted to this type of business. Like the freight market, this is a worldwide business. With its international contacts, the Baltic could hardly be otherwise. The result is that, as the Exchange itself claims, a good 50 per cent of the world sale and purchase business passes through firms represented on the Baltic.

The Baltic still serves certain commodity trades too. The grain and oilseed (and paint) markets remain an important section of the Exchange's function, linking past and present. A natural, though essentially new, departure is the expansion of the air charter market, already given its special part of the floor.

As with other City markets, rivals to the Baltic have already sprung up abroad. New York has an active market and similar but much smaller shipping exchanges exist in Paris, Tokyo and, for more local traffic, Hong Kong. Despite these competitors and the growth of direct international communications by telephone and telex, well over half of truly international shipbroking business is still done in London. New York, the only other major chartering centre, may deal with something like a quarter, though it is limited mainly to business from and to the United States. The City's leading shipping brokers sensibly maintain offices in several of these centres and are active on their exchanges. At present few of them represent a direct danger to the Baltic.

All these markets face a similar danger, though the Baltic has its own troubles to contend with. All have suffered from the recession in freight rates over the past decade (certainly since 1956). All have suffered and will continue to suffer from the tendency of individual governments to protect their merchant fleets and thus to organise work for their own vessels direct rather than on world markets. All will suffer from increasing governmental interference with the free movement of international commerce, especially over the oceans. And all are suffering, as mentioned earlier, from better communications and specialised types of shipping, both of which often tend to persuade shipowners to make long-term deals direct with industry, thus depriving these exchanges of the day-to-day business on which they thrive. But only the Baltic can and may suffer from the decline in Britain's share of the world's merchant fleet.

Decline in freight rates

These influences must now be looked at more closely. First, there is the recent recession in freight rates. On the face of it the expansion in world trade over the last decade should have brought in a similar rise in shipping business and hence in turnover on the Baltic and other similar exchanges. International trade has been rising at well over 5 per cent a year lately and has doubled in the past ten years. The persistent expansion since the war has been quite remarkable. The use of the world's shipping services, however, has not always kept pace and even where it has, neither the world's main maritime nations nor the shipping brokers that serve them have necessarily benefited to the same extent.

This apparent paradox needs some explanation. There should, of course, be a direct link between the expansion in world trade and the amount carried by sea. It is believed that something like three-quarters of the world's trade by value moves across the oceans. In 1961, for example, some 1,130 million metric tons of cargo was transported by sea. Of this 560 million tons was dry cargo and 570 million tons tanker cargo. But, of course, the main expansion in world trade in the past decade has been among the industrialised nations. This movement has two implications. First, although there has been a dramatic increase in the sea transport of certain bulk commodities such as petroleum, iron ore and bauxite, it has been in these trades that the large ship has had most impact in reducing freight rates. In other commodities the increase in world trade has been smaller. Secondly, the real expansion in trade has been in Europe, where the development of the Common Market gave such a stimulus to trade in industrial goods. Naturally, most of this took place across land frontiers and was hardly reflected at all in sea transport.

Moreover, although shipping business has expanded in this period (though not to the extent that world trade might indicate), the tonnage available to move these cargoes round the world increased faster, while ship efficiency has been transformed out of all proportion by the increase in size, speed, and, in tanker and bulk carriers, by much faster turn-round as a result of improved terminals and better ship design. Hence the recession in freight rates and the periodic laying up of such a large share of the world's maritime fleet.

Since 1956, when the recession in freight rates really set in, the size of the world's merchant fleet has grown by close on 40 per cent. Some national fleets have expanded greatly. The Japanese fleet has doubled in the last six years and the Norwegian has nearly doubled in the last ten. The Dutch fleet has increased by 50 per cent and the German rather more in the same period. For a time the use of flags of convenience, for tax and other reasons, pushed up the size of the Liberian and Panamanian fleets, but neither has grown much in the past few years. On balance, however, the world's fleet has been growing faster than the expansion in world sea trade in recent years.

Thus freight rates have been low and competition brisk. At the same time shipowners have had to face subsidised competition from several quarters, quite apart from needless restrictions. The Baltic and other chartering markets have naturally suffered from this general pressure on shipping earnings. But they have a wider stake than this. Since they are concerned with international shipping, they are equally involved with the question of whether world trade is free enough for their members to benefit. The Baltic, dependent as it is on the freedom of international trade and on the continuation of a high level of free chartering, is slowly being undermined by the encroachment of government interference, by the new methods of regulating world shipping, and by the replacement of all-purpose tramps by specialised ships sometimes built for employment negotiated directly with the industrial user.

State intervention

Government interference with international shipping comes in all sorts of guises. Some fleets will get inflated payments from their government for undertaking special jobs, whether the normal carriage of mail or of particular government cargoes. Some may get cheap capital for expansion. Some governments own fleets. In other cases governments insist on a stated share of their trade going in their own ships. Discrimination in practice takes all forms, but in most cases it simply adds to the cost of sea transport. Where it affects the Baltic particularly is where it interferes with the free fixing of shipping charters.

In most cases[1] it happens to be the poorer nations who invariably want to support their domestic fleets or to build them up. But the main culprit in recent years has been the United States. American shipping and shipbuilding have never managed to be competitive. The reason lies somewhere in the middle of the last century (when Britain's venture into steam left the American shipbuilding industry lagging behind) and somewhere in the high wage rates of American industry. Whatever the reason, subsidies are needed both for building and running American ships.

It is perhaps hardly surprising, though none the less depressing, that the United States should have decided to introduce a strict rule whereby 50 per cent of its post-war aid should be carried in American ships. Since its introduction this rule has been given wider coverage by the inclusion of commercial cargoes financed by US agencies and of surplus farm products. This stranglehold on American business has been bad enough. What has been worse has been the assumption among poorer nations that what is good enough for the US is certainly good enough for them. Bilateralism has been given an unexpected but deplorable shot in the arm. If this rule were driven to its logical conclusion, it has been estimated[2] that the Norwegians

[1] See pp. 97-98.
[2] Viscount Runciman, International Banking Summer School, July 1961.

(who own the second largest merchant fleet)[1] would be able to employ only 1½ million tons. This, of course, is an extreme example. But the dangers of the American restrictions to international commerce, and hence to the Baltic brokers, are plain.

These have not been the only restrictions introduced by the United States. The attempted interference with foreign lines in the spring of 1964, by obliging them to produce stipulated documents, brought a rumbling crisis to a head overnight. The dispute was apparently over so-called 'dual' rates. These are highly complex, but the basic American suspicion was that the conference lines were arranging rates detrimental to American exports. This suspicion, based on the well-known and understandable American bias against monopolies and trusts, was allowed to get completely out of hand. The result was that the Federal Maritime Commission virtually gave member lines of the conference trading to America three days to produce their documents and to change their contracts. As Sir Errington Keville[2] put it:

'Reduced to its simplest terms, the Americans were trying to tell a British exporter and a British shipowner what kind of contract form they would adopt for the shipment of British goods from a British port in a British ship.'

The reaction was immediate, not only from Britain but from the major shipping nations of the world. Government backing was forthcoming, too. American efforts, ostensibly against the liner conference system, were in effect aimed at trying to usher in a system of even more complexity by further documentation. This showdown, in which the Americans quickly backed away, making it clear that shipowners had 90 days (and not three) to produce documents, had a useful result. It brought together the European shipowners' organisations. And it increased co-operation between shippers and shipowners. Thus out of the uproar came the formation of the Committee of European Shipowners and, following two meetings of the European transport ministers, an official resolution praising the liner conference system as 'indispensable' to world trade. As a leading shipping spokesman commented at the time:

[1] Of 13¼ million tons.
[2] At Master Mariners' Conference, May 1964.

'Behind this spirit of co-operation . . . lies an implicit belief that no government has the right to exercise unilateral control over rates of freight and that shipping should be allowed to get on with its business instead of being surrounded by regulations with which compliance is almost impossible.'

Nationalism in shipping

This co-operation was to come in useful and to provide the basis for action when the real opposition was met at the United Nations Trade and Development Conference in Geneva in the early summer of 1964. The under-developed countries came together at this meeting for the first time as a group. And they soon voiced their complaints to the richer nations. In the case of shipping their views were fairly clear. They had little to complain about in the volume of world shipping. There was no shortage of vessels for their exports. What they complained about was the pattern of world shipping, the lack of their own ships, the cost to their balance of payments and the way in which the present structure of shipping worked against their interests. What they clearly wanted was both help and encouragement to build up their own fleets; preferential treatment to offset what they regarded as the high cost of world freight rates.

Some of the under-developed nations already have merchant fleets in the making; others have similar ambitions. Provided that they are efficiently run and earn a return, without restriction or subsidy, few of the main maritime nations can quarrel with these developments. What is less easy for them to swallow is the argument that only subsidised fleets of their own and preferential treatment in their operation will lighten the freight content of the balance of payments of the under-developed countries. There was much detailed argument on this score in Geneva, the main shipowning nations putting forward estimates to show that the financial advantages of a maritime fleet (to the balance of payments) were hardly as large as the needy nations apparently thought. Yet whatever figures were produced, the under-developed countries were clearly convinced that the present liner conference system and their lack of merchant fleets were working against their interests. The main maritime nations, undoubtedly shocked by some of the outspoken remarks as well as by the conviction of so many of the under-developed, put up a strong rearguard action, finally narrowing down the real area of conflict to two main issues, the role of the liner conferences and the criteria for the development of shipping services by the poorer nations.

It will take more than this, however, to ward off the determination of these developing countries to push ahead with their ideas of national subsidised fleets. Much can obviously be done to meet their complaints about the workings of the liner conference system, but little, beyond repeated argument, seems possible to counter some of the assumptions that subsidised fleets of their own would relieve their payments problems. The difficulty is that many others will suffer from the increasing restrictions that often accompany economic nationalism of this sort. There is still a close relationship between rising shipping costs and the lack of freedom in picking up return cargoes and in competing for any cargo from any port. And this rise in general costs is bound to affect the return from shipping on which much of the private investment in the industry is still based.

The basic fact is that world shipping remains privately financed and operated. Private money and capital has been, and still is, sunk into the shipping industry at risk. As a recent Chamber of Shipping annual report[1] calculated, the replacement cost of the British flag fleet alone would be in the region of £3,600 million. The comparable cost of the world's privately-owned merchant fleet would work out at no less than £20,000 million—accounting for well over three-quarters of the world's total fleet.

The threat to the Baltic and to the scores of London broking firms that support it is plain. Any new or growing national fleet not directly required by growth of overseas trade will tend to reduce still further the proportion of tonnage which can participate freely in international commerce. More restrictions on the handling of national cargoes are inevitable because young nations believe they should have their own ships to carry their own trade. If to these efforts of the under-developed countries are added the expansionist plans of the communist countries, the danger could be even more serious. Russia alone is reported to be doubling the size of her maritime fleet to something like 10 million tons (gross) by 1970 and to 21 million tons by 1980. The main impact on world shipping will naturally depend on whether Russia's own trade will expand rapidly enough to utilise the whole of the planned capacity, and on

[1] Chamber of Shipping of the United Kingdom, *Annual Report, 1963-64.*

whether the fleet is used without due regard to cost. If Chinese, as well as Japanese, plans for increased fleets are also allowed for, the encroachment on the free movement of goods might be serious.

The outlook

Yet there are people on the Baltic who do not despair. Russian and Chinese shipping demands have consistently been met by Baltic brokers. The recent chartering of grain ships for Russia, for example, was a major business operation. Russia and to a lesser extent China have never ruled out the use of the West's financial or other markets, provided the cost suited them. They have used London's financial mechanism to finance their trade, London's bullion market to sell their gold and, just as readily, London's chartering market to provide their shipping. The Baltic still has its optimists.

In the view of many leading brokers, the main challenge has (and will) come from a change in chartering habits among countries already convinced of the need for freedom in international commerce. Both methods of chartering and the types of vessels in use have been changing rapidly since the war. Technology and finance have been tending to push developments in the same direction: towards specialised ships and longer-term charters. Before the war the freight element was a fairly small share of the cost of individual commodities; as a result speed and turn-round time were not so important. The surplus of world shipping also helped in supplying the right ship at the right price. There tended to be a buyers' market in shipping space.

This is no longer so. Crew wages and conditions have improved considerably and ships themselves are far more costly to build. Moreover, in spite of occasional depressions in freight rates, seldom more than 5 per cent of the world's tonnage has been idle. As a result, charterers who have known their requirements some months and years ahead have been forced to think in quite different terms. With their monetary margin much narrower, they could no longer take their chance on the Baltic on a day-to day basis to quite the same extent. More and more of them either attempted to enter into long-term contracts or decided to buy or build their own ships, sometimes in partnership with shipowners. This policy protected them against the uncertainties of the tramp market and left them free to fall back on the Baltic for their marginal, or less predictable, needs. It assisted the development of specialised ships, bulk carriers and others designed for particular trades and reduced the relative importance of the general purpose tramp. It had one other important effect. If a powerful industrial firm, a major oil or steel company, wanting to move raw materials round the world, would undertake to charter a vessel for an agreed period, above, say, three years and sometimes up to 20 years, this charter could be used as the security for a bank loan, thus considerably facilitating the building of new tonnage. All these influences reinforced the moves away from the all-purpose tramp.

Purpose-built shipping fleets

The oil trade has been the major example of an industry building vessels to suit its own purpose. Just over one third of the world's oil is carried in tankers owned by the oil companies themselves, the rest being transported in vessels on short or long charter or voyage by voyage. Long-term planning has also been forced on other trades. The world's steel industries have built specialised ore-carrying fleets for their own purposes. This has arisen not only from the remarkable expansion of the traffic in ore (10 million tons in 1938, 30 million in 1950 and probably over 120 million tons in 1963), but also from the rise in world-wide steel-making capacity (in the Soviet Union as well as in the under-developed countries) leading to longer hauls. Coupled with the urge to keep costs down, specialised ships on long charter have more and more been the solution. And what has been done for ore-carrying has also been accomplished more recently for molten sulphur and liquid ammonia.

The encroachment of longer-term charters on the day-to-day business of the Baltic has been persistent since the war. Little more than 10 per cent of the oil and a similar share of the ore traffic is now arranged on short charter. Fortunately, this development does not mean that the Baltic brokers have been squeezed out of business to the same extent. The oil companies, for one thing, have sensibly maintained their contacts with Baltic brokers in drawing up their longer-term contracts. They have kept their relationships with their shipping brokers more or less intact. The business is different; the advice needed is different; the relationships are as close as ever. Much the same has happened in other trades, too, though some of the more conservative-minded brokers have been slow to adapt themselves to the changing situation. This sluggish response, observable elsewhere in the City, is discussed in Part II, Chapter 12.

The changing pattern of chartering and the increase in specialisation have not been the only dangers to Baltic brokers. The improvement in communication throughout the world has also tended to persuade shippers and charterers to make deals direct with each other. Only the more alert brokers have been and will be able to deal with this development; the rest may suffer the fate of firms in other parts of the City which fail to change with the times. Some broking firms already have branches in other countries in an effort to keep abreast of events. One leading shipbroking firm even had the joy of sealing a deal in Rio de Janeiro not long ago between a major Brazilian charterer on the one hand and a good proportion of the Brazilian tanker fleet on the other. This was broking at its best. It was not arranged on the Baltic Exchange. Many other deals of this sort may not be done on the floor of the Baltic. But what the Baltic stands for—its standards of fair dealing and its ethics of performance—should continue to make such deals possible, wherever they are consummated.

The British merchant fleet and the Baltic

The Baltic was built up on the back of the British merchant fleet in the 19th century, when the fleet was over half of the world's total. Now, in spite of a continued increase in tonnage, its size relative to the world fleet has dropped to $14\frac{1}{2}$ per cent from 26 per cent in 1938 and about 50 per cent at the turn of the century. The British fleet has grown absolutely from $17\frac{1}{2}$ million tons in 1938 to $21\frac{1}{2}$ million tons in 1963, and the business attracted to the Baltic has continued to rise. The share of international business has also grown despite the changes in pattern and the adverse trends discussed above. The Baltic remains very active and is plainly doing more business than ever before, although some of it does not get on to the floor of the Exchange. Virtually all ocean-going tankers have been dealt with by office-to-office telex or telephone for some years, even for single voyages. This method is also used for some dry-cargo business and longer-term business of a financial character, in which money for shipbuilding may be involved. But the principle on which the business is negotiated and the standards of performance automatically accepted throughout the world not only in documentation but also in unwritten and even unspoken intent, are as much part of the Baltic as if it were conducted on the floor of its market. Furthermore the personal meetings, morning and afternoon, on the floor of the

Exchange continue to prove the most effective way of matching supply and demand for dry cargo tonnage for single voyages and medium-term contracts.

The Baltic also continues to thrive as a centre for the exchange of information, as a pool of expertise and as an acknowledged and respected authority for fair and honest dealing. Coupled with its uses in arbitration and the improvement of standard terms in charters, all these qualities stand behind the brokers, whether they remain on the floor of the Exchange or go aggressively after business throughout the world. Whether they will protect the more sleepy partners is another matter.

TABLE III
GROWTH OF BRITISH AND WORLD MERCHANT SHIPPING TONNAGES, 1850-1962

	World fleet [a] (m. tons gross)	British fleet (m.tons gross)	British fleet as percentage of World fleet
1850 [b]	1.98	1.02	52
1890 [b]	11.1	5.5	50
1910 [b]	23.4	10.76	46
1920	53.9	18.1	34
1939	68.5	17.9	26
1948 [c]	67.2	18.0	27
1962 [c]	127.7	21.7	17

[a]   Great Lakes tonnage excluded.
[b]   Tonnages reduced to steam equivalent by treating 4 tons of sailing tonnage as equivalent to 1 ton of steam tonnage.
[c]   US Reserve Fleet, 13.1 million tons in 1948 and 12.3 million tons in 1962, excluded.

Source: **Professor S. G. Sturmey,** *Journal of Institute of Bankers,* **April** 1964.

CHAPTER 8

LONDON AS A CAPITAL MARKET

HARDLY ANY of the City's functions have changed quite so much as its role as a source of long-term capital for foreign borrowers. This is not entirely a post-war phenomenon. Even in the 'thirties, the ability of foreign governments and industrialists to raise funds on the London market was being limited both by a shortage of capital and by specific government controls. But it is only since the war that the real shortage of capital for foreign borrowers has become quite so prominent. As indicated in Chapter 1, while Commonwealth countries have been able to raise fairly sizeable funds in London, only a handful of foreign loans had been floated until recently.

The City's role in providing long-term capital has been affected in two ways. One has been the decline in the amount of domestic funds available for investment overseas. The other has been the relative decline in the proportion of Britain's capital exports that has taken the form of a market issue of securities. In other words, for several years the country had less to spare for investment abroad, and what was available tended to be invested in ways which have often by-passed the City.

The extent to which London had become the prime supplier of long-term investment capital for foreign borrowers was touched upon in Chapter I. In the years immediately before the 1914 war, funds were leaving at the rate of some £200 million a year. There seems little doubt that they were mostly raised by the issue of securities on the London market. It is estimated that of almost £4,000 million of British capital invested abroad in 1914, only about £300 million was made up of 'direct' investment. The whole of the balance was believed to be traceable in the form of security issues of one form or another.

The City's role in these operations was highly important. The merchant banks and private banking houses, which less than a century earlier had been risking their own money in the development of trade and of foreign lands, were by this time advising foreign governments about raising loans on the London market. While continuing to finance trade by the acceptance of bills of exchange, they introduced an under-wrote foreign government and foreign industrial loans in London. The countries with which the City's merchant banks have had relations of this sort can be traced to this day; many of them are still the paying agents for these old loans: Roths-childs for Brazil, Hambros for Norway, Barings for the Argen-tine, and so on.

Decline in overseas lending

Throughout the 1920s, the London market remained fairly active. Both in 1927 and 1928 the amount of new overseas issues exceeded £150 million per annum. But by 1931 the total had dropped to under £50 million. It is now clear that this was the turning point. From 1932 to 1937 the average annual amount of overseas issues in London was only £34 million. Towards the end of the 1920s overseas issues formed almost a half of total issues on the London market. In the middle 'thirties they had fallen to no more than 19 per cent. This decline was due to economic and political disturbances abroad, culminating in some defaults on outstanding loans, and the restriction of foreign loans in 1932 and extended in 1936. In April 1936, the National Government established a new advisory committee, which later became the Foreign Trans-actions Advisory Committee, under Lord Kennet, to examine and control proposals for overseas issues. At the outbreak of the war it was changed into the Capital Issues Committee which restricted foreign issues closely during the war and throughout the early post-war years. Not only have the authorities con-tinued to keep a close check on foreign lending since the war; surplus funds for investment have also been scarce. Thus, the post-war record has, if anything, been worse than that of the 'thirties.

Table VIII, based on figures compiled by the Midland Bank, brings out the further decline in the share of London's capital going abroad since the war.

The total for foreign countries has been extremely small since 1954, it was non-existent in 1956 and it recovered only in 1964. Although Commonwealth countries have been getting a slightly larger share of the total amount going abroad, only in one of the recent years did the share approach the average rate of the years from 1933 to 1938. This decline does not necessarily mean that the Commonwealth is being starved of capital compared with the immediate pre-war years. On the contrary, the flow of long-term capital to the sterling area has been extremely strong in recent years, strong enough to persuade many people to call for restrictions to control it. But it has largely taken the form of 'direct' investment, rather than of issues on the London market. In other words, in contrast to the period when London was the main centre for the provision of long-term capital, the bulk of our investment abroad nowadays is investment by firms (and government agencies) rather than issues in the London market. The City's role has shrunk even more than the fall in the country's total foreign investment suggests.

Effects on the City

It is therefore hardly surprising that the institutions that make up the London capital market should also have changed somewhat over the past 20 or 30 years. They include stockbrokers, issuing houses, merchant banks, clearing banks and mining finance houses, as well as the various institutional investors from the large insurance companies to the pension funds and investment trusts. Many have been forced to take on new tasks and new institutions have sprung up.

Few perhaps have been affected by the shift from foreign to domestic issues quite so much as the merchant banks. Although most of them have become extremely active in domestic issues, the relative absence of foreign loans in London has left its mark on the merchant banks in another direction. As we saw in earlier chapters, after the disappearance of the sellers' market within a few years of the end of the war, the demand for longer export credits became a thorny problem for the merchant banks, the clearing banks and other City institutions. In many ways, this demand for capital goods on five years' credit and longer was the result of the tremendous drives towards industrial development in all parts of the world. But, whereas part of the capital needs of the developing countries was in former times satisfied by long-term loans on the London market, in the post-war era it began to take the form of a demand for the delivery of capital goods on longer export credit terms. The merchant banks have been prominent in

TABLE VIII

NEW CAPITAL ISSUES, 1933-8 to 1964

		1933-38*	1954	1955	1956	1961	1962	1963	1964
HOME:	£m	131.0	410.0	525.1	264.6	553.5	565.2	534.6	464.4
% of all issues		80.9	87.0	92.6	89.4	90.9	93.4	90.2	91.4
COMMONWEALTH									
Public Bodies	£m	9.5	35.1	17.5	13.8	19.7	10.9	39.5	11.6
Companies	£m	16.8	19.3	22.4	17.6	29.2	18.1	14.3	10.9
Total	£m	26.3	54.5	39.9	31.3	48.9	29.1	53.8	22.6
% of all issues		16.2	11.6	7.0	10.6	8.0	4.8	9.1	4.4
FOREIGN	£m	4.7	6.6	2.2	—	6.3	10.7	4.6	20.9
% of all issues		2.9	1.4	0.4	—	1.0	1.8	0.8	4.1
TOTAL OVERSEAS:	£m	31.0	61.1	42.1	31.3	55.2	39.8	58.4	43.4
% of all issues		19.1	13.0	7.4	10.6	9.1	6.6	9.8	8.6

* Yearly averages.
Source: Midland Bank Review, February, 1965.

TABLE IX

FOREIGN BOND ISSUES IN EUROPE AND USA, 1959-63

($ million)

	Germany	Netherlands	Sweden	Switzerland	UK	US gross amount offered		Total
						Canadian issues	Other	
1959	34	—	—	107	98	496	284	780
1960	14	—	12	132	82	278	287	565
1961	3	146	7	218	112	324	301	625
1962	25	28	2	140	62	544	596	1,146
1963 (first half)	25	—	19	91	38	695	466	1,161
TOTAL	101	174	40	688	392	2,337	1,934	4,271

Source: A Description and Analysis of Certain European Capital Markets, US Treasury Department for Joint Economic Committee, US Congress, 1964.

filling the new gap as best they can. As it has turned out, the clearing banks have generally had to provide the bulk of the funds to meet these longer-term export credits, but the merchant banks have often played a useful role in working out the details, drawing once again on their intimate knowledge of overseas territories, gained from close personal contact with correspondents abroad.

New opportunities from Europe?

Now the wheel seems to be turning full circle again. Spurred on by the Bank of England, the City has been dusting off the old machinery and seeing whether it cannot really play an old role in a new way, to everyone's benefit. Europe, it is said, now has the savings and the spare money, but no capital market to speak of;[1] London, on the other hand, has the market, the mechanism and the old skill, but hardly enough spare capital. Why not put London's skill at the disposal of Europe's savings and allow London to earn an honest penny for its effort? The experiment is still young, but several important moves have been made to promote the extension of the City's security market over a wider field. Two events combined to put some drive into these efforts. The first was Britain's attempt to join the Common Market; the second the criticisms by the American administration of the European capital market. The lowering of currency barriers, following the introduction of convertibility in 1958, led to a growing interest among European investors in the shares of other countries. The prospect that Britain might join the Six added to this interest, and the general European prosperity confirmed investors in their faith. It was equally the combination of this rising tide of European wealth and the continuing series of European borrowings on the New York market, at a time when the dollar was still in the convalescent stage, that finally led to strong American criticisms of the failings of the European capital markets. These views were forcibly expressed by Mr. Douglas Dillon, Secretary of the US Treasury, in an important speech in Rome.[2] His major point was quite simple. The progress in removing the deficit in the US balance of payments, he said, was being threatened by the increasing amounts of long-term foreign

[1] The reasons for the absence of the right machinery in Europe are complex: the breakdown in the 'thirties, the war, the absence of an equity-minded investing public and the memories of the lost fortunes due to excessive inflation, etc.

[2] American Bankers' Association meeting, May 1962.

borrowing on the New York market. He called for the Europeans to cut down their borrowing in New York and to get their capital markets in working order. As a further protection for the American market, the United States Government eventually imposed an interest equalisation tax on foreign issues, thereby raising the cost of borrowing in New York. How far this foreign borrowing had gone (particularly the rapid increase during 1962 and the first half of 1963, compared with the corresponding issues in Europe) is shown in Table IX.

The first result of the American action (even before the legislation for the equalisation tax was passed) was a rapid reduction in foreign issues in New York. The second was the immediate re-appraisal of the London and Continental security markets. Why, it was asked, had so many European issues been made in New York, particularly when in some years as much as one-half or more of European bonds issued there were bought by Europeans themselves? In some cases the answers were easy: European investors found it convenient because interest paid to non-residents was exempt from the US with-holding tax.[1] Others were simply keen to evade taxation at home or wanted to keep part of their assets in dollars. But, whatever the reason, one thing seemed clear to the Americans: the trend would not have developed had Europe's capital markets been as flexible and efficient as that in New York. A subsequent investigation undertaken for the Joint Economic Committee of the US Congress[2] concluded that not only were Europe's capital markets generally inefficient, but that many legal and fiscal restraints were imposed on the flotation of new security issues. Apart from London and Zurich, which the report said had 'regularly accommodated a significant volume of new security issues by foreign borrowers', the efforts of other exchanges had been marginal:

'Germany, which does not impose restrictions on capital movements, has provided only relatively small amounts for new foreign security issues because of high issue costs and the high level of interest rates prevailing there. The Netherlands permitted a substantial volume of foreign issues in 1961, but no foreign issues in 1959 or 1960, and only a very

[1] The authorities stipulate that a certain proportion of the interest payable is withheld as tax, subject to claims by individuals. Foreigners can claim under double taxation agreements where they exist.
[2] *A Description and Analysis of Certain European Capital Markets*, US Treasury Department, 1964.

small amount in 1962 and 1963. France permitted no foreign security issues until late in 1963, apart from franc area issues, while Belgium and Italy have opened their markets to limited borrowings by international institutions but to few others.'

In contrast to these criticisms, the London market came in for praise both for its smooth machinery and for its costs of operation: 'London capital market facilities are among the most highly developed in the world'. The report also found that the low cost of making an issue (second only to New York) 'reflects the efficiency and extensive development of London's market facilities'.

The Bank of England's own conclusions[1] after a recent survey were not dissimilar. It found that the American market was appreciably bigger; that the costs of dealings in Switzerland, Holland and Italy were lower than in London; and that only a fraction of London's overseas issues since the war had gone outside the Commonwealth. Yet it found much encouragement, and concluded:

'It is clear that New York is pre-eminent in providing by far the widest and most competitive market in securities, with London easily next in importance . . . The U.K. market does not suffer from the structural limitations present in some Continental markets . . . There is no reason why the U.K. should not play a useful part by acting as a financial entrepôt, in which funds mobilised from a variety of sources are channelled into foreign loans issued on the London market.'

In spite of the size of the American market—especially the so-called 'over the counter' market which operates outside New York and American Stock Exchanges—the number and range of securities officially dealt in on the London Stock Exchange is remarkably high. Nearly 10,000 securities are quoted daily in its own Official List. This total is about nine times as large as Wall Street's 1,100 listings, and compares with a few hundreds of shares dealt in on the Continental stock exchanges. Yet even this is only a fraction of the total number of securities that can be dealt in on the London market. Under a special rule, members are allowed to deal for their clients in any security quoted on almost any recognised stock exchange in any country of the world. Thus an investor, British or foreign,

[1] *Quarterly Bulletin,* June 1963.

may use the London Stock Exchange to buy or sell virtually any security he likes, provided only that a recognised market for it is in existence anywhere in the world. No other market enjoys so much freedom.

Scope of the London Stock Exchange

Some idea of the scope of the London market is provided by the statistics published annually by the Stock Exchange. They show that the precise number of securities quoted in the Official List was 9,175 on 30 March, 1962; the nominal amount of capital represented by the securities was £33,621 million, and the aggregate market value £50,224 million (or about twice the British gross national product). Included in these huge totals were 597 gilt-edged stocks (securities issued by British and Commonwealth governments, local authorities, etc.) and 307 foreign government or similar loans having a combined nominal value of £21,597 million and a market value of £15,919 million, and 8,687 securities issued by companies with an aggregate nominal value of £9,696 million and a market value of £29,149 million. By comparison with these figures, the numbers and value of securities quoted on the various Continental stock exchanges fade almost into insignificance.

The nominal value of the foreign stocks, bonds, etc., which, for purposes of the Stock Exchange statistics, are incorporated with British Government and other gilt-edged securities, was as much as £1,707 million, but, as the total included the Czarist loans repudiated by the Soviet authorities (and, therefore, almost worthless under present conditions), the market value was only £221 million. No corresponding separate details are available of the foreign shares, or the shares of companies operating entirely abroad. But their number and value are substantial. They include Dominion and Colonial, Indian, American and other foreign railways, foreign banks, utility companies and mines working in Australia, Canada, Rhodesia, East Africa, West Africa, South Africa, Malaya, Mexico and many other countries. In addition, they embrace 295 securities of rubber companies (some registered in Great Britain, some in the country where they operate), 271 of tea or coffee companies and 33 of oil companies.

Reduction and revival in foreign stocks

Before the First World War—and indeed even just before the Second—the number of foreign stocks officially dealt in and quoted in London was much larger than at present. The reduction was primarily due to three separate causes. In the first place, huge quantities of British-owned foreign securities, especially British-owned dollar securities, were mobilised by the government and sold to help to finance the two wars. Second, numerous loans matured and were not replaced. And third many foreign operating companies, including the Argentine railways, were expropriated or nationalised by the governments of the countries in which they worked. Owing to balance of payments and other difficulties at various times since 1954 and the consequent restrictions on lending money abroad, the reduction in the number of foreign securities resulting from these causes could not be made good.

Apart from recent issues in London, considerable progress has also been made in what is technically known as the 'introduction' of foreign shares on to the London market. For many years the shares of various international companies such as Unilever, Royal Dutch Petroleum and Philips Lamp Works have been officially quoted in London. Comparatively recently this list has been extended by the granting of official quotations for a number of the best-known Continental companies. And the list seems likely to grow continually, because this cross-fertilisation of share markets is becoming increasingly popular among British as well as foreign investors who wish to increase the geographical spread of their portfolios.

Before an official quotation is granted, the Stock Exchange requires a market to be created in the shares in London. Normally this is arranged through the purchase of a block of shares in the foreign company, frequently by a merchant bank, and subsequently placing them with British investors. Simultaneously, a prospectus is published in British newspapers so that the general public have the opportunity to examine the information required to assess the investment merits of the share. These prospectuses, like all others, have to be submitted for detailed scrutiny by officials of the Share and Loan Department of the London Stock Exchange, who insist on the strict observance of stringent rules drawn up for the benefit of potential investors. The Share and Loan Department does not pass judgement on the merits of the shares: but it does demand that the prospectus contains all the relevant details which an investor needs before he can make a proper assessment for himself. Only when these conditions have been fulfilled will the Stock Exchange Council grant permission for the shares to be quoted on the London market.

This insistence by the Council on full disclosure of relevant information is one of the main factors limiting the number of foreign shares quoted in London. Often much of the information it demands is not made available by the foreign company to shareholders in its own country.[1] But the Council will normally accept nothing less than it demands from British companies whose shares are quoted on the London Stock Exchange. For instance, it needs consolidated accounts, that is, balance sheets and profit and loss accounts that include the figures of subsidiary companies as well as the parent company itself; profit statements covering at least ten years wherever possible; certification of the accounts by qualified, independent auditors; and details of material contracts, including directors' remuneration. Apart from the United States, there is probably no other country that requires the disclosure of so much information for the guidance of its investors.

British requirements are certainly far more exacting than those in Continental countries. On the Continent, more reliance is placed on the sponsors of a new issue (or of an application for permission to deal) than on the statistical and other details disclosed in a prospectus. In Britain, the information must be laid bare for all to see, though the quality of the sponsor is often taken as a guide to the quality of the investment. Many Continental countries consider there is no reason why they should change their method of approach, which they consider satisfactory, and publish information hitherto undisclosed simply in order to obtain a London quotation. Nevertheless, several leading European companies have obtained a London quotation. They include the Banque de Paris et de Pays Bas (France), Farbenfabriken Bayer, Farbwerke Hoechst, August Thyssen-Huette, Volkswagen, Commerzbank and Kunden Kreditbank (Germany), and Montecatini and Snia Viscosa (Italy). In addition, London quotations have been granted to several continental unit or similar trusts, including Robeco, Eurofund, Interunie and Vereenigte Besitzt (1894).

Buying and selling foreign securities in London

For the British investor, the procedure for buying or selling these shares, or of any other foreign share whether quoted in London or not, is the same as for the purchase or sale of a

[1] 'In law and even in common practice the contents of most European company accounts approximate to the position in this country before the 1948 Companies Act.'—Harold Rose, *Disclosure in Company Accounts*, Eaton Paper 1, IEA, 2nd Ed., 1965.

British share. He simply instructs his stockbroker either directly or through his bank, solicitor, or similar representative, to buy or sell the shares. After the order has been completed, he draws a sterling cheque to cover the cost of the shares, or receives a sterling cheque for the shares he sold. He does nothing more except, perhaps, sign a few papers under the broker's instructions. All the rest of the work, which seems complicated to the uninitiated, is done for him by the broker.

If the investor wishes to buy marketable non-sterling securities he, or his broker, is allowed under British law to buy in London a special type of currency with which to pay for them. This currency is variously known as investment, security, switch or premium dollars. There is a recognised market for these special dollars in the London money market, where they can be bought and sold freely. Their price is not fixed but is determined by supply and demand. Accordingly, the investor must recognise that when he buys a foreign share he is assuming an exchange risk as well as a stock market risk. The non-sterling securities may not be held directly by the investor who has bought them. He must leave them in the care of an authorised depository, usually a British stockbroker, banker or solicitor. And dividends received on the foreign shares must be converted into sterling immediately. Although all this seems complicated, it is no real deterrent to a would-be British investor in overseas securities because he is not directly concerned with the mechanics of the transactions he initiates, although of course he must pay for them.

It is also in London's interest to see that this traffic in international securities is 'two-way'. Just as a market for foreign securities has grown up in the London Stock Exchange, so markets for British securities have developed in many foreign financial centres. A whole host of prominent British shares are now being dealt in in the United States by American 'depository receipts'. Shares in the British company are bought on the London markets, usually by an American bank, and deposited in the vaults of the bank's London office. The London office notifies its American office of the purchase and the American office issues depository receipts against them, which are bought and sold 'over the counter' like shares. The London office receives the dividends and any other distributions made by the British company, and arranges for their payment in dollars to the American holders of the depository receipts. Whenever the American demand for depository receipts exceeds the number of shares deposited in the London office's vaults, the London office buys more shares on the London market. Conversely, when the demand is less the excess shares are sold on the London market. This method of dealing in British shares has a number of advantages, not least of which are that it avoids the physical transfer of the shares to and fro across the Atlantic, thus saving considerable time and expense, and that transfers of depository receipts in America escape United Kingdom stamp duty. Somewhat similar methods have been adopted for dealing in a small but growing number of leading British shares on several continental markets. They include Imperial Chemical Industries, Courtaulds, Bowater Paper, Great Universal Stores, Elliott-Automation and Electric and Musical Industries.

Obviously Continental investors buy many other British shares directly through the London market. Their number has increased materially in recent years and appears likely to grow further: this is one of the reasons why the London Stock Exchange Council in 1962 broke with tradition by allowing broker members to open branch offices abroad. But, until recently, any extension of Continental buying of British shares was hindered by fiscal and other obstacles. Chief among them was, and probably still is, the stamp duty on all purchases of shares, in spite of the reduction in the rate from 2 per cent to 1 per cent in the 1963 Budget. This impost has long been a very real handicap and discouragement to foreign investment because it increases costs considerably. Lord Ritchie of Dundee, chairman of the Stock Exchange, was reflecting virtually the whole of London financial opinion when he stated in a lecture delivered to the International Banking Summer School held in England in July 1961:

> 'The Chancellor who imposed this tax made no secret of the fact that he regarded it as a political move and not primarily for the purpose of raising revenue. It is to my mind incomprehensible that nothing has been done by successive Chancellors to remove it altogether, or even to reduce it. The situation has even arisen in some cases where business in some leading British securities can be conducted by over-seas investors more favourably in stock exchanges abroad than in London owing to this tax.'

Even stronger condemnatory words were used by Mr. Maudling when, as Chancellor of the Exchequer, he cut the rate of the tax in his 1963 Budget. He said:

'The 2 per cent rate of duty is substantially higher than in any other country and has many unfortunate effects. It drives business, and therefore invisible earnings, from London. It is a strong disincentive to investment in Britain by people in other countries. It discourages investment in productive industry, not least by the smaller investor. It tends to raise the cost of issuing capital.'

Halving the tax has halved the force of this argument but it remains true that it is driving business, and therefore invisible earnings, from London.

The tax on overseas investment

A further barrier to overseas investment in British securities is the method of charging tax on them. Dividends and interest paid on the majority of British stocks and shares are taxed at source at the standard rate; that is, tax at the full standard rate, which is appreciably heavier than the withholding taxes[1] imposed by other countries, is deducted before the dividend or interest is paid to the investor, whether he is resident in Great Britain or not. Non-residents can claim repayment of the tax but the paper work involved is tedious, sometimes complicated, always time-consuming and irritating. For the institutional overseas investors, such as investment trusts and insurance companies, who have staff experienced in making these claims, the task may not be too onerous. For the relatively small private investor, however, it is frustrating to say the least and often a sufficient deterrent to make him fight shy of British securities.

Fortunately, two other serious hindrances to foreign investment in the British market have been largely removed. The 1963 Budget lifted the ban on bearer securities imposed at the beginning of the Second World War as part of the emergency measures to conserve the nation's financial resources. Bearer securities have always been attractive to foreign investors accustomed to them—the bulk of investments overseas are in bearer form—and who like the secrecy that attaches to them. Removal of the ban should, therefore, increase the popularity of British securities with Continental and other overseas investors and thereby improve the United Kingdom's invisible earnings.

[1] See footnote p. 108

Simplifying share transfers

The other hindrance has virtually disappeared as the new procedure for transferring shares from one investor to another has got under way. The former system was archaic, cumbersome, complicated, frustrating, and above all, time-consuming. It frequently led to costly delay between the execution of an order on the floor of the stock exchange and the actual physical delivery of the securities to the purchaser. Although the new holder's rights to all future dividends and other distributions were completely safeguarded from the moment the shares were purchased on the stock exchange, the delays in delivery—and the paper work frequently involved—were irksome to all investors and often unacceptable to foreign investors not accustomed to them. The new system is much simpler. Sellers no longer need to sign so many documents, the signatures do not require witnessing, much labour is avoided and much time saved. For foreign investors in particular, this is a significant convenience.

New overseas borrowing

This new improved mechanism has already been put to the test. From small, tentative beginnings following the announcement of the new policy by the Governor of the Bank of England in March and October, 1962, discussed in Chapter 10, the number of new foreign issues in foreign currencies grew considerably throughout 1963 and 1964.[1] The first step came with an Iceland loan at the end of 1962. It was the first bond offering by a non-Commonwealth government in more than ten years and only the fourth since the war. It also allowed potential investors to opt for bearer certificates if they wished, a notable relaxation of exchange control. Then, five months later, came the first offering of a foreign currency issue since the end of the war—the first of many. It was for $20 million for Belgium. It was placed privately and was for only three years. In July of the same year followed another dollar loan, this time for Autostrade, an Italian private company to finance motorways. This was a longer-term issue. It was also the first to be quoted in Luxembourg. Then came a Japanese sterling conversion issue and, in November 1963, the controversial 60 million Swiss francs for the City of Copenhagen. The Swiss authorities made a strong protest about the use of Swiss francs, fearing it might affect interest rates in Switzerland and interfere with their control of the Swiss capital market. They also dis-

[1] See Table X at the end of this chapter.

liked the international status it might give to the Swiss franc. No other Swiss franc issues have followed, but the flow of dollar issues has continued regularly.

In 1963 the amount of foreign issues was close to the equivalent of $100 million, the majority in US dollars. This was followed by a total of no less than $350 million in 1964, with again most of the issues designated in dollars. The City's mechanism was working smoothly again and the cost to the gold reserves was negligible. Since United Kingdom residents could subscribe to the foreign currency issues only by buying investment dollars from the restricted pool at the current premium (between 9 and 10 per cent at times during 1963 and 1964), few in practice subscribed and those who did had no impact on the central gold reserves. The only people able to subscribe with free dollars were the banks sponsoring the issue, and this facility was given simply to support operations during the issuing period. It has been estimated that, in most cases, up to 95 per cent of these foreign currency issues have ended up in foreign hands. In short, London has performed a useful service at negligible cost to the reserves and has earned valuable foreign exchange for its efforts. The sponsoring banks get commissions for the various services they offer. Each issue will vary, but commissions of 2½ per cent are common, with part of this having to be shared out among the other members of the issuing consortia. The upshot is that for the issues of some $350 million in 1964, City banks must have earned up to £2½ million ($7 million).

There are, of course, two problems being faced. One is the difficulty of using the flexible machinery of the London market in a way that does not strain the British balance of payments. The other is the revival of European capital, through Europe's own market machinery, in order to take the burden off New York (or at least to even out the burden between the two continents). In this context, London naturally regards herself as part of Europe. London, therefore, has to take account not only of the role she can play, but also of the actions and intentions of her counterparts (rivals perhaps) on the Continent. The encouragement of foreign currency loans in London puts London's skills to good use at little risk. It successfully taps European savings and helps to take some of the pressure off the New York market. But it does not necessarily tap Continental (or even British) savings to the same degree that a sterling loan in London or a Deutschemark loan in Frankfurt would do. It is not surprising, therefore, that thoughts (and some actions) have been moving in that direction too.

Loans in domestic currencies

In London, the first step was to bring members of the European Free Trade Association on to the same footing in raising money in London as members of the Commonwealth. Thus, Austria, Portugal, Switzerland, Sweden, Norway and Denmark now have the right, given the technical permission of the Bank of England in the timing of the issue, to raise capital in the London market. Since Switzerland is unlikely to need money and the Scandinavian countries were already being treated on much the same financial basis as the Commonwealth, the concession largely concerned Portugal and Austria. It is one thing, however, to change intentions: quite another to put them into operation. The growing overseas deficit plainly reduced the possibility of opening to any significant extent the London market to sterling issues for foreign borrowers in 1964. An interesting exception was the £4 million City of Turin loan, issued towards the end of the year, designated in sterling with an option to holders to take principal or interest in pounds or Deutschemarks. Here was a new way of straddling the London and Continental markets, worked out and backed up by S. G. Warburg. An alternative idea with the same ultimate aim of reviving Continental capital issues has been suggested by Dr. Hermann J. Abs, managing director of the Deutsche Bank: the European parallel loan.

'I would define a European parallel loan as the simultaneous floating of several loans of one issuer in Europe with each participating country raising one loan in its own currency, the terms and conditions of all the loans being uniform as far as possible and only differing where absolutely necessary. Such a parallel action would accumulate the available resources of the European capital markets involved. As each issue would be made out in the currency of the country concerned, the loan would be acceptable to all groups of investors . . . In spite of their plurality, the European capital markets could then represent themselves as one market well capable of raising a total amount not falling short of that which the United States market could provide.'[1]

At the time of writing (March 1965), no practical test of such an issue has been possible. The difficulties are, of course,

[1] *The Times*, 11 March, 1964.

obvious. There are many administrative obstacles in different markets: exchange control varies; interest rates differ; transfer guarantees would need to be examined; and all the legal problems arising out of potential default need to be looked at closely. The main objection is that, by recognising the differences between individual capital markets in Europe, the parallel loan might tend to perpetuate them rather than shift them.

In addition, different currencies still persist throughout Europe. One way of getting round this diversity has been to issue loans in dollars. Another has been to make issues in terms of units of account.[1] This has been particularly encouraged by the Kredietbank in Brussels. It has been highly successful, if judged by the volume of such issues. But opposition is growing, not only from some central banks, but also from practical bankers who are increasingly worried about the full implications of so many issues with different legal backgrounds and about the complexities of trying to roll up a score or so of different currency values into one unit of account.

What a member of the London Stock Exchange has to realise now is that, in spite of all these difficulties, the Continent is not standing still. It is attempting to improve its various capital markets. It is trying to remove obstacles. Most important of all, the Common Market members are progressively putting their stock exchanges on a similar basis. Every member of the Six has now agreed to allow its investors to buy and sell stocks and shares in all the other member countries of the Community. The idea of establishing what would in effect be an EEC capital market that would supply the needs of all member countries is being actively canvassed. So, too, is the possibility of unifying the Community's stock exchanges, each one functioning separately but operating according to a common set of rules, regulations, standards and practices. Such a combination would create a formidable competitor to London. Individual Continental markets remain restricted, having difficulty in dealing in large blocks of shares quickly and without violent effects on prices. They need wider share ownership and much more participation by the public; the existing heavy concentration of shareholdings in the hands of banks and holding companies restricts marketability and tends to exaggerate price movements. But close co-operation among the bourses, together

---

[1] The issues were made in several countries at the same time and were denominated in units of account made up of, say, 17 national currencies. It was a way of giving an international value to the issues.

with the adoption of unified laws for taxing investors and, perhaps, common financial and monetary policies could improve the quality of the service the Continental markets provide.

Three imperatives

To sum up, London will have to keep in touch with all these developments in other capital markets, keep open its communications with the rest of the world, and increase its internal efficiency. Under the first head comes the ability to consider outside ideas, like those of Dr. Abs, to see whether London cannot co-operate with others or cannot adapt their plans to suit her circumstances. This is the way that Dr. Abs' views of parallel loans should be dealt with, not dismissed outright as coming from a rival stable.

Under the second head it is a matter of maintaining physical contact with other bourses by whatever means are available. London brokers are already linked by telephone, telex and cable with all the principal overseas bourses—those in Europe, North America, Japan, India, Australia, New Zealand, Hong Kong, Singapore, South Africa and South America. They conduct arbitrage business with about 25 other stock markets.

Advertising, size and efficiency

Finally, there is the question of London's internal arrangements to meet the challenge from abroad. The proposal to integrate the London and provincial stock exchanges into a National Stock Exchange may in fact be one of the signs of this awareness. The integration has been slow in coming mainly because of the difficulties of putting London's arrangements for protecting the public against defaulters on to a wider national basis. There is a large compensation fund for this purpose in London: the funds in some of the provincial centres have been less adequate. Another reason for delay has been London's natural desire not to give any appearance of domination. But diplomacy can be pursued (as in this case) at the cost of efficiency.

London also has much to do itself. The simplified transfer system, the cutting of stamp duty and the return of bearer securities all have needed and received the Council's support and all should help London to meet competition from abroad.

Yet the obvious restriction on competition among brokers, the ban on advertising, has not yet been removed. It is high time that the nettle was grasped. There is no reason why advertising by stockbrokers should descend to the tipping of shares or outright 'share-pushing'. The Council of the London Stock Exchange could control the quality of advertising. If it is claimed that this would give the large broking firms too much of an advantage it must be recognised that the trend towards larger firms already exists. Bigger units can provide the research and other services now needed to compete with foreign centres and to offer improved facilities for domestic clients.

The idea that large broking firms necessarily ignore the needs of the small investor is amply disproved by American experience. Since the City's clearing banks and merchant banks can advertise without harm to their services, stockbrokers should be allowed to do the same.[1] This may appear to be a small issue in the overall problem of improving the efficiency of the London market. But since private complaints from recent foreign borrowers have largely concerned the operations of the broking firms (rather than the issuing houses), any move, however small, to strengthen competition among brokers should be made. The broader questions of how far London's capital mechanism should be used to export growing quantities of Britain's savings and how far it should be confined to entrepôt operations are left until Chapter 12.

[1] One of the strangest anomalies is that Merrill Lynch, the biggest American stockbroking firm, is allowed to advertise the services of its London office in undertaking investment in American securities; yet London brokers doing the same business cannot.

PART II

ANALYSIS AND APPRAISAL

CHAPTER 9

THE CITY'S EARNINGS

I. INDIVIDUAL MARKETS

A. INSURANCE

AS WE SAW in Chapter 5, the insurance market's total premium income is known in some detail. It is also known in broad outline what proportion of this business comes from abroad. But to move from these percentages to the actual foreign earnings of the market is a hazardous exercise. This may explain why the British Insurance Association has never made an attempt to do so regularly. The only post-war figures for the insurance market's foreign income have been the following:

(a) an estimate of £33 million by the British Insurance Association in March 1949;

(b) a figure of £40 million quoted by the Association continuously since devaluation in September 1949;

(c) the same figure of £40 million by the Economic Secretary to the Treasury in December 1957; and

(d) a figure of £50 million by the chairman of the British Insurance Association in the same month.

How these figures were arrived at has not been revealed, and no recent estimate has been made by the Association. My own estimate[1] for the year 1958 was about £70 million. By 1963, as shown in some detail in Chapter 5, these earnings had probably grown to about £85 million.

This figure needs a little explanation. It is based, it will be recalled, on the average rates of underwriting profits in recent years. In the United States, for example, for which an average underwriting profit of 1.0 per cent was adopted, the rates in individual years have varied from profits of 8.8 per cent in

[1] *The City's Invisible Earnings, op. cit.*, p. 54.

1949 to *losses* of 8.6 per cent in 1946 and of 7.6 per cent in 1957. Lloyd's rates of underwriting profits have varied similarly. Thus, the foreign income of the insurance market varies widely from year to year. It is quite possible, for example, that the figure for 1956 (when underwriting losses were made in the United States) was little bigger than that for one or two of the early post-war years. The £85 million estimate is therefore the average annual profit which the London insurance market can expect to earn on its overseas operations, provided that the premium volume remains at the present level. The earnings for individual recent years may well have varied from £40 million to £90 million.

Earnings and remittances

Secondly, although this figure of £85 million is what the insurance market is estimated to have earned overseas, it does not necessarily square with the amount of foreign exchange remitted to this country from abroad. For example, the company remittances from the United States in 1956 amounted to $17.2 million (roughly £6 million) compared with estimated annual earnings of £18 million. The difference lies in the amount of money ploughed back abroad which may be larger than that remitted. Lloyd's underwriters also leave a good deal of their premiums abroad. Their dollar trust funds in the United States are known to have risen from $43 million (about £11 million) in 1939 to $463 million (£165 million) in 1963 (see Table XI). The importance of the dollar holdings of the companies

TABLE XI
LLOYD'S TRUST FUND IN USA, 1939 and 1963

1939				$'000	£'000
Trust Fund in New York	...	...	...	40,000	10,000
Deposit in Kentucky	...	...	...	350	87
Deposit in Illinois	...	...	...	2,350	587
			TOTAL	42,700	10,675
1963				$	£
Trust Fund in New York	...	...	...	445,000	158,000
Deposit in Kentucky	...	...	...	500	178
Deposit in Illinois					
Trust Funds	...	...	...	2,500	892
Non-Trust Funds	...	...	...	15,000	5,714
			TOTAL	463,000	164,784

was amply revealed during the war years when the British Government obtained a loan of $425 million (£106 million) from the United States Reconstruction Finance Corporation against the collateral of dollar securities of $530 million (£132 million), of which $202 million (£50 million) was accounted for by the shares of US subsidiaries of British insurance companies. The loan was repaid out of the dividends from the securities and from the remittances of the British insurance companies. The insurance companies alone repaid some $169 million to the RFC in the ten years between 1941 and 1951.

Quite apart from their direct value, the investments built up abroad have markedly appreciated in recent years. The capital appreciation in the United States alone has been estimated at an average of about £8½ million a year in the 13 years 1950 to 1962, over and above the underwriting and interest earnings. And, of course, the investments appreciated because of the devaluation of sterling in 1949.

B. BANKING

Foreign earnings within the banking system can be studied under three headings: income from all types of lending, from acceptance credits to longer-term finance; secondly, from foreign exchange and arbitrage transactions; and, thirdly, from other services.

Commissions are earned by the banks not only on transactions where foreigners borrow in London but also on transactions where the banks simply act as intermediates in facilitating payments. Both generally come under the description of bankers' documentary credits. Whereas the former involve what are known in their various forms as *acceptance* credits, the latter are described simply as *sight* credits (that is, they require payments in cash). In both, the bank receives a commission for its services. With a sight credit, the bank acts as intermediary between the buyer and the seller. The seller wants to be certain that the documents of title to his goods do not get into the hands of the buyer until he has been paid; and the buyer wants to be assured that his money will not be paid over until the documents have been checked. The banks earn commissions depending on whether the credit is 'confirmed' or not. Where the banks are asked to make their payments so many days after 'sight', that is, where the foreign trader wants credit, there is a different scale of commission.

In addition to these commissions, the banks earn interest on the credits extended to foreign borrowers. On a straight-forward loan or overdraft, the interest payment is a clear earning of foreign income. But with an acceptance credit the earning is not so clear-cut because of the discount on the bill of exchange. On an acceptance credit financing the movement of goods between third countries (from, say, the Far East to Germany), the rate of discount is earned basically by whichever institution holds the bill to maturity, whether a discount house or a clearing bank. But, when the exporter is British, it is often difficult to see whether the bank or the exporter earns the foreign exchange. Sometimes, the exporter will add the discount charge to the cost of his goods. The opposite is true when British importers get credit on a three months' bill; the discount charge may then be added to the cost of the goods by the foreign exporter. Thus, while the banking system earns commissions on all these transactions, it is never entirely clear where the final cost of the interest (or discount) charge will be borne.

Income from advances and acceptances

It is now possible to be more accurate than a few years ago about bank earnings, either by way of interest or discount, or by way of commissions. Since the Radcliffe Report's strong recommendations about the need for more financial information, more has been published by the Bank of England in its *Quarterly Bulletin*. The latest contribution by the Bank is a breakdown of the foreign lending of the British banks. The details are shown in Table XII.

TABLE XII

FOREIGN LENDING BY BRITISH BANKS
(£ million)

	Advances & Overdrafts	Acceptances
1962 December	318	177
1963 March	364	181
June	340	203
September	354	200
December	351	209
1964 March	399	240

Source: Bank of England Quarterly Bulletin, September, 1964.

It is possible to make a rough analysis of the banks' foreign earnings from these figures. For the whole of 1963, the total of foreign advances and overdrafts kept around an average level of £350 million. Bank rate was maintained at about 4 per cent during the year. The interest charged on advances was at least 1 per cent higher, so that interest earnings during the year were about £17½ million. The corresponding total of foreign acceptances was around £200 million on average and the average interest rate just below 4 per cent, thus yielding £7½ million. Acceptance commissions, etc., might add another £3½ million. Thus the total so far is £28½ million.

Banks in London pay interest on foreign money deposited with them. This is a particularly important part of London's function as an international banking centre. London's banks and institutions are in reality financing some of their business by making full use of foreign deposits. But in the post-war years these strictly banking (or even trading) deposits have tended to be lost among the extremely large total of sterling balances built up by several countries during and after the war. While it would be wrong to charge the interest payments on these £4,000 million worth of sterling balances against the banking system, it seems right to deduct at least the interest payments on what may be termed 'normal' banking deposits of overseas customers in arriving at a figure of the banks' invisible earnings. These foreign deposits are probably between £150 million and £200 million in normal times. The interest paid on some of the deposits might amount to £5 million, thus reducing the total earnings from foreign credits to about £23½ million.

Income from foreign exchange and arbitrage transactions
The second group of services offered by London banks includes foreign exchange dealings and all types of foreign arbitrage transactions. Almost every sort of bank is concerned in these activities. As we saw in Chapter 3 the expansion in the exchange business since convertibility in 1958 has been remarkable. Many people have the impression that profits have risen as fast as turnover. But competition has increased too, keeping margins exceptionally narrow. It is still a bone of contention in the City whether the foreign exchange market earns much foreign exchange itself. The share of foreign earnings in the total income of the market is difficult to measure with precision. Strictly, any transaction with a foreign centre which cuts down, however marginally, the cost to a United Kingdom client of a

foreign exchange operation ought to be counted. But foreign income arises mainly where a London bank (or authorised dealer) undertakes arbitrage between two foreign centres and where a London bank renders services for a foreign client. Yet there is little doubt that turnover has increased faster since 1958 than at any time since the end of the war. In that year (before convertibility) I estimated[1] that the net foreign earnings of all the banks from foreign exchange dealings might be between £2 million and £3 million. There is little doubt that this could easily have doubled since then. On top of this, the creation of the market in foreign currency deposits, the so-called Euro-dollar market, has added considerably to the earnings of the London banks. In view of the size of London's business (about £1,300 million),[2] and taking account of the interest payments made on these deposits as well as the earnings from re-lending, etc., it would be surprising if another £4 million were not accruing to London banks from this new market. This makes close on £10 million from foreign exchange dealings (including the Euro-dollar market) alone. Total earnings so far come to £$33\frac{1}{2}$ million.

Finally, there are earnings from the thousand and one other services rendered to foreign customers by the banks, from security transactions to the booking of travel and theatre reservations for visitors, as well as the earnings from the gold dealings of the five bullion firms[3] (bound to be lower than the £250,000 estimated for 1956 because of the fall in central bank business). The total foreign income of the London banks can conservatively be put at about £35 million.

Until the end of 1963, this would have been as far as we could go in estimating the banks' earnings. But, thanks to the efforts of the Board of Trade in compiling details of earnings from direct investments abroad, it is now possible to go a stage further and include for the first time the earnings of the London banks from their branches overseas. The only clue to these figures so far published was an obscure footnote to an article on direct investments abroad in the *Board of Trade Journal*.[4] It stated quite baldly that banking and finance accounted for 5 per cent of the estimate of £221 million as the earnings of overseas branches, subsidiaries and associates of

---

[1] *The City's Invisible Earnings, op. cit.*, p. 44.
[2] See Chapter 3.
[3] Shee Chapter 4.
[4] 15 November, 1963.

British firms. In other words, the overseas branches of British banks earned between £13 million and £14 million in 1962, in addition to the foreign income of the banks already estimated above at about £35 million. It brings the banks' total earnings to just short of £50 million.

C. MERCHANTING

The amount of foreign exchange earned by the City's commodity merchants has not been estimated by them since the pre-war years. The figures for 1937 and 1938 are worth recalling. The British Federation of Commodity Associations,[1] comprising 40 separate trade associations, investigated the turnover of members for both years. It particularly asked for details of transactions resulting in the shipment of produce and raw materials direct from foreign, Dominion and Colonial ports of origin to destinations outside the United Kingdom. These were shipments which did not touch British shores. The results of 26 members of the association showed that an average turnover of £248 million per annum was achieved in 1937 and 1938.

Post-war rise in commodity markets

Since this figure did not take account of several markets, the Federation estimated that the total 'invisible' international trade handled by all members in 1937 and 1938 must have been of the order of some £400 million per annum. It added that the total for the country as a whole must have been far higher. In the event a later estimate has put it as high as £500 million, of which about £100 million was attributed to the London Metal Exchange. Moreover, these figures did not include the business negotiated between subsidiary houses abroad (such as in Hong Kong or Singapore) with foreign ports, even though the profits earned by them eventually found their way back to London in the form of dividends to parent companies.

Nothing comparable in the way of official statistics has been undertaken since then. Some idea of the growth in individual metal markets can be gained from the turnover figures shown in Table XIII. In virtually every commodity the rise was marked up to 1961. But it will be seen that the total Metal Exchange turnover has not really reached the pre-war level, in spite of individual peaks. To some extent, this can be explained by the

[1] *Federation Review*, May 1944.

TABLE XIII

TURNOVER ON LONDON METAL EXCHANGE, 1936-62
(in thousand long tons)

	Copper	Lead	Zinc	Tin
1936	457	335	248	82
1937	711	482	594	101
1938	475	387	296	91
1957	467	201	301	61
1958	635	275	336	65
1959	772	395	335	43
1960	767	389	300	41
1961	796	429	374	98
1962	510	351	346	81

fall in outright speculation (by individuals who are not dealers in the market). But it mainly reflects the influence of governments on these markets. Even if the British authorities have got rid of many exchange restrictions, other governments have not done so to the same extent. Moreover, stockpiling by the United States and controlled sales of commodities by other governments (such as copper in Chile) have also tended to curb the turnover in London. In other commodities (such as tea), important markets have developed spontaneously abroad.

Success of new wool futures market
Yet, in spite of this generally unfavourable background, the experiment of opening a brand new market in London has been a marked success. The first London wool futures market was opened on 29 April, 1953. At the time wool futures markets established before the war were operating in Antwerp, Roubaix and New York. After only eight months, the average daily turnover in wool tops futures in London exceeded that in New York. And in the first twelve months, the turnover in London exceeded that in Antwerp and Roubaix combined. By 1961 London had managed to gain about three-quarters of the business, as Table XIV shows.

To move from the figures of individual markets to a figure for them all is difficult, but some idea of the commissions could be gained at one time from details given in the Bank of England's annual report. The report for 1958, for example,[1]

[1] These figures are the most recent.

TABLE XIV
LONDON'S SHARE OF THE WOOL FUTURES MARKET,
1954-63
(contracts of 5,000 lb.)

	London	New York	Antwerp	Roubaix	London's share of total %
1954	18,977	25,078	5,863	4,648	35
1955	14,623	20,732	4,528	4,151	33
1956	21,762	17,488	5,308	4,406	44
1957	37,007	18,746	5,061	5,143	56
1958	40,718	13,490	7,745	8,723	57
1959	56,356	13,289	8,022	11,449	63
1960	53,809	7,186	6,254	8,037	71
1961	53,154	3,153	7,567	7,381	74
1962	29,734	1,200	8,127	4,739	67
1963	47,795	784	6,410	8,200	74

stated that the total value of commodities sold to countries outside the sterling area under commodity scheme arrangements for payment in sterling or foreign currency was approximately £519 million in 1957 compared with £424 million in 1956 and £393 million in 1955. The figure of £519 million is believed to have included foreign sales of the coffee, sugar, cocoa, tin, zinc, copper, lead, copra, cotton, grain and rubber markets. It did not include trade in wool nor in other commodities for which no marketing scheme existed. Nor did it include foreign sales transacted by some of the City's larger merchanting houses, which to some extent perform the same functions for processed and semi-processed goods as do the commodity markets for the raw product. It was felt that in 1957 as much again might be allowed for all these different activities: thus, a total of close on £1,000 million might not have been an over-estimate of the activities of the City's commodity markets and merchant houses.

Decline in turnover since 1957

The dismantling of some of the exchange controls has naturally led to an absence of annual turnover figures. There is little doubt, however, for the reasons set out in Chapter 6, that the total turnover is now below its post-war peak. The equivalent total for the £519 million in 1957 was probably little above £350 million by 1963. As a result, the turnover of the general merchanting houses in semi-processed and processed products may well have exceeded that in raw materials for the first time in many years, leaving a total turnover of between £800 million and £900 million. If, in addition to this fall in turnover, account is taken of increasing competition and the consequent squeezing of commission and profit margins, foreign income from merchanting has plainly declined in the past few years. The average rate of commission may have dropped below 1 per cent in many trades (in sugar it is said to be below $\frac{1}{2}$ per cent). Even if allowance were made for the higher profits made by merchants when acting as principals (by buying and selling rather than taking a commission) and for the fact that the profits of merchants on foreign account are larger than their normal accounting profits (since overheads in London are payable in sterling), it would hardly be surprising if the total foreign income from merchanting had dropped to between £20 million and £25 million. The corresponding figures for 1956, estimated in the same way, were between £25 million and £30 million.

D. SHIPPING BROKERAGE

The main difficulty in estimating shipping earnings is in deciding which figures to take. There are several to choose from. A net figure of income from shipping has always formed part of the Balance of Payments White Paper, varying in recent years from a credit of £134 million in 1952 to a debit of £32 million in 1960. In 1963 the debit had narrowed to £11 million. The weakness with these figures is that they are struck after deducting the amount we as a nation spend on using foreign ships from the total we earn by putting our ships at the service of foreigners. If we want to concentrate on the earnings of Britain's fleet, the best figures are those compiled by the Chamber of Shipping. Since the war, the Chamber has conducted full-scale inquiries in 1947, 1952, 1958 and 1962. Its estimates show a remarkable rise and fall in these earnings: from £60 million in 1947 up to £221 million in 1952 and then down again to £135 million in 1958 and £72 million in 1962. Details of the recent figures are shown in Table XV.

Whichever figures one takes, they are still large, in spite of the recent decline. But what part of them can the City of London itself claim? More specifically, should the earnings of the 'Queen Mary' and the 'Queen Elizabeth' be included with those of the brokers on the Baltic Exchange? Should the cost of using a British tramp ship be included as well as the ship-

TABLE XV

INVISIBLE EXPORTS FROM UK SHIPPING
(£ million)

	1958*	1959†	1960†	1961†	1962*
Receipts from abroad:					
Freight on UK exports ...	150	148	148	148	135
Freight on cross voyages	339	328	337	341	348
Passage money from non-UK nationals	51	49	50	46	47
Time-charter hire ...	23	24	24	28	32
TOTAL	563	549	559	563	562
Disbursements abroad:					
Bunkers	99	92	89	89	88
Canal dues	18	18	23	23	23
Port & other expenditures	174	181	186	195	199
Time-charter hire ...	137	149	172	180	180
TOTAL	428	440	470	487	490
NET CONTRIBUTION TO INVISIBLE EXPORTS	135	109	89	76	72

* Full inquiries.
† Sample inquiries.
Source: Chamber of Shipping, *Annual Report, 1963-64.*

broker's commission? If one is to stick to a strict calculation of earnings which arise largely within the City's boundaries (and are earned mainly because of the City's unique mechanism), the answer is obvious. Attention must be confined to the Baltic Exchange itself.

Apart from the grain and oilseed markets (included in other sections of our estimates), the main earnings on the Baltic arise from the commissions earned in dealings with foreigners by ship-brokers and charterers' agent. Yet no official figure has ever been put to this income. If the turnover of the Baltic could be guessed with reasonable accuracy, an allowance for the average commission rate might produce a rough estimate. Unfortunately, no regular turnover figures are maintained. The only post-war estimate of the Baltic's turnover—essentially a private one in 1953-54—put it at some £300 million annually, including dry-cargo and tanker business.

Rising turnover, narrowing rates

After allowing for the changes in freight rates in the next couple of years and the larger volume of business, a figure of £400 million was probably reached by 1956. On that basis, I put the Baltic brokers' earnings at from £15 million to £20 million.[1] Since then, turnover has continued to rise. Although the British merchant fleet's contribution has fallen, Baltic brokers concern themselves equally with the fixtures of foreign tonnage. If account is also taken of their earnings from firms undertaking long-term contracts outside the normal business of the Baltic, the total turnover of most Baltic brokers has clearly continued to rise. It could easily have doubled between 1956 and 1963. That is certainly the impression of some of the large, active broking firms. If at the same time commission rates have narrowed, giving brokers a smaller cut of a far larger cake, their net foreign income might have risen from £15-20 million in 1956 to £20-25 million in 1963.

In the absence of reliable figures, these can be little more than guesswork, and to many members of the Exchange they may seem a particularly small sum. But three points are worth emphasising. First, they are meant to represent earnings of *foreign* exchange only (that is, they exclude brokerage earned from British owners); secondly, they include only commissions on dry-cargo and tanker business; thirdly, they do *not* include foreign earnings from the vessels themselves.

II. TOTAL INCOME

It is now possible to sum up the various estimates of the City's earnings. No regular official figures have been published. Some early unofficial estimates seriously underestimated the City's income.[2] The basic official framework was provided in an answer in the House of Commons on 19 December, 1957. It was suggested that in 1956 the City's foreign earnings amounted to roughly £125 million, made up as follows: insurance £40 million; merchanting £30 million; brokerage £30 million; and banking £25 million. Some preliminary ideas of how these figures would have turned out in 1957 were given in the House of Commons on 24 April, 1958. It was suggested that the total would be

[1] *The City's Invisible Earnings, op. cit.,* p. 79.
[2] Professor A. C. L. Day suggested £20 million to £30 million.—*The Listener,* 21 November, 1957.

broadly similar, with probably a little more from merchanting and slightly less from insurance. Since then, hardly any official estimates have been issued. The last to appear was the Central Statistical Office's estimate that the City's foreign earnings amounted to £150 million in 1961. This was published in the *Report of the Committee of Inquiry on Decimal Currency* in September 1963.[1]

If these official estimates, which are now out of date, are taken in conjunction with the outline of individual markets in this chapter, a more up-to-date picture begins to emerge. The details are shown in Table XVI. For 1956, my private estimates[2] were higher than the official ones. This largely reflected a higher estimate for the insurance earnings. As was explained at the time, if allowance were made for this higher insurance figure and for the extreme conservatism of some of the official figures (at least three of the four sections were given to the nearest £10 million), the City's earnings in 1956 were likely to have been nearer £150 million than the £125 million given in the House of Commons. By 1961, the official estimates had reached this level. My own latest estimates put the earnings for 1963 higher still. As will be seen, the insurance earnings have risen again. While income from merchanting activities in the

TABLE XVI

ESTIMATES OF THE CITY'S EARNINGS
(£ million)

	Official		in earlier chapters W. M. Clarke		
	1956	1961	1946	1956	1963
Insurance ...	40	—	20-25	- 70	- 85
Merchanting ...	30	—	5-10	25-30	20-25
Brokerage* ...	30	—	10‡	15-20‡	20-25‡
Banking ...	25	—	5-10	25-30	45-50**
TOTAL	125	150	40-55	135-150	170-185

* Includes shipping, underwriting, security deals and agency and head office fees.
** Includes £15 million estimate for overseas earnings of bank branches abroad for first time.
‡ Shipping brokers.

[1] Cmnd. 2145.
[2] *The City's Invisible Earnings, op. cit.,* p.93.

commodity markets is put somewhat lower, brokerage earnings in shipping have continued to expand. The major change, however, is accounted for by the inclusion for the first time of an estimate of £15 million for the earnings of bank branches abroad. The banking income has also benefited substantially from the expansion in foreign exchange turnover and the creation of the Euro-dollar market. The result is that the City's earnings must now be close on £185 million. However one looks at it, this is a sizeable contribution to the balance of payments.

Invisible earnings since the 1850s

Before comparing this figure with other parts of the current balance of payments, we may usefully consider how it has changed over the past century or so. Estimates of 'invisible' income relating to shipping, insurance, brokerage, banking and other commissions go back in one form or another to just over a century ago. In making what was clearly the first detailed attempt to quantify this invisible income in a paper read to the Royal Statistical Society in 1882, Sir Robert Giffen pushed his estimates back to the year 1854. His object was not merely to make the estimates, but also to point out that 'invisible' income should really be taken into account in looking at the yawning trade gap which was tending to cause alarm and despondency even at that time. He estimated that shipping freights brought in £60 million a year, which, together with £20 million for insurance, banking and other brokerage commissions, made £80 million ('which is really, to use a phrase which I have tried to make familiar, an invisible export'). For the years 1854 to 1856, he put the annual shipping freight earnings at £25 million, insurance and other commissions at £8 million, making a total of £33 million. Later, private estimates were made by Sir Robert Giffen in another paper in 1899, by Sir George Paish in a paper in 1909, and particularly by C. K. Hobson in his book *The Export of Capital*, published in 1914.

Since these early figures were based largely on the assumption that insurance, shipping and banking charges arose almost entirely from the movement of goods, they are not entirely comparable with later figures. But they provide a rough guide to their importance in filling the trade gap. It seems clear that in the 1850s these commissions were providing as much 'invisible' income as the interest from capital invested abroad. But by the 1880s, Sir Robert Giffen was already suggesting that, while commissions and shipping freights brought in £80

million a year, interest earnings might be anything from £75
million to £105 million. By 1913, shipping freights and commissions were bringing in £119 million, while income from overseas investments had risen to no less than £210 million.
Although the value of the pound had depreciated somewhat
by 1938, the figures for that year were somewhat similar to
those in 1913. While net income from overseas investments
amounted to £200 million, earnings from shipping, insurance
and other commissions totalled £135 million. With the fall in
real terms of the income from foreign investments, the contribution from the City of London was again growing in
importance.

Following the further forced sales of foreign investments
during the last war, the City's contribution has still further
helped to fill the trade gap in the post-war years. The income
from foreign investments had dropped to £100 million by 1945.
Thus, as this contribution from the past declined, so the contribution from the present, the City's current earnings, became
more valuable. Since then, both have recovered strongly. While
the income from foreign investment had once again moved
well over the £200 million mark by 1956, the contribution from
shipping, insurance, banking, etc., had also increased substantially. It is quite possible that the City's earnings at least
trebled between 1946 and 1956. This is almost certainly true
of insurance. If an estimate is made on the same lines as in
Chapter 5 (that is, a figure based on the average underwriting
results of nearby years), the result is a total insurance income
for the year 1946 of some £23 million. This compares with the
average figure of £70 million for 1956. For merchanting, since
only the fur, rubber and wool markets had then been re-
opened, it is unlikely that income in 1946 was more than
£5 million to £10 million, against the official figure of £30
million for 1956. Brokerage income, made up mainly from the
Baltic, is unlikely to have been much more than £10 million,
against £30 million ten years later. As for banking earnings
(with the foreign exchange market closed and trade at a low
ebb), it would be surprising if they brought in more than, say,
£8 million. All in all, the City was doing well if it earned more
than £50 million immediately after the war. Thus, while the income from foreign investments doubled in the first decade after
the war, the City's earnings from insurance, brokerage, merchanting and banking probably increased at least three times
over the same period.

The importance of 'invisibles'

Since the middle of the 1950s, income from both sources has increased further, that from foreign investments probably rising faster than that from the City's services. By 1963, so far as one can estimate, earnings from direct investment abroad had increased by four times[1] since the end of the war and the City's earnings over three times. This expansion has been a major contribution towards balancing Britain's overseas payments. Both foreign income from investments and the City's earnings form part of the country's total 'invisible' earnings. Their importance can be seen from Table XVII. In only two of the 12 years 1953 to 1964 did visible trade alone produce a surplus in payments. In six of the remaining years, the surplus provided from 'invisible' earnings converted a deficit on trade into an overall surplus: and in the others the contribution from 'invisibles' made the final deficit far lower than it would otherwise have been.

TABLE XVII

CONTRIBUTION OF INVISIBLES, 1953-64

(£ million)

	Total payments	Visible trade	Total invisibles (net)	Government spending abroad (net)	Invisibles excluding Government spending
1953	+151	—244	+395	— 58	+453
1954	+121	—204	+325	—126	+551
1955	—157	—313	+156	—139	+295
1956	+209	+ 53	+156	—192	+348
1957	+216	— 29	+245	—147	+392
1958	+345	+ 41	+304	—224	+528
1959	+140	—116	+256	—233	+489
1960	—275	—404	+129	—286	+415
1961	—22	—149	+127	—335	+462
1962	+90	—98	+188	—363	+551
1963	+96	—80	+176	—387	+563
1964	—374	—553	+179	—431	+610

Source: Preliminary Estimates of National Income and Balance of Payments, 1959-64, HMSO, March 1965.

[1] Because of the new figures now published by the Board of Trade for direct overseas investment, it is not possible to compare the £100 million figure for 1946 with later figures. Adding in a notional figure of £100 million for oil earnings on top of the £312 million for 1963, gives a total of between £400 million and £450 million.

On the face of it, however, the contribution of total 'invisibles' has been falling away. In 1953 and 1954 they were worth well over £300 million net annually. By the 1960s, they had dropped to almost half that amount. Part of the explanation, of course, lies in the decline in net shipping earnings. From a surplus of over £100 million in 1952, shipping has declined until it has produced a deficit every year in the 'sixties. Travel too has been producing a bigger deficit year by year. The main deterioration, however, has come from government spending abroad. As the Table shows, it has increased from £58 million net in 1953 to no less than £431 million in 1964. This additional spending overseas has gone on economic (i.e., non-military) grants (particularly since 1958), on the upkeep of embassies and other administrative units, but above all on military establishments. There is no doubt that this general increase in official spending overseas is the root cause of the fall in total 'invisible' earnings in recent years. The final column of the Table, which shows what happens to 'invisible' earnings when government spending is excluded, reveals a remarkable buoyancy, especially over the past four years.

TABLE XVIII
UK BALANCE OF PAYMENTS, 1963
(£ million)

VISIBLE TRADE	—80
INVISIBLES	
Government spending ...	—387
Travel	—45
Shipping	—11
Private transfers	—12
Civil aviation	+23
Other services[1]	+219
Interest, profits & dividends	+389
	+176
TOTAL PAYMENTS BALANCE	+96

Source: Preliminary Estimates of National Income and Balance of ments, HMSO, March 1965.
[1] Including the City's earnings.

The City and the balance of payments

The conclusion is clear. Without the City's earnings of between £170 million and £185 million and without the contribution from investment overseas, the balance of payments would have been in almost continuous deficit. The figures for 1963 set out in Table XVIII show how far these two items more than offset heavy government spending abroad, still leaving enough to convert a trading deficit into a final overall surplus.

One final point. When it is considered that in producing earnings of some £185 million, the City runs up virtually no import bill, the contrast with other export industries is striking. It is true that banks, insurance companies and so on incur foreign expenses, but by and large these expenses have already been allowed for in the figures. In contrast, the import content of British exports generally is roughly 20 per cent.

CHAPTER 10

THE GOLD STANDARD AND STERLING

IT IS TIME to examine how the City operates as a whole. The first part of the book was devoted to a detailed outline of different parts of the City. The second part started with a detailed attempt to assess the City's total earnings. This chapter is concerned with the conditions under which the City's machinery developed and worked best, with how far those conditions have gradually re-appeared since the war, and with the prospects of restoring them (or conditions closely resembling them) in the future. We shall then be in a position, in Chapters 11 and 12, to consider what role the City can reasonably play.

Britain's industrial decline and the City

The City was at the height of its power and dominance in the decade before the First World War. The outflow of capital from the City to foreign governments and other borrowers abroad reached new records and the bulk of world trade was still being financed, through sterling, by London banks. Yet Britain's industrial lead and, to a lesser degree, her political strength were already on the wane. Some economists[1] would put the turning point several decades earlier. Whatever the date, the decline continued between the wars. In spite of Britain's changing role in the world, however, the City markets managed to survive. This survival has not been universal, as we have seen. The commodity markets are no longer what they were and several other sectors have been transformed. The capital market is functioning differently. But no other international financial centre has risen to rival the City. As financial power continued its westward course, it might have been

[1] For example, Dr. T. Balogh, *Unequal Partners*, Basil Blackwell, 1963.

expected that New York would come to take the place of
London. In spite of the powerful creditor position of the United
States for well over a decade after the second war, New York
did not readily step into London's shoes. The New York
capital market revived strongly only *after* Europe's economic
recovery was complete. Thus, the City survived not only the
acute difficulties of the inter-war period, but also the American
financial dominance and repeated sterling crises of the post-
war years.

It was not a narrow survival. Even during the worst currency
crises, the demand for pounds was persistent. The transferable
sterling markets which sprang up abroad were not organised
by the Bank of England; they emerged spontaneously from a
general demand from foreign investors and traders. The growth
of the Euro-dollar market in London is only the latest example
of the continued flexibility of the City in international financial
business. Now, as we saw in Chapter 1 and later, the Bank of
England seems determined to force the pace a little more.
Lord Cromer, the Governor of the Bank, has already outlined
the way in which he feels developments should go. Two
speeches setting out his aims for the City are worth analysing in
more detail than we have done so far. The first hint of a new
approach came in an address to the Manchester and District
Bankers' Institute in Manchester in March 1962:

'Up to the last war it was common practice for foreign
buyers, government or other, through . . . their London banking correspondents, to raise funds in the London capital
market to finance the manufacture, shipment and erection
of capital goods and equipment for themselves either as
principals or for their public. The borrower obtained the
funds from the investing public in the UK on a long-term
basis by offering bonds at interest rates commensurate with
their credit rating in London. Under this system, the manufacturer at home made what was to him a cash sale and did
not have to preoccupy himself with the provision of long-
term credit.

At the beginning of the last war, the Exchange Control
Regulations prohibited this type of lending to the foreigner
and this prohibition still exists today. Partly as a result, an
alternative system has had to be devised under which a
manufacturer is called upon to provide credit to his customers
and suppliers' credit has largely replaced buyers' credit.

In my belief, this new system possesses many disadvantages
not possessed by the older system. Industry could, I think,

fairly claim that the manufacturer's task is to manufacture and deliver his goods against something tantamount to cash payment. It raises many difficulties for the manufacturer to burden his balance sheet with credit given to his customers, nor . . . is he generally himself particularly well-equipped to assess the credit standing of his overseas customers. It is the task of the financial community to grant credit and assess credit risks and to relieve the manufacturer of these problems. The financial community should have, and generally has, the necessary facilities and international relationships, indeed it exists to serve this very purpose. Through the lapse of time and increasing unfamiliarity, reversion to the earlier system whereby foreign buyers themselves more freely used our capital and credit markets might not prove easy, but I would certainly hope that an attempt might be made.'

This theme was further developed in the Governor's traditional speech to the bankers and merchants of the City of London the following October:

'I want to see more foreign business attracted to our markets so that we can earn more foreign money. The time has now come when the City once again might well provide an international capital market where the foreigner can not only borrow long-term capital, but where, equally important, he will once again wish to place his long-term investment capital. This entrepôt business in capital, if I may so describe it, would not only serve this country well but would fill a vital and vacant role in Europe in mobilising foreign capital for world economic development. It would be to the advantage of British Industry in financing our customers. This type of business in general tends to be less volatile in its effects on the balance of payments than much other business now carried on.'

The City and sterling

This determined official effort to give the City's capital market a new lease of life has prompted varied reactions in the press: courageous, far-seeing, foolhardy, dangerous. Whatever else it is, it is yet another sympom of the City's determination to survive. If the Governor of the Bank can contemplate, apparently without much qualm, the possibility of the City gradually reverting to its older role of providing capital, other questions naturally follow. As we saw earlier, the City flourished when the pound was dominant and the British economy at full strength: traders were confident in holding pounds and Britain's prosperity provided a steady outflow of capital. Can it continue to survive the decline in both?

This question immediately raises the relationship between the City's activities and the role of sterling. For some critics,[1] the United Kingdom economy has for too long been over-influenced by the need to maintain the strength of the pound. Because of the natural insistence by the City on the need to maintain the value of the currency (*any* currency, if it comes to that), there has grown up an assumption that the City's activities are entirely dependent on the maintenance of the pound's stature in the world and that City people would give it priority over other economic ends—full employment, growth, etc. Some undoubtedly would. The depreciation in the value of money, however gradual, can hardly be expected to commend itself to anyone whose prime activity in life is the investment of funds, particularly anyone involved in investing them widely across the world, as City people so often do.

This, however, is to confuse two issues: the relationship between the City and the role of the pound and the relative priorities to be given to full employment and a stable currency. The issues are closely allied, but too often emotions blur the essential distinction between the two. And these emotions are as likely to be encouraged in (or by) the City as elsewhere. The most sensible approach is to explore the two questions separately, to consider first how far the City can (or should be encouraged to) exist with a pound that is no longer so dominant and then, secondly, to explore how the authorities (the Treasury, the Bank of England and the Department of Economic Affairs) should view the apparent conflict between a stable pound and economic growth. We shall concern ourselves with the first of these issues in this and the following chapter and with the second in Chapter 12.

The strength of the pound and the prosperity of the City were so much a part of each other during the second half of the 19th century and the short Edwardian years that is is natural to assume that one cannot exist without the other. Certainly they are closely related. Yet enough has happened in the past 50 years to suggest that the relationship is not as clear-cut as many people imagine. The current efforts to bring further support to the world's two key currencies, the pound and the

[1] For example, Andrew Shonfield, *British Economic Policy since the War*, Penguin Books, 1958.

dollar, and to refashion the world's monetary system are bound to have two major effects on the pound: if successful, they will reduce the dependence of the world on pounds and dollars as reserve currencies and, at the same time, they will bring new support to both currencies. Both will have important effects on the workings of the City.

The City and the gold standard

It is difficult to face these questions, however, without looking closely at the workings of the gold standard and the City's role in it. For some 50 years (it was hardly longer, though the germs of what followed were discernible immediately after the Napoleonic wars) the pound provided all the means of liquid payments the world needed, and the City provided the credit and financial services to go with it. For a further period of 50 years (since the 1914-18 war), the financial experts of the West have been searching for a viable substitute. Whether the City has fully realised it or not, it has a vested interest in the form the substitute eventually takes. And it is important to know what sort of an interest it had in its heyday in the working of the gold standard, and what were the principal features of this earlier system. The literature on the topic is voluminous. Only the basic features need concern us. Two quotations are relevant, coming from each end of the economic spectrum. One is by the late Dr. Per Jacobsson, managing director of the International Monetary Fund from 1956 until his death in May 1963, the other by Dr. Thomas Balogh, now economic adviser to the Treasury.

First, Per Jacobsson:

'It would be a mistake to ascribe the success of the system in the dynamic period before the First World War merely to the elaboration of certain techniques and to adherence to certain roles—however important these aspects were—for there were some more general factors which affected conditions in the period up to 1914 which no longer had the same effect in the period after the war.

In the first place, the one hundred years between the end of the Napoleonic Wars and the outbreak of the First World War constituted probably the most peaceful period that the world has ever experienced—at least, since the decline of the Roman Empire; and this is important because war has always been the enemy of monetary stability.

Secondly, the City of London was then the economic and financial centre, not only of the British Isles, but also of the entire trading world. Great Britain pursued a policy of free trade; and the banks and merchants operating in the City of London provided what was in effect a reservoir of credit, which was essential to the financing of international trade, and which helped to regulate the flow of funds and trade itself. It has often been pointed out, but most recently by Professor J. B. Condliffe, that, rather by a series of historical accidents than by design, the regulation of the country's currency reserves, and of the credit limit based upon them, had fallen into the hands of the Bank of England, the directors of which were merchant bankers whose activities and interests were international rather than national. In addition, the credits extended by the London banking houses to their customers all over the world meant that the City was clearly a creditor on short-term account in relation to foreign markets. It was this which made it possible for the Bank of England to pursue its policies with the backing of an astonishingly small gold reserve, which was never higher than about £45 million before 1914—or about $400 million at the present dollar price of gold.

A third factor was the acceptance by other countries of the financial indications that came from London, for the decisions taken in London largely reflected changes in the international, rather than purely national, financial situation.

A fourth factor was perhaps more fortuitous: that the output of gold, thanks largely to discoveries of new gold fields from time to time, proved on the whole sufficient under the existing institutional arrangements to provide an expanding basis for money and credit.

Under the propitious conditions of the nineteenth century, particularly those which were thus established in the monetary sphere, a truly remarkable expansion took place in the world economy. The value of international trade rose from about $4 billion in 1850 to about $40 billion (US billion) in 1913.'[1]

Now, Dr. Thomas Balogh on the same topic:

'Prior to 1914, the world was the sterling area. London financed international trade and provided more than half, possibly two-thirds, of all foreign lending. Both operations were extremely profitable (though the export of more than half of the nation's savings necessarily cut the rate of industrial expansion and is one explanation of the decline of Britain relative to the US or Germany). London's advantages derived partly from the fact that the vast fund of short-term

[1] Per Jacobsson, *The Market Economy in the World of Today*, The American Philosophical Society, 1961, pp. 22-23.

assets (trade bills) enabled Britain to dispense with a large gold reserve; the rest of the world provided us with reserves by borrowing short—and paid good interest for the privilege. Whenever London needed reserves, a rise in the rate of interest called funds and gold back to London. Long-term lending, on the other hand, served mainly to increase the production of food and raw materials; it cheapened British imports and thus contributed directly to British prosperity and influence.

. . . In striving for convertibility and the restoration of London's role as an international financial centre, people seemed oblivious of the fact that the rise of London to the centre of an international economy was based on Britain's *mercantile supremacy* as an Imperial Power and her *industrial leadership* as an initiator of mechanised mass-production. It was this double superiority which enabled London to become the world centre for short- and long-term finance, and added further cumulative gains. The play of the Gold Standard became a source of profit and activity contributed to maintaining the British balance of payments.'[1]

The first contains all the essential ingredients of the gold standard; the second sounds some vital warnings about romantic attempts to put the clock back. Since the gold standard conditions produced such an expansion in world trade and such stable price levels, it is hardly surprising that, with war once again at an end in 1919, efforts to re-create the earlier conditions were begun by the leading monetary authorities. It is also not surprising that they overlooked the fundamental changes that had taken place in little more than five years. It was not simply a matter of restoring an international monetary system, however necessary. Monetary confidence had been shaken to its roots. The war had brought new economic powers to the front, had indeed speeded up developments that could be discerned at the turn of the century: the new-found monetary strength of the United States and the growing industrial power of Germany. It was equally not surprising that Britain's changed role in the world should have been overlooked as much by British politicians as by others. The determination to re-establish the gold standard in its old form was equalled by the British determination to re-establish sterling's connection with gold. That the event itself was delayed until 1925 was largely due to the conviction of Montagu Norman, then Governor of the Bank of England, that the questions of war debts and

<hr>

[1] *Op. cit.*, Vol. 2, pp. 217, 25.

German reparations should be faced first. What is surprising, looking back, is the general contemporary consensus of opinion that the gold standard should be re-created. The idea was prominent at the Brussels and Genoa financial conferences (in 1920 and 1922) and the only real subject of current debate was the rate to be fixed for sterling.[1] According to the conclusions of the Chamberlain Committee early in 1925, there was 'no alternative comparable with a return to the former gold parity of the sovereign,' and the Committee cited support 'by the overwhelming majority of opinion, both financial and industrial, represented in evidence before us.'

Mr. Winston Churchill duly announced the return to gold (in effect the end of the embargo on gold) in his budget speech of 28 April, 1925. It was the start of a new, though not immediate, round of tragedy and frustration. Both the action and the rate of exchange, which formed the basic part of it, have been blamed[2] for the industrial stagnation that was soon to follow, both in Britain and the rest of the world, and for the further

---

[1] There were two separate issues: whether to return to the gold standard and, if so, at what rate of exchange. An interesting summary of the official attitude to these questions is given in Sir Henry Clay's *Lord Norman* (Macmillan, 1957, pp. 154-8):

'Contemporary criticism of the return to gold in 1925 turned mainly on the rate of parity at which the return was made. The Cunliffe Committee did not consider any alternative to the pre-war parity, and it does not appear that any alternative was ever seriously considered in official discussions of policy subsequently . . . In a long series of discussions with the Committee of the Treasury on the return to gold the Governor [of the Bank of England] never raised any proposal for devaluation; the Bank and the City would naturally attach great importance to the loss of prestige which devaluation would have involved, and the Treasury officials do not seem to have differed. The Brussels and Genoa Conferences recommended devaluation, but only in the case of currencies which had fallen so far from their pre-war gold parity that it would have involved prolonged deflation and long delays before a stable exchange rate was restored; their expert advisers took the same view and one of them pointed the moral: "For the United Kingdom, where the exchange is only depreciated some 20 per cent, the balance of argument is clearly in favour of a return to pre-war parity".'

The main unofficial opposition (to the parity rather than to the gold standard itself) came from Keynes's *The Economic Consequences of Mr. Churchill*. His criticism was 'against having restored gold in conditions which required a substantial readjustment of all our money values . . . Mr. Churchill's policy of improving the exchange by 10 per cent was, sooner or later, a policy of reducing everyone's wages by 2s. in the £.'

[2] Lionel Robbins, *The Great Depression*, Macmillan, 1934.

decade of financial distress. Far from turning the world back towards that tried monetary system on which the world's prosperity had been based for so long, the events of 1925 were soon succeeded by one financial disaster after another: the New York stock market crash; Britain's decision to leave the gold standard; the closing down of successive financial centres to foreign loans (many not re-opened for over 25 years); and a whole series of forced currency devaluations. Much of the blame has been put on the determination of the authorities, for prestige reasons, to re-establish the pound's pre-war parity with gold; there is much truth in this as Keynes saw at the time, but it is an over-simplified version of what was in reality the result of highly complex political and economic forces.

The search for alternatives to the gold standard was thus forced to go on—into the 'thirties and beyond. Once the cataclysms of 1930-31 were over, the main moves were defensive. There followed the building up of national barriers, the raising of tariffs, the restrictions on capital movements and soon, a gathering together of several countries round the pound: in effect the birth of the sterling area. This phase survived the war, or rather was transformed into a statutory financial area by the war, and was forced to continue in much the same way until well after the war.

Reform and reappraisal

Throughout these vicissitudes, as we have seen in earlier chapters, the City of London managed to show a surprising flexibility, switching from foreign business to domestic and back again. But behind most of these switches, and in the minds of many City bankers, there lurked the hope and belief that the re-stablishmnt of a strong pound and a stronger world monetary system would bring prosperity back to the City and to the country. This was a continuing faith rather than strict logic. Something of the sort lingers today, as the Bank of England's recent evidence to the Committee of Inquiry on Decimal Currency revealed. The Bank feared that any change in the name or character due to decimalisation of the pound (even the transfer of one £ to two 10s. units) would do irreparable harm both to the currency and to the City's operations on which so much of the country's 'invisible' income depends. It was a mistaking of the shadow for the substance, just as so many people had believed that the restoration of the gold standard or its nearest equivalent would automatically take Britain and the City back to the halcyon days before the First World War. They would not.

Sources of strength

Both the success of the gold standard and the corresponding prosperity of the City's financial markets were based on several important features. The half century before 1914 was a period of peace and stability and of important gold discoveries. Thus, monetary confidence was undisturbed by the general political climate and indeed strengthened by the flow of newly found gold. In modern parlance, there was no shortage of world liquidity. Both features—political stability and gold expansion —were sadly lacking throughout the 'twenties and 'thirties. Confidence was undermined by political strife and economic distress; and the world's central banks had not yet learned how to co-operate effectively nor how to increase monetary liquidity by a network of bilateral 'swap' arrangements.

Beyond these favourable world conditions in the second half of the 19th century, Britain also possessed several important advantages that helped to support the pound and develop the City's financial services. She was in the forefront of the Industrial Revolution and at the centre of a mercantile Empire. Geographically she was on the sea-lanes of the world; politically she had established herself as the world's major sea-power; and economically, her industrial lead enabled her to produce a growing surplus of capital which she invested abroad. Her increasing volume of manufactured exports paid for the necessarily large imports of food and raw materials. It paid Britain to be outward-looking; it also encouraged the City to concentrate on external services. The City grew up, firm in the knowledge that its primary task was overseas and that British industry, far from being short of funds, was generally capable of generating its own capital.

The City's supremacy was based, therefore, on a worldwide period of stability; a freedom of movement for capital; Britain's economic strength and a continuing fund of capital resources; on an arrangement whereby world liquidity needs were met by gold and the mass of short-term credit available in London; and on the monetary indicators which the disciplines of the gold standard enabled her to send out to the ends of the earth (by putting Bank rate up or down) which in turn kept the world system in step. In such a harmonised world, though hardly without its moments of panic and crisis, London could develop its flair and skill knowing that it could serve the world and still make a handsome living for itself.

Lost advantages
Few of these ingredients for success have survived two world wars and as many more monetary crises. Britain is no longer supreme economically; she is dwarfed both by the United States and the Continent of Europe. She has lost her industrial lead. Her spare capital resources are relatively small. Sterling, though still a world currency, has had its role usurped in part by the dollar, in part by International Monetary Fund quotas and drawings. Yet, in spite of the dollar's dominance for the first 12 years after the war (a dominance that led at least one leading British economist[1] to assume that it would last far longer), this shift in monetary power across the Atlantic was not accompanied by a similar shift of influence from London to New York. Wall Street and the other financial markets of Lower Manhattan have undoubtedly become a bigger noise in the world's monetary affairs than ever before, but their activities are as much concerned with domestic finance as with purely international monetary problems. Turnover in many New York markets is often higher than in money markets anywhere else in the world; yet turnover in international business in foreign exchange, gold, commodities, and shipping generally remains bigger in London. The reasons are important. They lie in the contrast between the use by the United States of its surplus capital resources and in the way that London goes about its business. They have a bearing on the future.

London's private v. USA's government channels
During the early post-war years, when the United States balance of payments was producing a persistent and embarrassing surplus, the days of the 'dollar shortage,' when dollars were a hard currency, the New York market might have developed into the type of capital exporting machine that London grew into in the 19th and early 20th centuries. Recent New York issues of $1,000 million a year are only a third of London's activity just before the First World War. New York did not develop as far as London partly because the flow of funds

---

[1] Sir Donald MacDougall in *The World Dollar Problem: A study in International Economics,* Macmillan, 1957, concluded that the US balance of payments was more likely to improve than to deteriorate over the next two decades.

went largely through government agencies. The need to re-build Europe after the war, the help required in the under-developed world, the increasing pressures of the cold war and, eventually the growing surpluses of American agricultural products, all tended to channel aid through official hands in Washington. In addition, further American funds flowed through the new international agencies—the International Monetary Fund and the International Bank. Once again the private channels of the New York market were not given the stimulus they might otherwise have received. New York's international business, of course, is growing all the time, but it has not so far made the spurt necessary to overtake London that might have been expected during the early post-war years.

Two further reasons for this have been the smaller share of trade in the American economy than in Britain's and the use made of her economic strength. The first gave New York banks and financial institutions a larger interest in domestic affairs than was ever possible in London, and the dollar became far more dominant as a reserve currency than as a trading currency. The second supported (if it was not the real cause of) this inward-looking complex. Whereas Britain, in her days of dominance, found good use for the influx of gold (as Sir Roy Harrod has said, 'gold was no sooner attracted than repelled'),[1] the United States hoarded a significant share of it at Fort Knox or beneath the Federal Reserve building in Lower Manhattan. The significance of this use of gold has been emphasised by Dr. F. V. Meyer:[2]

'Throughout history, there has been a tendency for gold to flow to the centre of the world economy: to Rome and Byzantium in ancient times, to London in the nineteenth century. Examples could be multiplied, but these are sufficient to indicate the choice before the United States. Rome and Byzantium hoarded treasure, London banked it. The treasure that went to Rome or Byzantium was spent on current entertainment and the "balance" went into the Imperial kitty. There it stayed until needed to finance war or other special activities of the State. Since the balance was not put into circulation, a Roman or Byzantium export surplus led to an import of treasure, but had no multiplier effects. The provinces of their empires were under constant pressure to supply treasure, a task that became increasingly difficult as

[1] *The Dollar*, Macmillan, 1953.
[2] *United Kingdom Trade with Europe*, Bowes and Bowes, London 1957.

little, if any, of such payments were used to augment the productive apparatus of the provinces or even of the metropolis. Nineteenth century London knew better. Gold flowed to London, but the Bank rate policy of the Bank of England saw to it that there was no accumulation of idle gold reserves.'

Writing in the mid-1950s, Dr. Meyer was naturally interested in the attitude of the United States (the new Byzantium to Europe's Rome?). As we have seen, and as the generous American post-war aid programme shows, the United States did not sit on all the gold it acquired. But the amount it did make available only partly channelled back through the market mechanism in New York. Now that monetary strength has swung back to Europe again, a similar question is being asked. How can Europe—in particular France and Germany—find ways of 'repelling' the influx of gold; that is of putting it to use in commerce? Once again, the conditions in which the City developed and flourished are missing from the scene and, once again, the world's monetary authorities are having to grapple with a liquidity problem that in effect owes part of its origin to the lack of any automatic repellent mechanism such as the City of London provided in the last century. The Continent's capital markets are sometimes efficient and small, sometimes large and rather rusty or occasionally non-existent. If the governments do not find ways of using their acquired wealth in the outside world (as the United States did to some extent in the 'forties and early 'fifties), the stresses from insufficient monetary liquidity in the world are bound to increase in intensity. Thus, at a time when monetary power has switched back from North America to Europe (perhaps more accurately, from the Anglo-Saxons to the Continentals), the really efficient capital exporting machinery is still centred in London and New York. It is hardly surprising that many City people should have been quietly asking themselves in the past few years whether London, with its unique skills and flairs, could not play a useful role in bringing the two continents closer togther, or at least benefit from any monetary attempt to do so. In seeking an honest answer, we must first examine more closely recent monetary developments. The strength of Britain's economy must await later scrutiny.

Towards a world monetary system?

The world's monetary system is slowly, sometimes painfully, moving back to the conditions in which the pound and the City once flourished. Convertibility was re-established among the leading European currencies at the end of 1958. Since then, money and capital have been free to switch from one side of the world to another with almost as much freedom as they had 50 years or so ago. The monetary defences of the 1930s (and some of the economic blocks that grew up behind them, such as the sterling area) have been changing their character. In spite of the decline in Britain's economic strength, the smaller surplus of capital for export, the fall in the dominance of the pound and in Britain's role in the world, and the consequent breaking up of a colonial Empire, the conditions in which the City of London apparently works best have been gradually re-appearing. They have emerged at a time when no other foreign currency has been able to play the role that sterling once played. Before discovering what these changes mean for the City's markets, it is necessary to see what they imply for the pound.

The moves to European convertibility at the end of 1958 were regarded at the time as highly risky ventures. The French were persuaded to strengthen their monetary system and devalue to support the concerted European monetary moves. External convertibility for the pound was swallowed by the critics largely because of the company the pound was keeping. What the French franc and the Italian lira could contemplate, so could sterling. But people remained uneasy. It is difficult to understand why. The economic recovery of Europe, it is now clear, had been accomplished by 1956 and was delayed for only a further 18 months by the oil repercussions of the Suez venture. Without that final European reliance on American help, European economic independence would have been widely recognised *before* the moves to currency convertibility rather than afterwards.

The exact timing of the re-alignment of economic power across the Atlantic is now unimportant. By 1959, the flow of gold from North America to Europe was persistent, the dollar was coming under suspicion and first the German mark, then the French franc and the Italian lira showed that each possessed a remarkable new pulling power. As currency restrictions were removed, large masses of capital began to flow across the Atlantic and across frontiers. A new disturbing element appeared on the monetary scene. Differences in interest rates as well as fears for individual currencies, it was soon found, could disrupt domestic economic policies far more than in the past. Central banks were forced to co-operate more closely. Private capital movements had to be offset by equivalent movements of public money among central banks.

What was attempted in the currency field had also to be applied to gold too. The monthly meeting of the central bankers at the Bank for International Settlements in Basle became a focal point of these co-operative efforts. Yet behind the co-operation there loomed a new struggle: between the monetary authorities of the United States and the monetary authorities of Continental Europe.

The strains that the new era of convertibility had begun to bring to the surface were largely put down to the weakening of the American balance of payments and the strengthening of European payments. In the efforts to tackle the West's growing liquidity problem (as much a problem of monetary imbalance as of a lack of international money), a distinct clash of interests arose. The United States saw the difficulties in terms of its own commitments as leader of the West and could hardly understand why the new prosperity of Western Europe was not being used to buttress the West's basic position, already established by the United States. Europe found it hard to see why the United States was so unwilling to put its economic house in order by reducing its overseas deficit and why it continued to insist on getting monetary help, expecting other countries to hold surplus dollars, rather than do so.

The clash was never seen to better effect than at the Vienna meeting of the International Monetary Fund in the autumn of 1961. This marked the first post-war monetary victory of Continental Europe. Both the United States and Dr. Per Jacobsson, the managing director of the International Monetary Fund, eventually got what they wanted: an agreement in principle among the leading Western nations to establish a $6,000 million borrowing fund to increase the resources of the IMF. But the agreement had some important strings. The money was to be used only on conditions laid down by the countries concerned, not at the discretion of the IMF, as originally intended.[1] More important, the Group of Ten (the countries lending the money) later met to hammer out the details in Paris under a French chairman. The Americans had got their new borrowing scheme; but only on conditions insisted on by the French.

---

[1] Britain was the first country to bring the borrowing scheme into operation—in October-November, 1964.

It was a landmark in the world's post-war monetary history.[1]
And it was not overlooked by the scores of City bankers who
thronged Vienna's hotels during that significant week. It confirmed them in their belief that, just as the role of the pound
was changing in the world, so should that of the City. It was
a time when Britain's proposed entry into Europe was also being
canvassed strongly. The City, founded on a political Commonwealth a century ago and based on a financial monetary block
for part of the 'thirties, for the whole of the war and for most
of the post-war years, was being forced to come to terms with
a new monetary era. It had to look beyond the sterling area;
it had even to look beyond the Continent of Europe. Could it
now serve the still wider Transatlantic community as well as
the Commonwealth? Could it become the centre of a wider
area of operations? Here are the same questions we have met
before, coming from a different direction.

Sterling loses its defensive wrappers

Any widening of the sterling horizon was bound to affect
the sterling area, the kernel of the defensive block conceived
in the 'thirties. After the collapse of the revived gold standard
in 1931, a group of countries (inside and outside the Commonwealth) decided to stick to sterling rather than gold. This
grouping was given some cohesion even during the 'thirties by
the first moves towards the control of capital issues in London.
But it was the introduction of exchange control regulations in
1939 and, particularly, the definition included in a statutory
order under the Defence Finance Regulations of the United
Kingdom in 1940 that brought the sterling area into formal
existence.

[1] There were other landmarks. As *The Times* wrote in a leading
article about the changing strength of Europe and North America on
22 January 1963:
   The rise of European strength can be shown in many ways . . . But
it can best be realised by two speeches of President Kennedy and a
simple set of figures. The more important speech was the President's
offer in Philadelphia last July of partnership with Europe—an outright
recognition of Europe as an equal. The other, though less important,
was equally significant. It was the remarkable Presidential use of the
American Telstar—an achievement in itself—to deny to a European
audience any devaluation of the dollar. The figures provide extra evidence of the obvious truth of Europe's recovery. Between 1951 and the
end of the third quarter of 1962, the gold and foreign exchange holdings
of continental Europe rose from $7,445 million to $24,420 million,
whereas those of the United States dropped from $22,873 million to
$16,532 million. And Britain's? Over the same period, they changed
marginally from $2,374 million to $2,798 million.

Let the Treasury explain how it continued after the war:

'When the United Kingdom's exchange control powers were consolidated, after the war, in the Exchange Control Act of 1947, the sterling area became known more technically as the Scheduled Territories. It comprises all members of the Commonwealth, except Canada; British Colonial Territories and eight other countries, Burma, Iceland, the Irish Republic, Jordan, Kuwait, Libya, South Africa and South West Africa, and Western Samoa.'[1]

During and after the war, this grouping of sterling countries continued on the defensive. Within the area, movements of capital were kept fairly free—particularly outwards from London, but transfers to and from non-sterling areas were rigidly controlled. It suited both Britain and the other members. Sterling area countries deliberately discriminated against other areas by imposing import control and by regulating currency movements. All members agreed to put their earnings of non-sterling currencies in the common pool in London. This helped Britain considerably at a time when hard currency resources needed to be used sparingly. Britain held the combined reserves on behalf of other members and gave each member an equivalent balance in sterling. Not only were members able to draw on these balances as and when needed, they also had the right to go to the London capital market when they needed, a facility denied to all other countries abroad.

Gradually the inward-looking features of this system began to be eroded, first by the world-wide moves towards freer trade, later by the corresponding moves in the currency field. The developed Commonwealth countries began to lower their import controls on dollar goods and the preferences on British goods slowly diminished. As American and European industrial capital moved to Australia, New Zealand, South Africa, India, Pakistan, etc., closer trading links were also forged. Even the younger nations of the Commonwealth—those given their sovereignty for the first time since the war—have turned to other countries for part of their trade—and aid. The help that colonial governments could give to the parent country in channelling trade (and orders) in that direction was unlikely to continue so automatically after independence. Thus, throughout the 'fifties, the share of Commonwealth trade in the world's total trade was declining for broad structural reasons (mainly

[1] The Treasury *Bulletin for Industry*, July 1963.

the rapid growth among the industrial nations themselves and the consequences of the fall in commodity prices), and Britain's share in Commonwealth trade itself was also declining.

There is much here to explain why Britain's share of total world trade has fallen over this period, often giving an over-exaggerated appearance of declining competitiveness. But that is another story. What we are concerned with here are the weakening links, both trade and financial, tying Britain with the sterling area. As freedom extended to trade relations, financial controls began to wither away too. Britain had con-tinually maintained little or no barriers on movements of money from London to the other members of the sterling area. This discrimination had important effects not only on the workings of the City but on the pattern of new direct investments abroad by British companies. Commonwealth (i.e. most sterling area) countries could raise funds on the London capital market and British firms were free to set up new fac-tories or take a stake in existing firms anywhere in the Com-monwealth. This was the position in the early post-war years. But even by 1952 certain exceptions were creeping in. British firms were given a green light of sorts for investment in Canada (not in the sterling area). It was not, as it turned out, a profit-able encouragement. A good deal of British money was lost in the Dominion in the ensuing ten years, and some prominent City houses burnt their fingers in this Canadian venture.

The concession was the first of many. By 1958, when the pound was declared convertible externally (i.e. for all foreign holders of sterling) British industrialists were freeer than ever before to direct their manufacturing investments to non-sterling areas. Some restriction was restored by Mr. Selwyn Lloyd in 1961, but it was not significant. Soon British investments in Europe were bounding ahead. Before long the anxiety was not whether the 1961 measures would put the clock back but rather, following Britain's official application to join the Common Market, whether Britain would be forced, on becoming a full member of the Six, to discriminate *against* the Commonwealth. In any future monetary crisis, it was asked in all seriousness in many parts of the Commonwealth, would Britain be forced to take restrictive action against all overseas countries (including the Commonwealth) in order to protect the enlarged Common Market (including Britain)? The answer from London was a clear no, but the question asked by several Commonwealth central bankers was reflection enough of the degree to which preferential treatment for the sterling area had been whittled down, and of the way many members of the area expected events to move. Many of these fears proved groundless. But later events have fully confirmed that sterling area treatment is now being extended to other areas of the world. It is, indeed, another way of saying that Britain is nearing a position in which it will no longer discriminate quite so much between one area and another in its external monetary relations. As we saw in Chapter 8, the EFTA countries have already been put on a similar footing to the sterling area countries in capital issues in the London market.

Effects on the sterling area

Before examining the wider currency effects of removing some of these protective wrappers from sterling (as well as the further international problems arising from this new world of currency convertibility), it is worth looking for a moment at the immediate impact on the future of the sterling area and, as a result, on the workings of the City. The tightly knit, defensive character of the sterling area was, as we have seen, based on the right of individual members to draw on the central pool of gold and exchange held in London and to get capital from the London market, and on the freedom of capital movements from London outwards to the rest of the sterling area. Part of these privileges, in turn, were dependent on members agreeing (or being willing) to keep their official reserves in sterling and to use it for their normal external transactions. If some of the preferential treatment is whittled down (by the Bank of England increasingly treating all countries alike), how far is this likely to affect the desire of sterling countries to bank their earnings in London in sterling?

The evidence so far points to a gradual lowering of the sterling content in the official reserves of several sterling area countries. Some like to see a little gold in the shop window as well as sterling. Others want to leaven the total with other currencies. This trend may continue. It is natural for newly independent nations to want some gesture of independence in this sphere too. And, as the privileges of sterling area membership appear to decline, other countries are likely to follow suit. On the face of it, this may have all the appearances of a currency problem for Britain. It might lead to a run on the central reserves at an inconvenient time, or at least to a depletion of the gold and foreign exchange content (in return for a corresponding decline in sterling liabilities). Since total sterling balances (or liabilities) are well in excess of sterling assets and gold, the presentation of all the sterling balances for payment in gold or other currencies at the same time would, undoubtedly, produce a major crisis for Britain. But it is precisely because of this knowledge that sterling area members are highly unlikely to take any such action on such a scale. A run on a bank hurts depositors most of all. Britain, as banker to the sterling area as well as to other holders of sterling, is in the position of a bank. Assets are inevitably dwarfed by liabilities. But the system works so long as everyone behaves himself, and so long as the banker does not take undue risks.

Even though it would pay no-one to bring on an acute sterling crisis by his own action, some decline in sterling holdings may well be seen in the reserves of sterling area members. It is easy to move on from this decline to the assumption that their use of sterling for trade and other purposes would decline by the same proportion. It is not, however, the experience of countries (Iraq is one) which have deliberately cut down the amount of sterling in their official reserves. This is an important point for the City and one we shall return to again in Chapter 12. It need not be assumed that the withering away of sterling area privileges, thus weakening the rigid sterling links between Britain and other members, will necessarily lead to a corresponding drop in the use of pounds as a trading currency, nor to an equally corresponding decline in the use of the City's services. On the contrary, if the sterling area can manage to keep some of its old features while being merged in a far wider currency area (virtually the whole world, including the Iron Curtain countries), the City will be able to regard the entire globe as its oyster—as indeed it always used to do before the convulsions of two world wars led to the building up of defensive currency blocks.

CHAPTER 11

LIQUIDITY AND SUPPORT FOR THE POUND

THROUGHOUT the persistent efforts to put the monetary clock back, which have been far more successful since the war than before, the City survived to an unexpected degree. No other mechanism developed on the same scale. Yet the City's very success has raised doubts whether it should be encouraged further. Although convertibility and free world payments have returned in greater measure than for a quarter of a century, two features are still missing from this familiar scene: a strong pound and a dominant British economy. Their absence is bound to reflect on the workings of the City's markets. Without them can the City make much progress, without undermining other parts of the economy? Both elements call for detailed consideration, the pound in this chapter, the economy in the next.

Liquidity and currency

The currency problem is sometimes posed entirely in terms of a shortage of world liquidity, sometimes solely in terms of the two key currencies, the pound and the dollar. In practice, liquidity and currencies are inextricably mixed together. What is certain is that the onset of convertibility at the end of 1958 brought with it larger problems of world monetary management than anyone visualised at the time. When the major European currencies had become convertible and the French franc (supported by yet another devaluation) had regained its strength, pushed along on a growing tide of Gaullist confidence and prosperity from the beginning of 1959, the world's exchange markets were looking healthier and more stable than for 20 or 30 years. It was a stability that was not enjoyed for long.

The rise of Europe was accompanied by a weakening of the American dollar. Both movements were part of the same phenomenon. With Europe out of the competitive race for most of the early post-war years, American exporters were able to capture the world's markets and keep them simply by the ability to deliver plentifully and on time. When European industry recovered, the pattern began to change. European delivery dates improved and, more important, European prices were found to be lower. For the first time since 1939 American traders were forced to look to their costs. The American economy, which had for long borne the burden of the cold war and the bulk of the world's aid to the underdeveloped world, began to feel (and show) the strain. As European currencies gained strength, the dollar lost its dominant place in the world. The American payments balance worsened and the outflow of gold quickened. Yet, as we saw in Chapter 4, it was not until the closing months of 1960 that the first sharp crack opened up in the world's financial centres. Suddenly, and almost without warning, a gold fever spread through Europe, making itself felt particularly in the London gold market.

How or why such a sudden demand for gold starts it is difficult to know. The dollar had been uncertain for some time; the Swiss authorities had taken measures to keep out foreign money; there was an election campaign under way in the United States; and the London gold market provided the opportunity to hedge against the dollar by buying gold. In two or three days many people were doing so. The price shot up from around $35 an ounce to over $40. The initial speculation fed on itself. Gold is one of the few commodities in the world in which a rise in price stimulates further demand.

The reasons for the outburst are less important for our purpose than the consequences. They were immediate. The Bank of England, which had managed the London gold market since its re-opening in 1954, quickly came to the defence of the dollar by offering large quantities of gold on the market on behalf of the United States Federal Reserve Bank of New York. The fever gradually subsided. But it was to be followed within a matter of months by quite a different onslaught, this time on the pound.

Following the upward revaluation of the German mark and the Dutch guilder early in 1961, speculation in favour of a further upward adjustment completely upset sterling. Short-term funds moved out of sterling and into German marks, Swiss francs, French francs and Italian lira on a substantial scale. The pressure on the pound in one day is said to have been close to $900 million of sales. As in the previous October, the leading central banks were forced to take quick defensive action. There was no time to get help from the International Monetary Fund. The central banks receiving the sterling in such large doses simply agreed to channel it back to the Bank of England. Immediate short-term credits were introduced and different arrangements entered into between the Bank of England and the other central banks.

Informality was the keynote. The 'gentlemen's agreement' of Basle had been born. The need to defend both the dollar and the pound—the world's two key currencies—within months of each other on a substantial scale had brought the lesson home in the right quarters. It was the start of the systematic central bank co-operation that has continued ever since—either in the monthly meeting of the Bank for International Settlements in Basle or in the monetary committee of the Organisation for Economic Co-operation and Development in Paris. Since that time, the central bankers have built up and introduced a gold pool under the day-to-day control of the Bank of England, one of the most successful of these co-operative ventures. No dangerous upsurge in the London gold price has occurred since the pool began to operate. The rise during the Cuban crisis was modest.

Similar co-operation in the foreign exchange markets of the world has not had the same success in keeping pressures under control. But it has enabled monetary crises to be tackled with far more confidence and effectiveness than was possible before. After the German revaluation came the Berlin crisis, the problems surrounding the Canadian devaluation, the onset of the Cuban crisis, the shock of Britain's rejection by the Common Market and, finally, the onslaught within weeks of a new Labour Government in the autumn of 1964. All put intense pressure on individual currencies. Each in turn brought co-operative action by the leading central banks. During the Canadian difficulties, the central banks managed to find $1,000 million in a matter of 48 hours for the defence of the Canadian currency. Towards the end of 1964 they found $3,000 million in less than 24 hours to protect the pound.

New techniques for supporting major currencies

This pragmatic approach to the world's monetary problems brought a gradual introduction of new techniques. There were straightforward credit facilities from one central bank to another; interventions in the forward exchange market; informal joint activity in the gold market; and the fresh acquisition of foreign currencies by the United States. All these official actions became difficult to follow from the outside.[1] One central bank would be on the telephone to another in a matter of minutes, if necessary, forestalling speculation.

Soon these techniques were followed by others, deliberately introduced by the United States Treasury. A new network of so-called 'swap' agreements was arranged with other central banks by Mr. Robert Roosa, then US Under-Secretary of the Treasury for Monetary Affairs. Under these arrangements, the US Federal Reserve Bank undertook to offer credit lines to individual central banks in exchange for equivalent credit lines from them. By the autumn of 1963, a network of swaps amounting to no less than $2,050 million had been agreed with 12 national currencies. At first they were arranged for little more than $50 million each. Later the individual amounts increased considerably. The American swap with France was pushed up to $100 million, those with Italy and Germany to $250 million, that with Switzerland and the Bank for International Settlements to $300 million, that with Canada to $250 million and that with Britain to $500 million. A new one was introduced in 1964 with the Bank of Japan for $150 million. The 'swaps' were eventually accompanied by American efforts to get longer-term arrangements by the issue of so-called Roosa bonds—debt certificates of the US Treasury, expressed in the currency of the country buying them. The sales started with one to the Bank of Italy at the beginning of 1962. Those sold so far have been generally for longer than 15 months, most of them for two years, with one, for exceptional reasons, going five years.

Beyond these specifically American arrangements have been the new commitments of the International Monetary Fund, with its $1,000 million standby credit for Britain, a similar substantial credit for Canada and the first standby authorisation of $500 million for the United States. And the IMF itself can now rely on further help because of the arrangement with the so-called Group of Ten.[2]

---

[1] Since the central banks worked in secret it became difficult for an outside observer to detect whether stability in any currency was natural or simply the result of official intervention.

[2] An agreement initiated in Vienna in September 1961, concluded in Paris in December, 1961, ratified by the US Congress in June, 1962, and effective since October, 1962, which established facilities allowing the IMF to borrow up to $6,000 million from Belgium, Canada, France, West Germany, Italy, Japan, Holland, Sweden, Britain and the United States.

In all these ways the world's monetary authorities have acted swiftly in placing a defensive ring around the major currencies of the world. But, according to Mr. Roosa, these new defences

'may not in the end be found to provide an adequate answer to the world's long-run need for liquidity, but they are a powerful bulwark today—making borrowed reserves available to supplement the owned reserves of the leading industrial countries which have joined the ring.'

What the sterling crisis at the end of 1964 brought home was the marked growth in the size of the attack on the reserve currencies under current conditions of exchange freedom. As *The Economist* said at the time, Britain needed external credits of $1,300 million to deal with the Suez crisis in 1956; $2,000 million in the 1961 crisis; and $4,000 million ($1,000 million from IMF and $3,000 million from central banks) at the end of 1964. It is hardly surprising that the City should want to know whether enough has now been done to defend the pound from sharp overnight attack.[1] Mr. Roosa has done what he can to put up a defensive barrier round the dollar. In doing so, he has also helped the pound. The new central bank co-operative arrangements, the IMF standby credit, the potential borrowings from the Paris Group of Ten and the swap agreement with the US Federal Reserve, quite apart from Britain's gold reserves and her second line of defence in the shape of dollar securities, may prove enough for the moment. Is it enough for the next ten years? This is the question, in a broader context, that has been occupying the world's monetary minds in the past 18 months. In the current jargon, is there enough liquidity in the world to cope both with the expected expansion in world trade and with the speculative shifts in short-term capital?

More international liquidity?

The pound, as one of the world's two main reserve currencies, is at the heart of the liquidity question. Basically, international payments since the war have been made in gold, dollars, sterling and a handful of other currencies.[2] But, in trying to discover whether there is enough of this world money to finance the expected growth in world trade, too many people have been

[1] See Appendix on how the pound is defended, p. 186.
[2] The connection between other currencies and gold has been provided by the willingness of the United States to switch dollars, held officially, into gold at $35 an ounce, and buy gold at the same price.

content to assume that the total of these various means of exchange should keep in step with the rise in trade generally. Calculations made on this basis have usually turned out to be depressingly pessimistic. Politicians in particular have been prone to do their sums this way. What they have overlooked is that world trade is generally financed by the domestic credit of individual countries through their own banks and that world currency as such (gold and foreign exchange) is used simply to offset the final balances left over between countries. As the 1963 annual report of the International Monetary Fund put it:

'The use of foreign exchange resources is limited to covering the differences that arise from time to time between the flows of receipts and payments. This means that there is no simple functional relation between the need for some aggregate of official liquid resources and the volume of world trade; in fact, it is the increased movement of short-term funds since convertibility that has required greater use of external liquidity rather than increased trade.'

There are various ways of estimating the world's total currency reserves. One way was shown by the United Kingdom Treasury. The details (confined solely to gold, dollars and pounds) were as shown in Table XIX.

TABLE XIX

WORLD MONETARY RESERVES, 1937-62

(in $ millions)

	Total	Gold	%	Dollars	%	Pounds	%
1937	30,000	26,000	86	1,800	6	2,300	8
1953	47,500	34,300	72	5,700	12	7,500	16
1962	57,400	39,200	67	11,900	21	6,800	12

Source: Treasury *Bulletin for Industry*, December 1963.

It will be seen that the proportion of gold has gradually fallen since before the war and the reliance on the two main currencies accordingly increased. The bulk of those pounds available as reserves was the result of the war and of dollars of the recent American deficits. The roles of sterling and the dollar have been reversed. Up to 1953, there were more pounds than dollars used as currency reserves; by 1962 (largely because of the continuing American deficits) there were more dollars than pounds. It is possible that other leading currencies (mainly European) made up a total about half that of sterling, though precise figures are not available. Beyond this, of course, there are the important gold and lines of credit ('tranches') of the International Monetary Fund that can be drawn upon by members in time of need.

The sum total of all these various reserves and credit facilities open to individual governments is set out in Table XX. At the end of 1963, it came to $87,000 million. Of this, $70,000 million was made up of gold, foreign exchange, the IMF gold tranche and the various US bonds and currency 'swaps' already in use. The balance of $17,000 million was accounted for by various types of credit facilities available, ranging from unused 'swap' facilities to the IMF tranches subject to negotiation. The main point of the Table is that little more than one-fifth of the total growth in world liquidity in the ten years from 1953 to 1963 was provided by increases in gold holdings. Even gold and foreign exchange together accounted for little more than a half of the total increase. Credit facilities were already providing a significant contribution to world liquidity.

At present these combined monetary resources are little more than adequate to cope with the swings in international payments. The conclusions of both the IMF and Group of Ten study group reports issued in the late summer and autumn of 1964 before the latest sterling crisis, were more reassuring. The Ministers of the Group of Ten stated that supplies of gold and reserve currencies were 'fully adequate for the present and are likely to be for the immediate future.' These resources were fully supported by a broad range of credit facilities. But the continuing growth in world trade and payments, the Ministers thought, would entail a need for larger international liquidity. This would call for an expansion in credit facilities and, in the longer run, might even call for some new form of reserve asset.[1] A new study group was begun, under the chairmanship of Signor Ossola, to examine the various methods of creating such assets. The IMF report on liquidity also concluded that liquidity was adequate, but did not hide its view that there would be 'persistent and substantial growth in the demand for international liquidity over the next decade'. The IMF was convinced

---

[1] A much less anxious view of world liquidity is taken by Professor Gottfried Haberler. He believes that part of the trouble with some countries is creeping inflation, not shortage of liquidity. See *Money in the International Economy*, Hobart Paper 31, I.E.A., 1965.

TABLE XX

WORLD'S RESERVES & CREDIT FACILITIES 1953 AND 1963

(All countries)

($ billions)

| | RESERVES | | | | | | | | CREDIT FACILITIES | | | | | | GRAND TOTAL |
| | Gold and Foreign Exchange | | | Other | | | | Total Reserves | Assured | | | Subject to Negotiation | | Total credit facilities | (Reserves & Credit) |
	Gold	Foreign exchange	Total	Gold tranche	Special U.S. bonds	Swaps used by other party	Total		Swaps unactivated	IMF stand-bys	Total	Other IMF tranches	Total		
1953	34.32	17.11	51.43	1.89	—	—	1.89	53.32	—	—	—	7.14	7.14	7.14	60.46
1963	40.20	25.07	65.27	3.94	.71	.29	4.94	70.21	3.16	.51	3.67	13.48	13.48	17.15	87.36
Change	+5.88	+7.96	+13.84	+2.05	+.71	+.29	+3.05	+16.89	+3.16	+.51	+3.67	+6.34	+6.34	+10.01	+26.90

Source: Group of Ten report on international liquidity.

that any further expansion in new facilities should make full use of the Fund's resources and machinery. At the annual meeting of the IMF in Tokyo a month or so later (September 1964), three things became apparent: that any agreement among the main industrial countries about the form of the world's future monetary system would be difficult to reach; that, in spite of certain difficulties over details, the quotas of the Fund should be increased by some $4,000 million or $5,000 million in 1965; and that the Group of Ten's borrowing arrangements, due for renewal not later than October 1966, would come under scrutiny at the same time.

Political pressures

Whatever the conclusions, there can be little doubt that demands for bigger currency reserves are bound to grow over the next decade. This rests on far more than the usual assumptions about expanding world trade. In a world of convertibility, capital movements, whether from speculation or international investment, are likely to increase rather than decrease and the swings between currencies almost bound to grow. There have already been signs of this in the size of the outflow from London, for example, during recent currency crises. The pressure on the pound is now far stronger than it used to be before convertibility. There is a further important point. In a political atmosphere in which full employment and growth are given the highest priorities, the internal disciplines which are likely to bring costs under control and, thus, payments deficits into balance no longer have the impact that they had. Whether these developments are desirable is discussed in Chapter 12. If this is accompanied by an international climate in which exchange rate adjustments are frowned on, trade controls hardly encouraged and exchange controls generally dismantled, it is bound to take longer for payments deficits and surpluses to be corrected. Few deficit countries, for example, are likely to succeed in bringing internal prices down. To attempt to do so is apparently considered by politicians to be political suicide. This is, of course, a matter of degree. A certain amount of deflation has been possible in several countries since the war. with only temporary political unpopularity. Both Conservative and Labour governments have administered significant deflationary doses in Britain. They have also, however, drawn the line at plunging the country into a long period of widespread unemployment. Even if the authorities discover how to manage the economy better, by avoiding the excesses of the 'stop-go' cycle, and even if they decide to operate the economy at a lower pressure of demand, the need to keep unemployment at a level significantly lower than the pre-war average would still make price and cost adjustments much more difficult (certainly less flexible) than they used to be under conditions of high unemployment.[1]

In general, therefore, we have to get used to the idea that once costs and prices get out of line in a country, it will take far longer than it used to do for the appropriate corrections to be made. This will, naturally, place a greater strain on the world's monetary resources. Debtor countries will probably need more help over a longer period.

What are the chances of the normal means of international payment increasing in line with these needs? On closer scrutiny they appear remarkably small. The increase in official gold holdings from newly-mined output has varied considerably in recent years, largely depending on the amount of private hoarding. Something like $1,500 million worth of new gold is available every year. But the annual average reaching official reserves in the four years 1960-63 was little more than $500 million compared with an annual average of some $700 million in the previous three years. With the lowering of international tension (particularly following the acute Cuban crisis of 1962 and the détente between Russia and America), the hoarding demand for gold may subside. The upsurge in January 1965 was a reminder that a steady flow of gold into official hands cannot be relied upon.

The dollar-sterling dilemma

The trouble is that any additional gold supply is likely to be more than offset by the reduction in the supply of surplus dollars. The American authorities are determined to bring their payments deficit under control as soon as possible. This determination was given a further stimulus by President de

[1] For a useful discussion of the effects of different levels of unemployment on costs and prices see the following: A. W. Phillips, 'The Relation between Unemployment and the Rate of Change of Money Wage Rates in the United Kingdom 1861-1951, *Economica*, November 1958; R. R. Neild, *Pricing and Employment in the Trade Cycle*, Cambridge University Press, 1963; J. C. R. Dow, *The Management of the British Economy, 1945-60*, Cambridge University Press, 1964; F. W. Paish and Jossleyn Hennessay, *Policy for Incomes?*, Hobart Paper 29, I.E.A., 1964; F. W. Paish, 'The Management of the British Economy,' *Lloyd's Bank Review*, April 1965.

Gaulle early in 1965. The more successful the Americans' efforts, the smaller the supply of dollars for the world's monetary reserves. Since additional dollars have been accumulating at a rate of $1,000 million a year, this will make a noticeable difference. Sterling holdings have already fallen over the past decade and there is no reason to believe that Britain will want to run its recent sizeable deficit in overseas payments for very long.[1] Thus, both the United States and Britain will be trying to cut down the supply of their currencies for use as world reserves in the coming years, rather than the reverse. Paradoxically the less successful they are (and thus the more dollars and pounds are made available to others), the bigger the strain on the world's monetary system since both the key currencies will, by definition, be coming under renewed pressure. Equally, the stronger they are and the stronger the British and American payments position, the more the world's monetary system will be in need of alternative means of payment.

Several solutions to this dilemma have been offered in recent years. They include a rise in the dollar price of gold, the introduction of flexible exchange rates,[2] a scheme for turning the IMF into a super central bank with credit-creating facilities, gold guarantees for the reserve currencies, as well as individual plans bearing the names of Triffin, Stamp, Harrod, Bernstein, Posthuma, Maudling, etc.[3] Since 1958, all have run the gauntlet of informed financial opinion. They have done so in a special way since the middle of 1964 because of the specific inquiries set in motion by the IMF and the Group of Ten. It is now

[1] Since both Britain and the US were running a combined deficit of the order of £2,850 million ($8,000 million) a year in 1964, other countries were unlikely to allow this to continue indefinitely.

[2] See Appendix C, p. 187.

[3] Professor S. Posthuma, 'The International Monetary System'; *Banca Nazionale del Lavoro Quarterly Review*, September 1963; Edward M. Bernstein, *Outlook for US Balance of Payments*, Hearings (December 14 1962), Joint Economic Committee, Sub-committee on International Exchange and Payments (Washington 1963); Hon. Maxwell Stamp, 'The Stamp Plan—1962 Version,' *Moorgate & Wall Street Review*, Autumn 1962, Philip Hill, Higginson, Erlangers Ltd, London; Robert Triffin, *Gold and the Dollar Crisis*, Yale University Press, 1960; Sir Roy Harrod, *Reforming the World's Money*, Macmillan & Co., 1965; Reginald Maudling, Statement to International Monetary Fund annual meeting, Washington, September 1962.

A summary of these and other plans for improving the international monetary system is contained in *World Monetary Reform*, edited by Herbert G. Grubel, Stanford University Press, California (and Oxford University Press, London), 1964. See also Appendix I to this chapter, pp. 184-185.

clear that several solutions stand little chance of acceptance by the monetary authorities of the world, unless forced upon them by unforeseen speculative events. Any change in the price of gold, the introduction of flexible exchange rates and gold guarantees for the reserve currencies, have all been rejected; the first by the United States, the second by most central bankers and the third by Britain and the United States. Apart from the windfall profits to Russia and South Africa as well as to speculators, and apart from the loss of American prestige involved, any rise in the price of gold is opposed by many central bankers because it might lead to credit inflation. The same fear is also prompted by the suggestion of flexible exchange rates. This would remove any need to keep a currency fixed to a certain level and thus relieve the necessity to maintain exchange reserves. Politicians could more easily pursue inflationary policies. Of the ideas that remain, we need to sort out the practical possibilities, assess their effect on the pound and their implications for the working of the City.

The four solutions

There are now two basic issues involved. One is the question of the role of gold and the method of switching currencies into gold and vice-versa. The argument is largely between those (like the French economist Jacques Rueff and his most recent adherent, President de Gaulle) who want a return to the strict discipline of gold payments to cover deficits and those who want to build on the present gold exchange standard. Jacques Rueff has gone to the point of recreating the ghost of 1929 again and warning the world of the monetary dangers it will run[1] unless some means are found to return to the discipline of gold. He feels that the world made a grave mistake when in 1922, following a resolution at the Genoa international monetary conference, central banks agreed to economise in the use of gold by maintaining reserves in foreign currencies. Thus was the 'gold-exchange standard' born. It allowed countries running deficits to avoid payments in gold—particularly Britain and the United States. It had one further effect. Since countries earning dollars and pounds, instead of receiving gold, were enabled to deposit them in New York and London, the deposits could be lent to national borrowers. As Rueff put it, 'the functioning of the international monetary system thus became

[1] See especially three articles in *Le Monde*, reprinted in *The Times* on 27, 28, 29 June 1961.

reduced to a mere children's game in which one party had agreed to give back their investments, after each game of marbles, to the party who had lost the game'. The previous discipline on a deficit country to deflate following a loss of gold was weakened.

This disturbed, and still disturbs M. Rueff. It does not disturb others. It can be argued that the excesses of the now gold-exchange standard inevitably led to the collapse of 1929-31. It can just as easily be argued that, without the gold-exchange standard, the unprecedented prosperity of the post-war years and certainly the widespread achievement of full employment policies in the western world would have been impossible. In short, without the use of national currencies as additional means of payment, the expansion of world trade over the last 20 years could not have taken place.

President de Gaulle, in spite of earlier assumptions to the contrary did not wholly accept Rueff's views. He criticised the gold-exchange standard. He wants a return to gold payments by countries in deficit. He has pledged that France will pay gold to meet her future deficits and will take gold from other countries. He has made it clear that France will gradually convert her dollar holdings (they once amounted to some $1,300 million) into gold. And he has urged the other industrial nations to do likewise. But his call for a return to gold[1] was not Rueff's pure doctrine. As M. Giscard d'Estaing, the French Minister, made clear a couple of weeks after the President's press conference, French policy also included the possibility of introducing other means of payment 'based on gold.' This was a plain reference to the composite reserve unit idea, the original Bernstein scheme[2] modified to French requirements. In French eyes this was a way of replacing pounds and dollars as international means of payment by some internationally accepted unit.

This brings us to the second of the basic issues facing the world's monetary authorities. The first, as we have just seen, concerns the role of gold. The second concerns the best way to supplement or replace the two main reserve currencies, dollars and pounds. There are in fact four basic ways of improving the use of the reserve currencies.[3] They are not mutually exclusive:

(a) continue the present system, while widening the co-operative credit arrangements;

[1] February 1965.
[2] Appendix I p. 185.
[3] A useful survey of the theoretical possibilities was given by Robert Roosa in the October 1963 issue of *Foreign Affairs*.

(b) enlarge the resources of the International Monetary Fund and make its facilities more flexible;

(c) establish a new grouping of some of the other leading currencies as a complement or alternative to the roles now performed by the pound and the dollar as reserve currencies;

(d) give the IMF the ability to create credit, or to co-operate in the issue of certificates with its guarantee attached, or to modify its articles sufficiently to provide additional banking assets.

All raise a fundamental question. As so many people have asked, are the pound and the dollar to get additional help automatically and without accepting any further discipline to put their economic house in order either by deflationary domestic policies or by reducing overseas commitments or both? There should be enough currency reserves in the world to avoid trouble. But, as Mr. Reginald Maudling put it in Washington in September 1963,

'the availability of liquid resources should not be such as to promote, or encourage countries to tolerate, the continuance of basically unsound domestic or international positions in the guise of temporary fluctuations. The basic dilemma is clear. If adequate resources are not available automatically or nearly automatically, their usefulness in times of trouble may be problematic; but, to the extent to which they are automatically available, they may present a temptation to refrain from the necessary corrections of policy.'

The Secretary General of the Organisation for Economic Co-operation and Development, Dr. Thorkil Kristensen, said much the same thing. 'How can we ensure,' he asked, 'that the results of this co-operation will be a suitable combination between the necessary financing and the necessary discipline? That is the core of the monetary problem.' Other countries have had other ways of putting it. Europe in particular has insisted that the problem of the shortage of world liquidity and the problem of improving the present gold-exchange standard should not be confused with the need to improve the American and British balance of payments. As we have seen, President de Gaulle has been most insistent on this point.

Grouping reserve currencies

So far most progress has been made in terms of the first two theoretical solutions. The third idea of trying to set up a new grouping of reserve currencies has many variants. It lies behind the Common Market's efforts to find economic union. The aim of the Treaty of Rome of giving complete freedom to the movement of capital, labour and services within the Community, with a view to the eventual integration of economic, fiscal and monetary policies, has naturally been followed by a similar attitude to currencies. The idea of a common European exchange reserve was aired by M. Jean Monnet in July 1961.

'It is certain that, if the West had a common currency, the problems that harry us now would not exist. Obviously, a common currency is not possible today, though the day when it may come in the Common Market is, I think, closer than most people realise.'[1]

Certainly it was an idea that seemed to have its attractions for Mr. Roosa, too, for at that time much of his thinking included the dollar on one side of the Atlantic and a large European currency (in which the pound would be merged) on the other. It was the time when Britain's application for entry to the Common Market was still being discussed in Brussels. Even since the rejection of Britain's application, the idea of forming a nucleus of other reserve currencies from Europe has persisted.

A European currency?

This solution, however, would not be achieved overnight. It is unlikely that much progress could be expected in merging monetary or currency affairs, until considerable economic integration had already been achieved. But the basic hope at that time was that any merging of the pound in Europe within the coming decade would lend support for sterling and open up a larger area of operations for the City of London. This attitude jumped many difficult fences prematurely. In particular, it assumed that Britain could manage to gain the help she wanted from Europe without giving Europe far more control over Britain's financial affairs than might be readily swallowed in London, let alone the Commonwealth. It was not always a realistic assumption, as any perusal of Article 108 of the Treaty

[1] M. Monnet's Action Committee for a United States of Europe passed a resolution in July 1961, for creating a European monetary reserve union.

of Rome[1] would quickly reveal. In short, many people who were enamoured of this European solution were more concerned with the fruits in the long-run than with the difficulties (perhaps humiliations, certainly weak negotiating positions) in the short-term. There was little doubt in authoritative quarters in the City that a good deal of deliberate and continuous education about the peculiarities of running a reserve currency lay ahead of any currency merger with Europe.

We have already referred to one further offshoot of the idea of creating a new reserve asset to supplement or replace pounds and dollars. This is the so-called French version of the original Bernstein plan that Composite Reserve Units (CRU's) should be created in the following way. The value of one unit would be equal to one US dollar, half consisting of US currency and the other half made up of the currencies of the other members of the Group of Ten (plus Switzerland) in proportion to their gold holdings. Each country would deposit an amount of its own currency proportionate to its share in the units being created. The French and Dutch, who have been pushing this idea in its revised form,[2] suggest that each country would guarantee its contribution against devaluation. Thus, the CRU's would be equivalent to gold, by having a gold guarantee, in contrast to dollars which do not. The scheme has the advantage of involving other currencies in replacing the reserve currencies. But it runs up against the weakness of yielding virtually nothing,[3] though Mr. Bernstein has offered ways of getting round this. Bigger defects appear from the methods of creating the units. Can other countries be included later? If so, how? In addition,

[1] Article 108 of the Treaty of Rome contains the following paragraph: 'Where a member state is in difficulties or seriously threatened with difficulties as regards its balance of payments as a result either of overall disequilibrium of the balance of payments or of the kinds of currency at its disposal and where such difficulties are likely, in particular, to prejudice the functioning of the Common Market or the progressive establishment of the common commercial policy, the Commission shall without delay examine the situation of such state and the action which, in making use of all the means at its disposal, that state has taken or may take in conformity with the provisions of Article 104. *The Commission shall indicate the measures which it recommends to the state concerned to adopt.*' (My italics.)

[2] The main French revisions are that the Bank for International Settlements should act as trustee instead of the IMF and that the units would earn no interest (i.e. like gold).

[3] The French regard this as an advantage in that it will prevent the deficit country from generating further internal inflation and would offset gold's present disadvantage.

such a system would hardly be automatic and would give the power of creating these units to a particular group of countries. Because of the inter-dependent nature of the units, this controlled creation would also give individual members of the group a veto over the others. It is not hard to see why some Continental countries, particularly France, find the prospect of introducing such a system to their liking. They would get a guarantee for any of their present foreign exchange, mainly dollars, replaced by such units; more important, they would also gain control over the future creation of reserve assets.

Should IMF create more credit?

The fourth idea of giving the IMF more credit-creating powers takes various forms. In some, it is linked with the issue of certificates guaranteed by the IMF. In others, the Fund is likened to a national central bank though on a world scale. The idea of a supranational bank with full credit-creating facilities is clearly before its time. It stands little chance of acceptance while central bankers and politicians want to maintain even a semblance of national sovereignty and while national fiscal and monetary policies could impede the overall policies of the super-bank. Varying interest rates in different centres, for example, could lead to difficult stresses. No doubt the world will get to a super bank in the end. But that time is not yet. What stands a better chance of acceptance is the idea of making fuller use of the gold tranche rights within the Fund. A more intensive use of what is called a 'super gold trance' would, it is emphasised by Britain and America, be the equivalent of creating a new reserve asset. In essence, this is not a new mechanism, but the more intensive use of an old one. The American authorities have been fully aware of its use for some time. When other countries draw an individual country's currency from the Fund, its drawing rights within the Fund are automatically increased. For example, in the early post-war years, other countries drew $1,300 million in dollars from the IMF. This system provided the United States with an additional drawing right up to this amount, a facility that was especially timely once the American payments balance began to deteriorate. The operation is simple. The original borrowing country has acquired additional foreign currency; the selling country has equally acquired additional reserve assets, highly liquid and fully transferable. All that is needed to make wider use of this credit-creating mechanism is a more intensive use of the Fund's facilities, coupled with the steady increase in Fund quotas, or at least in the quotas of countries whose currencies can be used in Fund drawings. This idea has the merit of supplementing the liquidity already in existence, without interfering in any way with the present machinery.

Gold certificates

Another variant stems from the idea of paying gold subscriptions to the Fund partly in the form of gold certificates. This has been developed by Mr. Maxwell Stamp.[1] It has one particular advantage over the ideas of Professor Robert Triffin[1] and others in that it has been modified to suit the outlook of the central bankers and finance ministers who will make most of the initial running in this field. The idea, basically, is that the industrialised nations should be persuaded to look on certificates issued by the IMF as equivalent to gold in their reserves and that they should be issued, in the first place, to the underdeveloped countries. It attempts, in effect, to solve two problems at the same time by providing credit to the needy nations and inserting extra liquidity into the reserves of the industrial countries, at one move. As Mr. Stamp has recognised, it is essential to sell schemes of this sort to the right people in the right quarters, and he was quick to advise Mr. Harold Wilson (who favours this scheme) not to try to do too much at the wrong (political) level. There is a limit to what central bankers and politicians are willing to accept at one time, but in my view the germs of a possible future solution lie in the direction outlined by Mr. Stamp. Yet even this is clearly running too far ahead of what is immediately possible.

The outlook

The characteristic attitudes of central bankers, and those already adopted by European bankers and politicians suggest that any sharp break with current arrangements by the introduction of large new schemes can be ruled out. The practical choice, as we shall discuss in Chapter 12, seems to be between the French CRU scheme and some extension of the IMF's gold tranche. Meanwhile, building stronger defences along the bilateral and multilateral lines of the past three or four years will go on piecemeal. Increases in IMF resources will be agreed and increased flexibility in the Fund's facilities are likely to be considered. A by-product will be further help for the pound.

[1] Appendix A, p. 184.

The outstanding question is what conditions will be laid down for this further help. In view of the events in Vienna in September 1961, these conditions may not be laid down beforehand. But it may be assumed that if the Europeans have their way, as they did in Vienna, the strings will be firmly in their hands. Further disciplinary arrangements have already been introduced under the guise of 'multilateral surveillance.' Both these techniques and the conditions of borrowing may be more important to the British economy than to the City of London itself. But, as we shall see in Chapter 12, the prospects of the City and the economy are closely intertwined. In general, the stronger the support for the pound, the better for the City. The fewer the crises, the more the confidence and the more trading pounds will be left permanently in the Square Mile. Moreover, to the extent that outflows of funds from London can be neutralised by central banking co-operation supported by longer-term defences (both inside and outside the IMF), the economy can continue to expand without putting on the brakes prematurely; and the City, for its part, can continue to go about its profitable business without interference from hastily imposed exchange controls. As we shall argue, the City has suffered as much from the excessive stop-go mentality of Whitehall as any other part of the economy.

The type of solution to the liquidity problem that the City will have to watch carefully is the possible introduction of other reserve currencies[1] (with or without the assurance of immediate transferability into gold). But, if the argument we have already deployed is tenable, financial rivals to the City would have to appear on the scene well before any other individual currencies could take their place alongside the pound and the dollar. In other words, it is unlikely that the establishment of new reserve currencies would lead to the stimulating of European capital markets on the City pattern. The evolution process seems to work the other way round: the encroachment on the City's activities would be felt first and it would then lay the foundations for the gradual establishment of other reserve currencies.

One aspect, however, is often overlooked. A new reserve currency or even a series of them, cannot be established overnight. They grow to be accepted gradually. There is not simply

[1] This was one of Sir Roy Harrod's main fears about the Triffin plan—that it would undermine the role of sterling and thus of the City (*Economica*, May 1961).

the obvious matter of confidence. Convenience is equally important. Both the pound and the dollar are backed by financial communities in New York and London that provide facilities for short-term investment. Money can be left overnight and still make a return. Reserves held in pounds and dollars can be both profitable and highly liquid. This is not so in Zurich, Paris or Frankfurt, or at least not to the extent that it is in London and New York. Moreover, the Swiss and German governments have generally acted in a positive way to keep excessive foreign funds out and to avoid any interference from this direction with the domestic economy. Both governments have been keen to prevent inflationary forces coming in by a flood of unwanted foreign funds. This is a natural reaction on a Continent that has suffered so badly many times from the evils of rampant inflation, not least internally in social injustice and the disruption that helped to impoverish the German middle classes and provoke the Nazi revolution. It is equally a reflection of the absence of a Continental centre with a mechanism (like London) for pushing out foreign funds in a different guise almost as soon as they have arrived or for absorbing them safely into the system. As Sir George Bolton, chairman of the Bank of London and South America, once told American bankers in New York,

'The dollar and sterling systems have become of world-wide use and importance, not because of the inherent strength of the USA or the British Commonwealth, but largely because of the stability of our social and political institutions, the strength of the banking system and the efficiency of our commodity and money markets. Until other currency systems can match these factors, dollars and sterling will remain without rivals.'

The City may now have to know how to avoid deciding whether to throw in its lot with the United States or with Europe. The future points in both directions. Should Britain, as Sir George Bolton has already persuasively argued on several occasions,[1] move closer to the United States? Or should it, as so many others have stressed, see its future solely in terms of Europe? Sir George's argument rests on two main grounds. One is that the pound and the dollar are bound to sink or swim together or, more accurately, to be under pressure alternately. What he foresees is both currencies being forced

[1] In a speech in New York on 25 October, 1962, and in an article in *The Times* on 20 September, 1963.

to surround themselves by exchange controls for self-protection, and London and New York operating inside these new boundaries. Secondly, he regards it as nonsensical for the two major centres of world banking, London and New York, to fight each other tooth and nail for customers and business in all parts of the world. More co-operation, he argues, would not only be more sensible but also more profitable. In effect, both arguments are simply a financial reflection of the political dilemma facing Britain. Politically the future must lie with Europe; yet in most major questions—in currency matters, trade, agriculture and defence—Britain often finds herself closer to American views than to European. Fortunately, in finance as in politics, there is a positive alternative combining both points of view: a trans-atlantic community bridging both sides of the Atlantic. It suits the City far better than any narrower solution, for it could then play its traditional role of banker to the world, embracing Europe, North America and the Commonwealth together. Such a solution will not necessarily be easy. Britain may often be forced to choose between America and Europe. But, as we shall see in Chapter 12, any solution to the problem of reducing sterling's role as an international reserve currency is bound to need the agreement of both Europe and America.

APPENDIX A

Increasing international liquidity

Four of the main plans are summarised below:

1. *Triffin[1] Plan*:

The ultimate aim is to make the International Monetary Fund a world central bank. The scheme would also reduce and ultimately end the use of dollars and pounds as reserve currencies. There are two versions of the Triffin plan. In the first member countries of the IMF would transfer to the IMF all their holdings of reserve currencies (dollars and pounds) and receive deposits in return—the equivalent of gold and as widely acceptable in international payments. It would be necessary, in the early years of the scheme, or in the modified second version, to require all members to hold a stated proportion of their monetary reserves in these Fund deposits. Professor Triffin suggests 20 per cent minimum at first. He recognises that a limit must be placed on the volume of subsequent Fund lending in any one year and suggests that it might be a total amount that, together with current increases in the world stock of monetary gold, would increase total world reserves by, say, 3 to 5 per cent a year.

2. *Stamp[2]*:

The purpose is not only to use the IMF more intensively but also to provide development aid for the poorer nations. Mr. Stamp's latest version (in which he has tried to meet earlier criticisms) is as follows: The Governors of the IMF should agree that the IMF be allowed to create credit. He suggests $2,000 million to begin with, in the form of Fund certificates expressed in terms of gold but not automatically convertible into gold. Member countries would agree to receive these certificates in settlement of international debts up to a total amount equal to their quota in the Fund. The Fund would lend the certificates in the first place to the International Development Association (the offshoot of the World Bank) for fifty years. IDA would lend the certificates in the normal way to under-developed countries. These in turn would use them in payment to the main industrial countries—which could use them in their reserves.

[1] Professor Robert Triffin, *Gold and the Dollar Crisis,* Yale University Press, 1960.
[2] Hon. Maxwell Stamp, *Moorgate and Wall Street Review,* Philip Hill, Higginson, Erlangers, Autumn 1962.

3. Bernstein[1]:

The main purpose is the creation of new reserve units, each equivalent to a gold dollar, consisting of a stated proportion of each of the currencies of the eleven leading industrial nations. It might consist of say, half in dollars and the rest made up in pounds, French francs, Japanese yen, etc. The proportion would depend on the country's role in world trade and so on. To create the units each participating country would deposit its currency with the IMF, acting as Trustee, to an amount equal to its *pro rata* share of the reserve units to be created. In return each country would be given a credit on the books of the Trustee denominated in reserve units. Participating countries would be able to hold their reserves in any form—gold, foreign exchange and reserve units—but gold holdings would have to be matched by a minimum amount of reserve units. The ultimate objective would be for each country to hold reserve units amounting to at least one half of its gold reserve. Thus total liquidity could grow in line with gold reserves, and other countries, besides Britain and America as at present, would participate in supplying additional currency.

4. Maudling[2]:

This is how Mr. Reginald Maudling, then Chancellor of the Exchequer, described his scheme at the IMF meeting in September 1962:[2] 'We might develop a system of co-operation between the leading trading countries in the form of a mutual currency account in the Fund. By this I have in mind an arrangement of multilateral character under which countries could continue to acquire the currency of another country which was temporarily surplus in the markets and use it to establish claims on a mutual currency account which they could themselves use when their situations were reversed. Such claims on the account would attract the guarantee that attaches to holdings in the Fund. We would hope that such a system would enable world liquidity to be expanded without additional strains on the reserve currencies or avoidable setbacks to their economic growth, and at the same time without requiring countries whose currencies were temporarily strong to accumulate larger holdings of weaker currencies than they would find tolerable.'

[1] Edward M. Bernstein, *Quarterly Review & Investment Survey*, Model, Roland & Co., New York, Fourth Quarter, 1963.

[2] Reginald Maudling, Speech to annual meeting of International Monetary Fund, September 1962. A fuller report of Mr. Maudling's proposals is in *The Economist*, 22 September, 1962, pp. 1123-4.

APPENDIX B

Supporting the pound

The value of the pound in terms of dollars, francs or any other country's money is governed by the continual exchanging of currencies to finance international transactions for industry, commerce, banking, and private individuals and also inter-governmental borrowing and lending.

If exchange rates fluctuated freely (and *all* currency transactions went through the foreign exchange markets) the quotation for the pound, that is, its price in terms of other currencies, would be a true reflection of supply and demand.

Nowadays, however, most countries maintain their spot rates of exchange within the narrow limits agreed with the IMF and rely on central funds to iron out the wider movements which might otherwise occur. In Britain, the government holds gold and foreign currency in the Exchange Equalisation Account. The Bank of England meets any abnormal demand for converting pounds into (say) dollars by supplying the dollars from this account and taking the pounds in exchange, or a demand for pounds in exchange for (say) francs by supplying the pounds and taking francs. These transactions are normally executed for the Bank by one or other of the commercial or merchant banks as purchases and sales in the foreign exchange market where the Bank of England at all times has to ensure that the rate of sterling against the US dollar remains within specific limits ($2.78—$2.82).

A persistent demand for foreign currencies in exchange for pounds would therefore lead to a continual drain on the gold and foreign money holdings of the Exchange Equalisation Account. If the Bank of England finds that the resources of the account are being unduly depleted by support operations, some action must be taken by the government. The alternatives are either to 'devalue' the pound by fixing a lower official exchange rate (and this by itself would be no cure for the underlying causes) or, if the deficit is thought amenable to correction by fiscal and other measures, to persuade other countries to lend gold or other foreign currency either direct or through the International Monetary Fund. Short-term borrowing of this kind from foreign central banks had to be used in November, 1964, while application was being made to the International Monetary Fund for longer-term help.

No details of the operation of the Exchange Equalisation Account are published from day to day though the monthly figures of the gold and exchange reserves give some indication of the position and more detailed figures are given in the Bank's *Quarterly Bulletin* some time after the event. But even the true strength of these so-called 'reserves' as shown monthly is difficult to assess as they can contain an element of short-term money finding a temporary home in Britain and do not take account of longer-term assets or fluctuating sterling liabilities.

APPENDIX C
Liquidity and flexible exchange rates
Different views of the liquidity problem from those outlined in Appendix A are held by several leading economists including Professors J. E. Meade, Milton Friedman and Gottfried Haberler. Professor Haberler has argued:

'My general conclusion is that the alarms about an impending scarcity of international reserves . . . have been . . . greatly exaggerated. International liquidity is not scarce now and has not been scarce at any time since the war, notwithstanding that the international reserves of some countries, notably of the United Kingdom, are smaller in relation to the value of their foreign trade than before the war.' *(Money in the International Economy.)*

The main point at issue for the City of London is whether flexible exchange rates could offset the need for gold and exchange reserves. If a deficit was appearing in a country's payments, the result need not be an outflow of gold or exchange but a depreciation in the exchange rate.

These arguments are resisted by most central bankers and finance ministers on three grounds: that fluctuating exchange rates would allow politicians to pursue inflationary policies, lead to bewildering changes in exchange rates, to the detriment of exporters and traders generally, and, in practice, lead to more rather than less speculation against individual currencies.

The issues are well explored in the following: J. E. Meade, 'The International Monetary Mechanism', *Three Banks Review*, September 1964; Milton Friedman, 'The Case for Flexible Exchange Rates', *Essays in Positive Economics*, University of Chicago, 1953; Sir Roy Harrod; *Reforming The World's Money*, Ch. 2, Macmillan, 1965; Gottfried Haberler, *Money in the International Economy*, Hobart Paper 31, IEA, 1965.

CHAPTER 12

THE CITY AND ECONOMIC GROWTH

ON BALANCE, we have argued, the City will gain from most of the attempts to build up defences round the major currencies. The greater the stability in the exchange markets, the more confidence in leaving trading pounds in London and the more business the City can expect to attract. This does not, however, dispose of the question of what priority should be given to the support of the currency, nor of the question of whether Britain should now deliberately shed the load of sterling as a reserve currency. The government has invariably wanted to have the best of all worlds: full employment, stable prices, a strong and stable pound, and now growth. Others have posed a stark alternative between full employment and growth on the one hand, and a strong pound on the other. What suited one line of policy, it has often been assumed, would not suit the other They were mutually exclusive. And the City would always put the pound first, growth second.

The City and the pound

This is an over-simplification. On the contrary, it is my belief that, far from benefiting from the attempts to protect the pound by over-restrictive measures, the City of London has probably been prevented from playing its full part in world monetary affairs. An over-readiness to apply the brake to the economy (often by using the wrong weapons) and, for a time, an over-reliance on monetary weapons alone[1] have done little good to the City's sensitive mechanism.

[1] Since 1951, when more flexible monetary weapons were re-introduced, the use of Bank rate, special deposit schemes, hire purchase controls, overdraft directives, etc., has too often been undermined by the lack of equal control on government spending.

Consider the capital market; here the City can offer three different types of services. It can provide a place where traders can keep their pounds for short periods, before or after doing business. It can operate as an entrepôt centre in capital funds, attracting funds from abroad for foreign issues and taking a small commission for its trouble (and its services). And it might, as in the past, provide capital funds for investment abroad. The succession of post-war crises and the abrupt 'stop-go'[1] policies of recent years have affected each of these roles differently. But all have suffered. The sapping of confidence has clearly obstructed, though not completely undermined, the leaving of surplus money for relatively short periods. Secondly, the tendency for each crisis to produce a still higher level of interest rates (before they have fully subsided to the previous level from an earlier crisis) has impeded the healthy two-way flow of money that any really important entrepôt centre should expect to handle. Finally, the lack of economic growth has undoubtedly prevented the production of surplus savings that could provide the basis for any active capital market.

There is a more fundamental City interest in post-war attempts to solve successive sterling crises by a series of restrictive measures In general, though apparently giving priority to the pound, they have not succeeded in providing a freedom of capital movement that could be relied upon. Certainly the extension of currency freedom to the point of convertibility for external holders of pounds admirably suited the City's operations. These are the conditions in which the City can operate most efficiently and profitably. But successive crises have invariably produced some back-sliding, even if only for a matter of six or nine months at a time. Concessions on the movement of capital have been withdrawn. More important, because of an inability or reluctance to anticipate the onset of another economic crisis, the measures have often been much more severe than they might otherwise have been. The basic criticism of excessive 'stop-go' measures is not their attempt to control the economy (some change in the pressures on brake and accelerator is bound to be necessary), but rather the ham-handed way in which they went about it. The freedom was too great at one point (e.g. the summer of 1958) and far too severely restricted at another (the

---

[1] 'Stop-Go' policies are necessary to cope with the natural waves of economic activity. The main criticism of British post-war policy is that the timing and the impact of the measures have tended to aggravate the underlying difficulties.

autumn of 1957): hardly the conditions of confidence in which the City can develop its monetary flair, for nothing kills potential financial business more swiftly than uncertainty. The way in which 'stop-go' policies led to bewildering changes in exchange control should have been enough to persuade the City to protest against them earlier than some of the progressive minds eventually did.

The fundamental problems

It is not enough, however, to deplore the various mistakes in policy. Behind them lie several fundamental problems that concern the City as much as British industry. If the series of restrictive measures the country has suffered since the war has interfered with the City's operations without at the same time curing sterling's ills, a far different approach is called for. The City has as much interest as any other part of the economy in getting answers to several fundamental questions.

Why has Britain continually run into payments difficulties since the war or seemed about to do so?

Why has she continued to lose her share of world trade?

Why have domestic prices often risen faster than those abroad and, even when they have not, why have *export* prices still tended to move ahead of her main competitors?

Why in recent years has she been at the bottom of the world's economic growth table?

Some of the answers are now becoming clearer. They partly lie in the situation in which Britain found herself after the war —exhausted with the war-effort, equipped with a growing social conscience and faced with the unenviable task of accepting the responsibilities of a first-class power with the economic resources of a second-class one. Couple all this with a pledge to maintain full employment, with the lack of the stimulation from an early post-war re-equipping boom (so necessary in Continental Europe) and with a pattern of trade, based on the Commonwealth, that kept her out of the booming industrial markets in Europe for too long in the late 1950s, and it is hardly surprising that exports so persistently trailed behind the rise in imports.

Sterling—a psychological brake on economic growth?

These circumstances explain a good deal. They show the extent of Britain's post-war difficulties, but do not fully explain why they were not overcome. It is easy to point to the precarious state of sterling (as well as to the determination of successive Chancellors, fully supported by the Bank of England and leading City figures, to defend it at almost all costs) and to assume that this sufficiently explains why the brakes have so often had to be applied prematurely. It is hard to see what else could have been done at a time when the pound was weaker than it is now, when exports lacked buoyancy, when the capacity of British industry was smaller, when the gold reserves were slender, and when central bank co-operation was still largely untested. Exchange rates might have been changed or freed and import controls introduced, but, without fundamental changes in industry itself, without a more competitive economy, without basic changes in the way that wages and other incomes are settled or the pace at which the economy was run, and without a reduction of her foreign commitments, it is hard to escape the conclusion that almost any growth in the economy would have brought itself to a halt sooner or later either through production bottlenecks or an uncontrolled wages-prices spiral, or both.

In short, anxiety about the currency was undoubtedly a psychological damper on the whole economy. But it was not the only one. This, admittedly, is to take a pessimistic view of the state of the British economy and of British industry in recent years. Recent evidence, however, confirms it. It has to be faced that economic expansion came to a premature, though temporary, halt in the summer of 1964, in spite of all the talk of growth throughout industry and in spite of the determination of the then Chancellor of the Exchequer to do nothing to obstruct further economic expansion. It also came to a halt, for the first time, before the onset of the sterling crisis. The complexities of the wage-bargaining process, the habits of unions and employers alike in coming to mutually convenient terms and the easy way in which sections of industry have passed on price increases to others—all revealed by the first investigations of the now defunct National Incomes Commission—coupled with the widespread obstacles to growth confirmed even by the first efforts of the National Economic Development Council have all underlined the difficulties still to be overcome if a steady growth rate is to be maintained in future.

Only now, therefore, is it becoming apparent what major obstacles lie in front of any attempt to get the British economy out of its post-war habit of lurching from one currency crisis to another. Several recent books have charted the main reefs,[1] revealing a number of areas that plainly require more attention and better management. One is the role of sterling as a major reserve currency; another the continuing size of Britain's economic commitments abroad, a direct reflection of her political commitments and of the difficulty of withdrawing from her former colonial dominance without leaving a trail of potential Congos behind her. Thirdly, there is the problem of making the economy flexible and British industry efficient. The City (and many of its critics) have concentrated their attention on the first—a natural reaction. In my view the others are equally important. Unless the economy can be coaxed back to health, unless overseas burdens can be reduced and unless sound economic growth can be based on a corresponding expansion in competitive exports, winding up the sterling area and freezing our sterling obligations (in other words, the abrupt ending of Britain's reserve currency role) would solve none of our problems. Currency crises would still recur.

Is the opposite equally true? Would an efficient and competitive economy, coupled with a marked reduction in our overseas commitments, enable Britain to continue operating one of the world's two reserve currencies, without any thought of international help? The City might be tempted to answer in the affirmative. In my view it would be wrong to do so. Prestige is naturally involved, just as it is involved in the reluctance to reduce our foreign and Commonwealth commitments in line with our economic strength. The Suez crisis, Britain's minor role during the Cuban episode, and the succession of sterling crises since the war should have been enough to persuade us to take on only those burdens we can shoulder and to realise what tasks are now beyond us. The role of running a major reserve currency and the competitive state of the economy both deserve closer scrutiny.

[1] Andrew Shonfield, *British Economic Policy Since The War*, Penguin Books, 1958; Michael Shanks, *The Stagnant Society*, Penguin Special, 1961; J. C. R. Dow, *The Management of the British Economy 1945-60*, Cambridge University Press, 1964; Samuel Brittan, *The Treasury Under the Tories 1951-64*, Penguin Books, 1964; Norman Macrae, *Sunshades in October*, Allen and Unwin, 1963; F. W. Paish, *Studies in an Inflationary Economy*, Macmillan, 1962; A. K. Cairncross, *Factors in Economic Development*, Allen and Unwin, 1962; Nicholas Kaldor, *Essays on Economic Policy*, Vols. I and II, Duckworth, 1964; Thomas Balogh, *Unequal Partners*, Vols. I and II, Basil Blackwell, 1963; Nicholas Davenport, *The Split Society*, Victor Gollancz, 1964.

Sterling as a major reserve currency

As we have noted in earlier chapters, people have left pounds in the City of London for two basic reasons: convenience and security. Since the war this convenience has persisted against heavy odds. The services in the Square Mile continue to attract trading money to London. They were the foundation on which the reserve currency role was based. They explain why money has flooded back to the City, often within months of a major currency crisis. They also explain the recent phenomenon of the London-based Euro-dollar market. Foreign traders and bankers find it inconvenient to run down their sterling holdings in London to too low a level. Nevertheless, the safety of keeping pounds in London has fluctuated sharply over the past 20 years Crises have blown up swiftly and the smallness of Britain's gold and exchanges reserves in relation to the sterling balances (they have largely reached their post-war size because of the cost of running the war) has continually forced governments (both Labour and Conservative) to take early restrictive action to protect the currency. If the City is to get any relief from the series of 'stop-go' measures, therefore, Britain's role as a reserve currency country needs weighing carefully in the balance.

It is becoming increasingly clear that the world cannot go on relying on the domestic currencies of two individual countries for a large part of its international means of payment. Apart from the unlikelihood, mentioned in Chapter 11, of more dollars and pounds being available in the next ten years, there is the simple point that the world needs something rather more sophisticated on which to base its future trade and payments. There is no need to deploy French anti-American sentiments to see the dangers and inadequacies of the present system. President de Gaulle can hardly be faulted in his criticisms of the gold exchange standard. Since dollars and pounds are held in other countries' reserves, any mismanagement of the economies of Britain and the United States (allowing them to generate too much inflation) is bound to have direct repercussions on the rest of the world, through these currency holdings. The opposite is also true. Any attempt to lend automatic support to these major reserve currencies, in order to help world trade, could allow the governments of these two countries to pursue unsound economic policies far too long. In an extreme case the choice might boil down to this: either the rest of the world is going to be drawn into detailed interference in British and American economic affairs or else the potential mismanagement of their economies may endanger world payments. In practice the potential expansion in world trade and the remarkable increase in the size of recent currency movements, quite apart from the shock of the sterling crisis of November 1964, have provided convincing evidence that the time has come to prepare major adjustments to the international payments system. In any event Britain clearly cannot carry her burden indefinitely. Three British possibilities, therefore, have to be considered: the winding up of the whole sterling area system; the imposition of trade and currency restrictions as a barrier behind which economic growth might be fostered; and the integration of the pound into a wider international system.

Winding up the sterling area?

There is no longer such a widespread assumption that the sterling area should be wound up as there was four or even five years ago. At that time there was a tendency to put most of the blame at its door and to suggest various extreme ways of cutting loose from these commitments. Now it is increasingly regarded as a less dangerous arrangement than it was.[1] For one thing, the sterling area's London balances have remained remarkably stable in recent years. For another, the economic and financial links with the Commonwealth plainly need to be strengthened rather than weakened further. This suggests that closer co-operation with the Commonwealth sterling countries is needed rather than any abrupt severing of financial relations. This change of attitude was finally reflected in Mr. Harold Wilson's remarkable speech at Guildhall on 16 November 1964, when he went out of his way to deny any intention of placing new exchange control obstacles between Britain and the sterling area. He went further:

'In past years there have been suggestions that we in Britain should turn our back on the sterling area, cultivate our own garden, and repudiate our obligations to other Commonwealth countries. Her Majesty's Government unequivocally reject this approach as harmful to Britain, harmful to the Commonwealth and harmful to world trade. I have

[1] Samuel Brittan, *op, cit.*, p. 284; Michael Shanks, *op. cit.*, pp. 201-3.

spoken this evening of the importance of preserving and improving our Commonwealth links, and not only on economic grounds: to turn our back on the sterling area would be a body-blow to the Commonwealth and all it stands for.'

That the sterling area reserve system would be costly to wind up (even if it were possible) and undesirable does not mean that nothing need be done to improve its workings. Closer economic co-operation among sterling area countries, particularly on matters of exchange control, would be in everyone's interest. It is remarkable that, apart from central banking contacts, nothing systematic has been established. Such a central body could reduce the strains on Britain's reserves (which is in everyone's interest as well as Britain's) during difficult periods. It is also time that Britain herself did more to draw attention to her financial strength than she has so far.

The relationship of liabilities to liquid assets of roughly four to one is known by virtually every Continental banker and is the essence of sterling's weak position. What is not so well known is that in contrast to nearly all Continental countries, Britain has a massive second and third line of defence. The Bank of England, to its credit, has at last worked out a financial balance sheet that makes sense. It is set out in Table XXI.

As will be seen, Britain's basic position is far healthier than most people suppose. In 1962 gold and exchange reserves were backed not only by official holdings of dollar securities worth £385 million but by private long-term investments (both direct and portfolio) of close on £8,000 million. There are also, of course, foreign investments in Britain. The effect is that because heavy official liabilities are more than offset by large privately-held assets abroad, Britain's total balance sheet turned out to be £1,700 million in credit and, as the Bank of England noted, this figure was probably an under-estimate. Yet until recently little effort had been made to publicise any of this except for a technical article in the Bank of England's *Quarterly Bulletin* (March 1964). The Chancellor of the Exchequer's reference to Britain's £11,000 million overseas assets in his April 1965 Budget was a welcome departure, as was the Prime Minister's similar reference in New York a few weeks later. There is no reason why the monthly gold and currency figures should not include details of privately-held assets, or at least of some of

TABLE XXI

BRITAIN'S BALANCE SHEET (end-1962)

(£ million)

	Assets		Liabilities
SHORT-TERM:			
Official			
Gold and currency reserves	1,002	Treasury bills, Government stock deposits at Bank of England and loans to local authorities	2,462
Private			
Banks and private residents	2,104	Banking liabilities (including hire purchase)	2,738
LONG-TERM:			
Private			
Portfolio investments	3,000	Portfolio investments in UK	735
Direct investments (except oil, insurance & banking)	3,500	Direct investments (except oil, insurance and banking)	1,400
Net assets abroad of UK oil firms	1,100	Net assets in UK oil companies overseas	700
Direct investments of UK insurance companies (US only)	350		
TOTAL	7,950	TOTAL	2,835
Official			
Government holding of dollar securities	385	Loans to UK	2,640
Other loans	684	IMF sterling holdings	517
IMF: UK subscription to IMF	696		
GRAND TOTAL (identified items)	12,821	GRAND TOTAL	11,192

them.[1] There is a more practical possibility. Instead of waiting for a crisis before pledging the £385 million worth of dollar securities against a short-term loan, why not arrange a stand-by on a semi-permanent basis and include both this and Britain's IMF gold tranche in the monthly reserve figures?

Financial and trade insulation?

The second type of solution, of Britain turning her back on the world and deliberately building a barrier both by exchange control and higher tariffs, is rarely suggested though it continues to raise its head in different guises from time to time. It is essentially a defensive reaction and was far easier to sustain before the other European currencies moved towards external convertibility in 1958 than it is now. At that time it appeared that Britain was pushing ahead towards currency freedom far more rapidly than the rest of Europe and far too quickly for her own good. It is less easy to blame Britain on this count when the Italian lira and the French franc are also convertible externally.

There is one element of this freedom, however, that not only continues to call for restraint but often receives it as in the April 1965 Budget. This is the excessive freedom, as some see it, on capital account. If the City were not so efficient in pushing out capital for investment abroad and if British companies were not so keen to invest overseas, it is argued, far more capital would be left for use at home and British industry would get what at present goes to its foreign competitors. This is a persuasive argument and deserves careful consideration for it crops up in different guises. It is also not a new one. Much the same thing was being said at the turn of the century when the City's capital exports were reaching their peak. It has raised its head again more recently since the Bank of England began to revive the idea of using the London capital market for foreign loans on the pre-war pattern.

Three main arguments have lately been deployed against

[1] It is true that this wider notion of Britain's reserves to cover the holdings of private assets abroad as well as gold and foreign currencies held in the Bank of England might entail a new concept of a country's currency reserves. Private investments overseas were sold in order to pay for emergency purchases (of US destroyers and other equipment) in the war. It may be objected that such a use by the government of powers of sale over private assets can be regarded as confiscation and that there is no parallel between war and peace. But this would be jumping too many fences prematurely. The only point of the inclusion of some estimate of Britain's private overseas assets every month would be to put strength into a useful 'shop window'.

the use of the City's capital market in this way.[1] The first is simply that British industry is in need of what is going abroad. The second is that, if there is money to spare, it should go to countries that need it (often those that cannot repay) rather than those that have the best credit-rating (usually the highly-developed countries). The under-developed have a case; the developed have not. The third is that if the next phase of expansion is brought to an abrupt halt because of the narrow reserve base on which Britain operates, then it is wrong to let the City deplete the gold kitty by reviving capital exports even on a limited scale.

These views would be easier to accept if foreign capital issues in London were bigger than they are. As was shown in Chapter 8, foreign currency issues probably amounted to some $350 million in 1964. But of this total only a small percentage represented British subscriptions. The bulk came from foreign investors. Criticism of the capital market would also be more readily accepted if British industry was demonstrably short of capital. A shortage of money for expansion is rarely mentioned as a bottleneck.[2] And the idea that the City is giving priority to the wrong borrowers misunderstands the role of private enterprise. If capital should be directed to the needy countries (without hope of repayment or on a long-term basis) that is surely the role of the government and its agencies.

Even a few sterling issues would not be the threat to the reserves comparable with the heavy outflow of government money on defence establishments abroad or with the continual outflow of direct investment by British industry. The tidal wave of payments in and out of Britain every year add up to close on £13,000 million. Britain's solvency depends on how these payments end up at the margin, with an annual surplus or deficit. To the extent that protection for the world's key currencies increases, the time available to transform a marginal deficit into a surplus (without dipping disastrously into the gold reserves) will be longer and the need to restrict capital payments that much less pressing. But improvements in the world's monetary system should not blind us to the fact that Britain can no longer squander any payments surplus without thought. This means that to the extent that the government's current spending

[1] See particularly an article on economic growth and exchange freedom by Andrew Shonfield in *The Director*, January 1964.

[2] What *can* be argued is that parts of industry *ought* to spend more money on capital re-equipment. The question to ask is why they do not do so.

abroad on military establishments as well as on economic grants cannot be reduced swiftly (the figures were discussed in Chapter 9), net direct investment abroad may have to be restrained. The slower the reduction in military commitments, the more other restrictions will have to be considered. In these circumstances there may be some case for considering both current and capital account in the same light. If foreign exchange is valuable, why should it be regarded as better to spend it on consumer imports or military objectives abroad than on an overseas investment that might produce a useful return (whether it is direct investment in a foreign plant or a foreign issue in the London market)?

Economic and political choices

Choices of this kind become necessary simply because of the changes in the flow of international payments. Restrictions on foreign payments are in their nature little more than short-term defences, buying time. Beyond them lie the fundamentals. It is not immediately clear why British industry, for example, seems to be more willing to expand abroad than at home. In some cases it is possible that initial overseas investments are in further need of finance. In others, export markets have been in danger and local plants have had to be built as a substitute. Moreover, money has sometimes had to be ploughed back abroad for further expansion. Local political pressure may also lead to excessive ploughing back of profits. Yet the movement of capital has been on such a scale that something more seems to lie behind it.[1] Many of these companies could have used at home the money invested abroad; some of them could have remitted more of their overseas earnings back to this country. Why did they not do so? Part of the answer may lie in differences in taxation.[2] The return abroad may appear bigger than at home, after allowing for tax treatment. Other opportunities abroad may also appear better than at home. When domestic growth has been confined to 2 or 3 per cent a year it is hardly surprising that industry puts money elsewhere. The reverse may equally be true. A bigger rate of growth at home might attract some of the funds now going abroad.

Before we leave these various views about imposing selective

[1] Direct investment abroad by UK companies has totalled £2,000 million since 1959.

[2] The Chancellor of the Exchequer deliberately tried to curb some of the tax stimulus towards overseas investment in his April 1965, Budget.

controls on capital movements, one final rather obvious point
needs to be made. It is occasionally represented that, were it
not for the City, many more restrictions might be contemplated
in controlling the outflow of funds and in restricting currency
movements. It is true that prestige occasionally persuaded the
authorities in the early post-war period to take off the wrappers surrounding the pound earlier than was wise. Whether
this was aimed at helping the City or was simply an over-
confident assessment of the economy generally is difficult to
judge. That it was mistaken is now plain. But this should not
allow the same argument to be asserted in quite different circumstances, when all European currencies have been made
convertible on current external account and when some
countries, notably Germany, have freed virtually all movements
of capital. The criteria to be used now should be fairly simple:
both trade and payments should be freed as far as the economy
and overseas military commitments will allow. As a major
importing nation, highly dependent on other countries for her
food and raw materials, Britain is the last country to maintain
restrictions longer than is necessary. She should also be the
first country to persuade others to follow suit. As a major importer and exporter of long-term capital she should equally
pursue a policy of freer capital movements. Both are in her
interests. That they are also in the interests of the City is only
another way of saying that the City is a financial reflection of
these free trade habits.

A new reserve currency?

There remains the third possibility: the idea of supplementing
the present role of the pound and dollar by the introduction of
some new international reserve unit. The various schemes—
Bernstein, Stamp, etc.—were outlined in Chapter 11. It is not,
of course, simply a matter of choosing the scheme that suits the
pound best. Other countries have their views too. And while
Britain's bargaining strength remains weak, it will be difficult
to take any real initiative. Nevertheless a way through the
various obstacles must be found. Two events, however, have
turned what was threatening to remain an academic issue into
a practical one. These are the last sterling crisis, particularly
the shock to the world's monetary system on 25 November 1964,
and President de Gaulle's monetary challenge to the United
States in February 1965. Some method must be found, therefore, of reconciling the views of the Americans and the French.

Up to 18 months ago the difficulty was that the division between British and American thinking appeared almost as wide as between British and French. The problem was whether the present gold-exchange standard needed changing and, if so, in what direction. The Americans, deep in their own currency troubles, were firmly against substituting anything else for dollars in the world's monetary reserves. Hence the cold shoulder given to Mr. Maudling's currency plan. The French have never hidden their view that the gold-exchange standard is in need of improvement, not by supplementing the pound and dollar but rather by replacing them.

Thus on the one side the United States was treating any effort to supplement the present reserve currencies as an affront to the dollar, and on the other side France wanted to move towards gold payments. Britain was thus discouraged from both sides. Now there are signs that both American and French attitudes are in the process of adjustment. The main shift has taken place in the American outlook. This is of immediate importance to sterling, for the pound's fortunes will depend largely on what happens to the dollar. The closer the British and American monetary authorities work together, the better. As the recent crises have shown, both currencies face the same problems and both depend on each other. The result has been a full realisation of their inter-dependence and a marked improvement in Anglo-American relations. This accord has been coupled, if not entirely caused, by a growing American willingness to consider schemes for supplementing the role of dollars and pounds. Hence the combined Anglo-American support for the super gold tranche scheme to be run by the International Monetary Fund, outlined in Chapter 11. These improved relations, which had made good progress before Mr. Maudling left the Treasury, emerged in full measure during the early months of the Labour Government. The understanding statements issued by the US Treasury about the import surcharge, the other economic measures, the sharp increase in Bank rate to 7 per cent and the $3,000 million borrowing arrangement towards the end of 1964 stood in marked contrast to the fierce round of criticism from every corner of Europe. The pound and the dollar were standing together for the first time. It was a sensible move that should have been made earlier, and should be developed more fully in future.

Yet this official Anglo-American unity in monetary affairs should not blind Britain to her important relations with Europe and should be a stepping stone to a broader monetary agreement with the Continent. This is easier said than accomplished. France still sticks rigidly to her modified Bernstein plan for composite reserve units. For a time, after President de Gaulle's press conference, it was assumed that the CRU plan had been superseded by his cry for a return to the gold standard. But if de Gaulle's speech is analysed carefully and read in conjunction with the statement of M. Giscard d'Estaing, the French Finance Minister, two weeks afterwards, it becomes clear that what the President implied by the gold standard was simply that France intended to pay gold to meet all future deficits and wanted to encourage all other industrial nations to do the same. This policy would be combined with the introduction of the CRU plan. At the time of writing French intentions about the flexibility of her CRU plan remain to be explored. It is possible that France will be willing to consider circumstances in which the proposed new reserve units might be additions to pounds and dollars rather than simply replacements. Britain should try to build on this concession and to treat criticism of the French plan in a constructive way. This will be all the more difficult in that so many parts of the French plan are aimed directly against the United States. For example, the French envisage that gold payments to meet deficits and the switching of currency holdings into gold should be adopted solely by members of the Group of Ten (mainly Europe, North America and Japan). This would mean that most of Britain's relations with the sterling area would be unaffected and only sterling officially held by Europe and North America would come into the new scheme. For the United States, however, the introduction of the plan would mean an immediate switching of Europe's dollars into gold and an end to the future holding of dollars by Europe.

The French plan, in short, is aimed against American dominance of the present gold exchange standard. How far, therefore, could Britain go in accepting such a scheme, without undermining the Anglo-American monetary co-operation recently built up so painfully? In resolving her dilemma Britain should be concerned to criticise the French plan for the right reasons. Since the implementation of the CRU scheme plus de Gaulle's ideas about gold payments would automatically reduce world liquidity, this would be a retrograde step at a time when the problem is how to increase the world's money not reduce it. The plan should be criticised on these grounds. It is also tempting to criticise the scheme because it gives the influential Group of

Ten nations the power to create new currency units and, because of the idea of having unanimity about decisions concerned with their creation, provides them with an important right of veto. It is not surprising that a French plan should give the French a bigger say in the operations of the international payments system. But this is no reason for rejecting it. Britain cannot expect to get support for the international role of her currency (nor America, for that matter) and still keep control of the international system firmly in her hands. This may be hard to swallow. Until it is understood in London, little progress can be expected. The elements of compromise are closer now than they have been for some time; but it takes two sides to make a bargain and Britain must be clear in her own mind that sharing burdens also means sharing responsibilities. She may prefer to share them with an international agency (the International Monetary Fund) but if Europe, the major source of help, is firmly against this course, a realistic attitude must be taken. On one point Britain must remain firm: any new scheme should add to international liquidity rather than reduce it.

Effects on City's earnings

The City's interest in developments along these lines naturally hangs on the question whether, without a sterling reserve system as operated at present, the City markets would suffer. The usual answer has been that a large part of the City's earnings would remain unimpaired. Shipping brokerage, insurance business, merchanting and so on could all proceed without much interference if, overnight, the pound suddenly reverted to a trading role rather than as a reserve currency. Banking earnings, it is argued, might suffer, but the loss would be a small price to pay for more economic freedom. There is little doubt that the links between the international role of the pound and the City's activities have been over-emphasised in the past. But it is highly questionable whether the ending of sterling as a reserve currency (or its gradual replacement by some other means of payment) would reduce the needs of individual traders to keep their pounds in London. Most of the discussions on this topic seem to begin from the wrong end. It is not so much that the City's earnings depend on the holding of pounds in London, though they do, but rather that the City's services lead to the holding of pounds. The question is not whether City earnings would continue or not if restrictions were placed on the reserve status of the pound or if some new international means of payments were to be introduced. It is whether, if the City's markets and institutions in total remain as efficient and delicate a mechanism as they still are, private investors and traders will not continue to leave their currency in London for their own convenience.

This, after all, is how the whole affair started in the first place. If, as the world's international monetary system moves into the modern age out of the equivalent of the stage-coach era (just as the domestic banking system did much earlier), sterling's role as a reserve currency is superseded by some new international device, the habit of keeping pounds in London on private account is unlikely to end. As we saw in Chapter 10, even when countries have left the sterling area or have reduced the proportion of pounds in their official reserves, their use of sterling facilities for trading purposes has not been reduced. In any event, the period since convertibility was established in 1958 has amply consolidated the growing use of the City's services. It is the City's usefulness both to Britain and to the world that attracts pounds to London, not the prestige surrounding a reserve currency. As we emphasised earlier, it pays Britain to pursue a policy of free trade and payments. The City reflects this policy by offering financial services to British and foreign traders alike and earning income for its efforts. Both the country and the City, therefore, should be pulling in the same direction. Government policies on exchange control towards trade and currency problems generally should be pursued because they will benefit the country, not the City. If they benefit Britain, which needs freer trade throughout the world to give her the opportunities to sell enough to pay for essential imports, it would be surprising if they did not suit, and benefit, the City too. Even if the role of dollars and pounds was gradually replaced by some new international unit in the world's monetary reserves, there is little doubt that traders and bankers would find it useful to leave pounds in the Square Mile. Traders will continue to need pounds, even if governments do not. Thus this combination of increasing help for the pound as a reserve currency and continuing use of pounds in the settlement of world trade would give increasing support to the City's operations.

Making the economy more competitive

This arrangement would also reduce the need to restrain the economy prematurely, as so often in the past. In itself this would not be enough. Far more would need to be done in making industry more efficient, the economy more flexible and the weapons used to achieve the ends more effective. The need for restriction because of the plight of the pound has often been reinforced by the apparent inability of the economy to expand at a steady pace. Both the timing of, and the type of, measures themselves have plainly added to the difficulties.[1] The immediate importance of the new Ministry of Economic Affairs, and the National Economic Development Council before it, lies not in its introduction of planning concepts or growth targets as in its promised efforts to search out the obstacles to growth and remove them and in its further promises to increase the capacity of the economy by acting directly on individual industries. To its credit in its earliest report, Neddy did not pose the old question of either growth or a stable pound, but showed how sound expansion must depend on competitive exports. The original 4 per cent growth rate target in the years to 1966 plainly depended on a corresponding expansion of 5 per cent in exports. Apart from numerous structural changes needed in industry, already pinpointed by Neddy, the basic necessity hammered home in several of its reports is the achievement of an improved competitiveness throughout British industry. This implies something more than efficiency. Costs can be influenced by the general atmosphere provided by the Government as well as by what happens on the factory floor.

Since the end of the 1950s the main inflationary impulse has been provided by the wages/prices spiral ('cost push') rather than by excessive demand ('demand pull'). The first has continued even in periods when demand has been remarkably moderate. This has been particularly true of Britain, but most other countries pursuing full employment policies have suffered from the continuous rise in costs and prices. This experience was enough to persuade the leading countries of Western Europe and North America to examine the problem together. The first joint effort was made by the Organisation for European Economic Co-operation in its examination of wages and prices policies, published in *The Problem of Rising Prices*.[2] Britain's experience, it became clear, was not unique. Full employment policies were, to a larger or lesser degree, having the same effect on prices throughout the free world. Prices had

---

[1] J. C. R. Dow, *op. cit.*, pp. 379-84.
[2] OEEC, Paris, 1961.

risen in Britain in every year since 1934, but whereas pre-war prices went down as well as up (they were lower in 1938 than ten years earlier), the post-war rise has been continuous. Between 1946 and 1958 the average annual rise was between 4 and 5 per cent. There is no precedent for such rapid inflation over the previous 100 years.

Full employment is the key to the puzzle. With it came an unprecedented prosperity; and with it also came new pressures leading to constantly rising prices. Full employment naturally puts additional strength in the hands of the unions; it also weakens the resistance of the employers to wage demands. Costs can be absorbed in higher prices and the general atmosphere of prosperity allows price increases to be passed on to the general public. And the unions are there to protect their members from most of the price increases by still higher wage demands and so on. It is hardly surprising that this dilemma led to a search for a way out: a method of replacing the former disciplines of the market place, without undermining the new-found prosperity. The germs of such a policy were to be seen in the immediate post-war efforts of Sir Stafford Cripps,[1] with his wage freeze and heavy deflationary Budget. Dividend limitation was part of the same programme. They were only temporarily successful. Eventually, many years later, came Mr. Selwyn Lloyd's 'pay pause;[2] yet another restrictive policy backed up by deflationary measures. Finally, out of this and under the guidance of Mr. Reginald Maudling, emerged the germs of a Conservative Government's incomes policy: an attempt to get both sides of industry to agree to voluntary curbs on wages and price increases.[3] But it was too late. The unions were unwilling to co-operate in an election year, particularly so soon after the restrictive policies of Mr. Selwyn Lloyd. It was left to the new Labour Government and particularly Mr. George Brown, First Secretary and Minister of the new Department of Economic Affairs, to turn the idea of an incomes policy into an agreed 'Statement of Intent,' signed by the government, the unions and employers in December 1964. This was followed

---

[1] A general warning about wage increases by Mr. Attlee, the Prime Minister on 4 February 1948, published later as a White Paper, and Sir Stafford Cripps's appeal for the voluntary limitation of wages, prices, profits and dividends on 12 February 1948.

[2] Mr. Selwyn Lloyd appealed for a 'pause' in wage increases and for dividend restraint on 25 July, 1961.

[3] February 1964.

in April 1965 by a further agreement about the machinery to be used and the criteria to be followed.[1]

So much for the official efforts. So far the rise in prices has continued. It is still too soon to know whether the effort to replace the old market disciplines by co-operative restraints will be successful. It is not too soon to harbour doubts about the measure of success to be expected. If employers and workers could be persuaded that, with the appropriate restraint, they would all ultimately be better off, a certain amount of progress could be expected. But there is the world of difference between the signing of an agreement by the representatives of unions and employers and what subsequently happens in wage bargains at factory level. This is where the pressures of the market place are inevitably felt and will be so long as free bargaining continues. This difference between intention and practice in a free economy is the major stumbling block in the path of a national incomes policy. There are others, such as the criteria laid down for exceptional increases in incomes and prices, which are likely to be too wide to serve any useful purpose[2] or too narrow to be workable. But the difficulties will inevitably lead back to the economic pressures being exerted at the point where wage bargains are being thrashed out.

It is at this point that two separate issues immediately emerge. What level of economic activity (or of unemployment) lead to a moderation of wage demands? And, without any change in this level of activity, what other sanctions can the Government

[1] The agreements were summed up in the White Paper, *Prices and Incomes Policy*, (HMSO, 8 April, 1965): 'In the Joint Statement of Intent on Productivity, Prices and Incomes, representatives of the TUC and the employers' organisations have accepted that major objectives of national policy must be: to ensure that British industry is dynamic and that its prices are competitive; to raise productivity and efficiency so that real national output can increase, and to keep increases in wages, salaries and other forms of incomes in line with this increase; to keep the general level of prices stable.

They have also agreed with the Government's proposals, set out in the White Paper on *Machinery of Prices and Incomes Policy* that: (i) the National Economic Development Council should keep under review the general movement of prices and of money incomes of all kinds; and (ii) a National Board for Prices and Incomes should be set up to examine particular cases in order to advise whether or not the behaviour of prices or of wages, salaries or other money incomes is in the national interest as defined by the Government after consultation with Management and Unions.'

[2] One of the four criteria for exceptional wage increases in the White Paper *Prices and Incomes Policy*—'where there is general recognition that existing wage and salary levels are too low to maintain a reasonable standard of living'—is broad enough for a varied interpretation by union leaders.

impose? Apart from changes in the structure of the trades unions (giving a larger say in the bargaining process to the central authority), the other suggested sanctions are invariably an interference or potential interference with the workings of a free economy. If, therefore, it is found from experience that the co-operative effort still needed cannot be produced either at all or with too long a time-lag, attention is bound to return to the level of activity. As we saw in the last chapter, several economists have recently been giving this relationship (between the price level and the level of activity or unemployment) some close examination. Mr. J. C. R. Dow has concluded that 'if unemployment were kept at 2 to $2\frac{1}{2}$ per cent, instead of the post-war average of $1\frac{1}{2}$ per cent, this would probably make a major difference to the rate of rise in prices.'[1] But he does not believe that this would necessarily lower the rate of growth of the economy. 'If the pressure of demand had been somewhat lower, and the margin of unused capacity somewhat larger, than in most of the post-war years, there could have been steady expansion of expenditure, output and output per head as rapid as that which in fact occurred.' Professor Paish, who shares these sentiments but would extend them further, has provided the connection with the pursuit of an incomes policy. He has concluded that if unemployment is below 2 per cent an incomes policy is bound to be ineffective because of the pressure of demand for labour. If unemployment is within the range of 2 and $2\frac{1}{4}$ per cent, other measures could be supplemented, but not replaced, by an incomes policy. If unemployment is above $2\frac{1}{4}$ per cent, he argues, an incomes policy would be unnecessary.[2] These are rough guides to policy, but they make an important point: that the level of activity cannot be ignored in any attempt to keep the rise in costs and prices within reasonable bounds. If an incomes policy provides a climate of opinion that accepts that a co-operative wages effort might help to replace the lost market disciplines and that keeps a damper on prices, it should help. But an incomes policy cannot be a substitute either for regulating the economy at a lower level than in most post-war years nor for the implementation of government policies that would sharpen competitive enterprise.

[1] J. C. R. Dow, *op. cit.*, pp. 361-403.
[2] F. W. Paish, 'The Management of the British Economy,' *Lloyds Bank Review*, April 1965; F. W. Paish and Jossleyn Hennessy, *Policy For Incomes?*, Hobart Paper 29, I.E.A., 1964.

Fortunately Mr. George Brown secured an important assurance from unions and employers in his 'Statement of Intent' agreement that goes far beyond any incomes policy. He got them to promise 'to encourage and lead a sustained attack on the obstacles to efficiency, whether on the part of management or of workers.' This is a weapon that in the right hands might be used with vigour. But it must be followed up with government policies designed to raise output and productivity and to sharpen competition. If, as is becoming clearer, it is difficult to restrain incomes in conditions of high activity in a free society, more effort must be made to push up the other element of the productivity equation—output. All this implies many things: a fuel policy that does not set out to buttress the coal industry at the expense of oil, gas or electricity; a more vigorous attempt to root out restrictive practices within industry and to enlarge the official bodies undertaking this; a determination to press ahead with the abolition of resale price maintenance and to reduce the number of exceptions; a continuing examination of the tariff protection provided for individual industries, with a determination to lower it once the Kennedy round of trade talks gives signs of producing reciprocal tariff cuts too small and too late; efforts to bring British industry into close alignment with Europe on standards, weights, measures, etc., not with political motives in mind but simply the need to keep close to a potential domestic market of 200 million, on which so many technological innovations could be based; and so on.

This necessarily brief outline of the problems facing Britain at home has been given for a good reason: to show that, even without the difficulties and burdens of running a world currency, and without the added burdens of overseas aid and military commitments, Britain would have enough to contend with in making herself as competitive and prosperous as her main industrial rivals. Her overseas commitments have simply given added meaning to a problem she would have had to face in any case. The winding up of the sterling area and even the writing off of all the outstanding sterling balances, were all this possible, might have helped. They would not, in themselves, have solved Britain's economic growth problem. Nor will they do so now. They would not make British industry efficient overnight. And they would not resolve the problem of how to contain the continuing pressures of cost inflation.

Conclusions
It is time to sum up. Whether it has fully realised it or not the City has a clear vested interest in a successful outcome to the world's liquidity talks, in Britain's efforts to hammer out an incomes policy and, eventually, in the achievement of sustained economic growth. The first is easier to accept than the rest. The growth we are talking about is not growth achieved at any price: that way lie untold difficulties and distortions for any country, whether it has a world currency to concern itself about or not. But with sound sustained growth not only might British industry be persuaded to invest more funds at home, but the success would feed on itself. The more growth, the bigger future domestic investment would become. If this in turn lowered the volume of money being attracted into plants and factories abroad, the pressure on the whole capital account might be considerably eased, thus providing more scope for the City's activities. An inflow of foreign direct investment (as opposed to volatile short-term funds) would have the same effect. A successful growth policy would help the City in other ways too. It would probably lead to a growing surplus of savings available for use in the City, some of which might spill over into the City's external operations. Moreover, a successful expansionary programme would presumably be based on a substantial expansion in exports that in turn would (or at least could) lead to a further lowering of capital barriers and, eventually, to the freedom on which the City's activities have always thrived. But that is running too far ahead.

The world in which the City grew up has changed radically. Yet the conditions in which it works best are, to a modest extent, beginning to be reproduced in other ways. It is far too soon to talk of a return to a more stable atmosphere in world affairs, but the Cuban crisis may have been a turning point. Certainly the period in which the United States, Britain and the Soviet Union agreed to a limited test-ban treaty and went some way towards lowering the international temperature happened to coincide with an easing tension in the gold market and with a corresponding reduction in gold hoarding. The modern equivalents of the gold discoveries and the widespread use of sterling credits to oil the wheels of world trade in the second half of the last century are the increasing use of the IMF's resources, the recent moves to increase the defences of the world's key currencies, and the creation of credit by bilateral swap arrangements. Although convertibility has provided more financial freedom at home, several markets, as we have seen, are now suffering from restrictions imposed by foreign governments. These are unlikely to improve and the City must make the best of it. It must now exist more by its wits than by its superior strength. So far it has shown every sign of doing so. Skill based on British economic power and geography has been replaced by inherited flair, financial habits and (most important of all) a fund of world-wide contacts.

Can this skill cope with the changing demands made on it? The question must be answered in three separate areas—in financing world trade, in establishing a new type of capital market and in meeting the growing needs of British industry itself. The volume of world trade financed in pounds, though it has fallen from about one-half immediately after the war to a third, is still remarkably high. It amounts to between £15,000 million and £20,000 million (i.e. a third of £50,000 million) Over a half of this is concerned with trade that does not touch Britain's shores. Although the amount of sterling used in the world's monetary reserves is not as high, proportionately, as it was, the volume of pounds kept in London for trade and investment purposes by private individuals and concerns has continued to increase. According to the old sterling balance figures, the total of non-official sterling rose from £725 million in 1952 to over £1,000 million ten years later. The figures worked out on the new basis from 1962 onwards are shown in the Table XXII (p. 212). They show that non-official sterling holdings in London rose from £1,560 million at the end of 1962 to £1,920 million in September 1964. (This date was chosen because later figures are complicated by the onset of the sterling crisis and by the need for foreign help.) Thus the total of what might be termed trading pounds, at £1,920 million, was not far short of the total of sterling held in official reserves throughout the world, i.e. £2,444 million. This is an important point to bear in mind in assessing the effects of using other currencies or other media in exchange reserves on the use of sterling for trading purposes and on the activities of the City. The evidence strongly suggests that the City will continue to attract business even in the face of a decline in the use of the pound in the world's exchange reserves. This was certainly the conclusion of the Radcliffe Report[1] when it commented in 1958 that the City's invisible earnings were unlikely to be 'perceptibly less

[1] *Committee on the Working of the Monetary System, op. cit.*, para. 659.

if the settlements that now take place in sterling came to be made, under a different system of payments, in some international currency such as "bancor".' Since this was written, the City has managed to attract to itself the larger share of the $5,000 million worth of Euro-dollars—adequate proof of this judgement and of the City's continuing flexibility.

This flexibility is now being tested to the full in the efforts to revive Europe's capital markets and to cream off as much of the business as possible to London at a time when the amount of surplus capital is limited because of payments difficulties. As we saw in Chapter 8 the City's ingenuity is being taxed to the utmost in devising ways of linking London issues with similar ones in different European centres.

TABLE XXII

GROSS STERLING LIABILITIES

	£ million	
	December 1962	September 1964
Grand total	4,386	4,983
of which:		
a Central monetary institutions	2,220	2,444
b International Organisations	606	619
c Other holders	1,560	1,920*
i Sterling Area	868	1,026
ii Western Europe	407	478
iii North America	109	139
iv Other Areas	176	277

* Of this £1,920 million, some £1,653 million were held in current and deposit accounts, £56 million in U.K. Treasury bills, £79 million in commercial bills and promissory notes and £132 million in British Government stocks,

Note: In September 1964, Britain's gross sterling liabilities of £4,983 million were offset by sterling claims of £1,069 million, leaving *net* liabilities of £3,914 million.

Source: Bank of England Quarterly Bulletin, March 1965.

It is an ingenuity that must do nothing to undermine the City's services to British industry. Fortunately industry can manage to find most of its capital needs from its own resources. In 1962 it found no less than £2,140 million from self-financing. There is, of course, a limit to what should be provided in this way. Too great a reliance on self-generating capital tends to produce some rigidity in the pattern of industry, by starving promising new firms of capital through the capital market. Charges that the City was devoting far too large a share of its resources to foreign borrowers than to capital-starved firms at home could quickly revive. Such criticisms, however, can hardly be supported at present. The City has rarely devoted more of its time to the domestic affairs of British industry than in the past ten years. The return of Rothchilds to Manchester is symptomatic of this post-war development. The City is already meeting the challenge voiced by Mr. Harold Wilson at the head of Chapter 1.

From now on the City will have to rely more on its skill and flair than at any time in the past. As a recent observer of the City scene put it:

'To the casual visitor it is the tradition (in dress, manner and furnishings) that is most striking. But coupled with this is an informality that only the man who has tried to do a financial deal in London and, say, New York will readily appreciate. And this is as true of the discount houses and stock exchange brokers as of the traditional merchant banks and Lloyd's underwriters. All of them willingly undertake transactions every day often running to hundreds of thousands of pounds by word of mouth alone. It is a place for quick decisions.'

If it is to keep its position in the world, it must remain so. Foreign bankers confirm that in this respect the City remains basically the same as they knew it before the war. Two important influences are still at work. In the first place the City of London is not 'lawyer-ridden like New York' and deals can still be done by word of mouth rather than by detailed documentation; secondly, the City contains within its Square Mile all the services required for even the most complicated transactions.

The City has always placed great faith in its own integrity ('My Word is My Bond' was the title of the Stock Exchange's first film about itself), but it would be idle to ignore that more and more legal requirements have been imposed between institutions and their clients. This has been a natural development arising from the desire of various governments to protect the public against abuses of one sort or another. The Board of Trade has been extremely active in this way and so has the Share and Loan Department of the Stock Exchange. New issues on the stock market are subject to far more regulations now than they were 30 or 40 years ago. The same trend has been seen in other markets. Many abuses have been prevented, but it is quite possible that cumulatively these regulations have tended to slow up many transactions. Yet in the face of a growing amount of paper work the City still comes out of most comparisons with other centres with high marks.

The City's compactness is equally coming under a little more stress as more institutions consider whether they would really be better off outside the Square Mile. Transport conditions are getting to the point where some firms suspect that it would be far easier to recruit office staff in the country than in the City, and the more agreeable working conditions outside are clearly tempting. A few insurance companies have already been persuaded, but they are the exceptions. Most City institutions have resisted a trend that seems to have made further headway in New York. The ties with other institutions have so far proved far too close and the advantages of proximity far too weighty. If the major oil and shipping companies still find it pays them to maintain large offices inside the Square Mile (presumably because of the large financial transactions they are continually having to arrange) then the banks, insurance companies and other City institutions may be expected to stay too.

Criticisms of the City

So far so good. The flair, the compactness, the desire to serve domestic industry; all are present in the Square Mile. Yet too many awkard questions can still be asked about City ways of doing things; and there is probably, even now, too much insistence on the *mystique* and too little recognition of the major changes taking place not only in British industry but even in Whitehall. The City's job is by its nature technical, complex and highly confidential. But a customer's secrets need not be an excuse for keeping the whole mechanism out of sight, nor for reacting over-emotionally to constructive criticism.

Let us be more concrete. The discount market is one of the major assets of the City; it possesses an unrivalled ability to place short-term funds overnight, something that an international monetary centre must be able to do if it is to attract funds to oil the wheels of trade. Thus, because of the activities of the discount houses, it pays people to leave pounds in London until they want to use them to finance trade, insure goods or buy commodities in any of London's markets. Yet, because of historical necessity (some of it based in the 1930s rather than in the 19th century), the twelve members of the discount house syndicate get a privileged position at the Bank of England and at the weekly tender for Treasury bills because of their promise to 'cover the tender' (that is, undertake to take up all the Treasury bills on offer), a practice that remains as difficult to explain as to defend. It is no coincidence that the arrangement for a syndicated tender for Treasury bills was introduced in 1935. As Mr. Wilfred King has rightly commented,[1]

'It was born of slump and abnormality and its originating cause was the rate-restrictiveness of the clearing banks, in not lending money at a flexible rate throughout, but insisting that the basic rate must never drop below a given point.'

Thus the banks agreed not to buy bills in the market at a rate below the minimum money rate, and not to tender for Treasury bills at the weekly tender. All this is highly technical jargon but the consequent competition among the discount houses for the Treasury bills every week became so fierce that they too decided to carve up the tender among themselves, agreeing on the price at which they would all tender. And so, in spite of the introduction of a more flexible monetary policy in 1951, it has continued. It is more than time to consider, therefore, what parts of this system can be defended and what parts can eventually be discarded without damaging the City's services to foreign investors and traders. The element that needs close examination is the assumption that the weekly Treasury bill tender needs to be 'covered' by the discount houses, for it is this arrangement that is said to have led, inevitably, to the 'syndicated' tender and other rigidities.

There are three ways of supporting this arrangement: that it helps to provide government finance; that it furthers the official manipulation of short-term interest rates; and that it is an important factor in providing an efficient market in Treasury bills. The Radcliffe Report was already somewhat doubtful about the first two in 1959 and spoke caustically of 'the outmoded supposition that government finances would be gravely imperilled by failure to place all the offered Treasury bills.' In fact if the habit of covering the tender were dropped (and with it the syndicated bid), this would bring in a demand for Treasury bills from many other quarters that, at present, find little incentive to do so. That it would provide the authorities with a fluctuating demand for Treasury bills and thus an added

[1] *The London Discount Market Today,* Ernest Sykes Memorial Lectures, The Institute of Bankers, 1962.

difficulty in manipulating short-term interest rates is not disputed. But, as Mr. King has pointed out,[1] this would not be as bad as it appears, for official control of the banking system and of interest rates has now shifted to medium- and long-term interest rates. The discount market is no longer the main vehicle for the transmission of official policy it used to be. It is in practice providing a mechanism for evening out the ups and downs in the flow of short-term funds and an efficient market in Treasury bills and commercial bills. This is now its main *raison d'être*, particularly in maintaining London as an international financial centre. As the Radcliffe Report concluded:

'It would not be beyond human ingenuity to replace the work of the discount houses; but they are there, they are doing the work effectively, and they are doing it at trifling cost in terms of labour and other real resources.'

In short, their efficiency is what counts, not their *mystique* and not their *privileges*. Would the discount market work less efficiently without its restrictive practices and its privileges at the Bank of England? I believe not. It would also make it far easier for some of its friendlier critics, who know its true worth to the City in providing an unrivalled market for short-term funds from home or abroad, to defend it.

Let us turn to the clearing banks. As we saw in Chapter 2, these are the institutions now wielding the monetary power in the City. Yet here too restrictive arrangements prevail; and calls for an end to them can still produce some heavy arguments. The major cartel agreement among the clearing banks is their arrangement on rates offered for deposits. None of them offers any interest on current accounts. The rate on seven-day notice deposits, however, is fixed among them at a uniform level varying with Bank rate (usually 2 per cent below it). Efforts to get the banks to vary these rates among themselves and certainly *vis-à-vis* other institutions ran into heavy weather early in 1964. Although some agreed plan was reached between the clearing banks and the Bank of England, it was apparently turned down by the government, partly on monetary, partly on political, grounds. While the debate was going on a variety of defensive arguments were produced by leading bankers. Some suggested that if the banks competed for the public's money by raising their deposit rates, either individually or collectively, many of the banks would simply be paying more for money that would

[1] *Ibid.*

have come to them in any case. Others took the view that the banks would simply lead to competition with the government, by channelling off money that would otherwise go into Treasury bills, etc. Some again raised the question of the cost of such an operation and were doubtful whether it would be profitable. It is significant that few of them examined the advantages of the added flexibility that freedom from the cartel agreement would bring. What is plainly needed is for the individual banks to have the ability to offer special rates to special customers for special deposits. This would give them added competitiveness at home and would bring them into line with international banks abroad.

Since the Conservative Government turned down the bank proposals (they have not been published, so it is difficult to know how restrictive or otherwise they remained), several significant moves have taken place. Some of the banks have attempted to get the same flexibility in another way. They have turned to subsidiary companies or have set up special banks outside the cartel arrangement. As we mentioned in Chapter 2 the Midland Bank has formed Midland and International Banks with the help of three overseas banks. Barclays Export Finance Company was established in the middle of 1964. Finally, early in 1965 Glyn, Mills and Co. formed its finance company. Some of these new institutions are to concentrate on foreign business. Others will be concerned with a wide range of operations. All have one thing in common: they have the ability to raise deposits on any terms they wish. And so have several banks already in existence: Westminster Foreign Bank, Lloyd's Bank Europe, etc.

It is encouraging to see competition breaking down rigidities in this way, but it would be even more encouraging to see the competition operating directly among the major banks rather than through some of their back doors. Yet all is not lost, for the clearing banks are slowly beginning to realise their immense monetary strength and to see how to use it in areas that have so far been the preserve of others. They are already encroaching on the overseas banks; they have already moved into the field of export credits; they could, as they did until the 1930s, move back into the Treasury bill tender every Friday; and they could just as quickly move into the new issue field. The City would benefit by their activities in all these fields—whether they compete directly or by way of a further strengthening of interests with the merchant banks and the overseas banks.

Much the same type of criticism could be made of other

parts of the City. The Accepting Houses Committee has a restricted entry (there are 17 at present) largely based on the size of the applicant and on his general spread of business. Membership does not affect the attitude of the Bank of England in buying commercial bills from a merchant bank (its criteria apply to members and non-members alike). But, as explained in Chapter 2, it must not be overlooked that the Accepting Houses Committee, or at least its chairman, has direct access to the Governor of the Bank of England at all times.

Some parts of the City, therefore, are still more equal than others. The Stock Exchange still prevents advertising by its members, in contrast to the London offices of American broking firms. Examples could be found from most corners of the City. In every case there are reasons of varying plausibility for the restriction. In some it is claimed that the institutions are providing services to the authorities; in others that the public is being protected. The need to be assured of adequate monetary resources is particularly the reason given for the emphasis on financial backing, rather than expertise, in controlling entry to certain City jobs (on the Stock Exchange and at Lloyd's). All these arrangements ought to be regarded for what they are: restrictive practices that could be against the public interest and might well rebound on the City itself.

In the past the City has thrived on its ability to remain efficient, however incomprehensible its operations might appear to the outside world. The view that this is no longer enough must be based not only on a feeling that the City's image is in need of an overhaul, nor on the many lessons learned at the time of the British Aluminium affair. It must be based on the close analysis of individual City markets such as those in the early part of this book. In one area after another, it became clear that the threat to the City came not from home but from abroad. In shipping, commodities, capital issues, insurance and banking it is the encroachment of foreign competition or foreign restrictions that will count from now on. In shipping, insurance and commodities, the under-developed countries are increasingly going to reduce the freedom of movement on which so many of the City's activities have been based. In capital issues it will be a simple case of European (as well as American) competition. And in banking, industrial and under-developed countries will create new and different problems. Competition is becoming more intense: it cannot be in the City's long-term interests to preserve outmoded practices on grounds of tradition unless they stand up to scrutiny, not as providing protection but as ensuring efficiency. The City has much to gain, and the rest of the free trading world with it, from the attempts to improve the international payments system and to revitalise Britain's economy. But the City has a job to do too in fitting itself for a new competitive age.

SHORT BIBLIOGRAPHY

References to appropriate books have been made as footnotes in the text. But a brief guide to the main City landmarks may be useful. One of the most readable accounts of the world of finance in the century after the Napoleonic wars is contained in P. H. Emden's *Money Powers in Europe in the nineteenth and twentieth centuries* (Sampson Low, 1937). A more economic treatment of Britain's role in financing overseas development is given in C. K. Hobson's *Export of Capital*, Dr. Bowley's *England's Trade in the Nineteenth Century* (Allen and Unwin, 1922) and Mr. C. K. Cairncross's *Home and Foreign Investment, 1870-1913* (Cambridge University Press, 1953). More specifically on the City are *The City* by B. Ellinger (King, 1940) and the post-war edition of Sir Oscar Hobson's *How the City Works*. More recent guides to what goes on in the Square Mile are Paul Ferris's *The City* (Gollancz, 1960 and Penguin Books, 1962) and a part of Anthony Sampson's *Anatomy of Britain Today* (Hodder and Stoughton, 1965). Both are extremely readable and provide some of the atmosphere of the place.

Sections of the City's institutions have been individually studied. All the 'Big Five' clearing banks have had their histories written, the main post-war volume being R. S. Sayers' *Lloyds Bank in the History of English Banking* (Oxford University Press, 1957). The Bank of England has its two-volume coverage by Sir John Clapham, *The Bank of England—A History* (Cambridge University Press, 1944), as well as Sir Henry Clay's *Lord Norman* (Macmillan and Co., 1957). The leading theoretical work in the field is R. S. Sayers' *Modern Banking* (Oxford University Press, 6th Edition, 1964). In insurance there are H. E. Raynes' *A History of British Insurance* (Pitman, 1950) and Mr. D. E. Gibbs' *Lloyd's of London* (Macmillan, 1957). The best historical account of the money market remains Mr. W. T. C. King's *A History of the London Discount Market* (Routledge, 1936). An excellent post-war outline of the work of the discount market and the role of the bill of exchange is contained in *The Bill On London* by Gillett Bros., one of the twelve discount houses (Chapman and Hall, 1952). The Stock Exchange is well served by the authoritative *The Book of the Stock Exchange* by F. E. Armstrong (Pitman, 5th edition, 1957), and also by a more recent study, *The Stock Exchange: Its History and Functions*, by E. Victor Morgan and W. A. Thomas (Staples, 1962). In a wider context Mr. Norman Macrae's *The London Capital Market* (Staples, 1957) is an economic and financial analysis of the capital generating machinery. The Radcliffe Report, *Report of the Committee on the Working of the Monetary System* (Cmnd. 827, HMSO, 1959) and the symposium *Not Unanimous: A Rival Verdict to Radcliffe's on Money*, edited by Arthur Seldon (IEA, 1960) are invaluable references.

The role of the pound has not been neglected since the war. A simple and useful account of the sterling area is given in Mr. Paul Bareau's *The Sterling Area and How It Works* (Longmans Green, 2nd Ed., 1950). Since then there have been Mr. A. C. L. Day's *The Future of Sterling* (Oxford University Press, 1954), Mr. Philip W. Bell's *The Sterling Area in the Post-War World* (Oxford University Press, 1956) and Mr. Judd Polk's *Sterling— Its Meaning In World Finance* (Harper, New York, 1956). A recent small, though admirable, addition has been Mr. Christopher McMahon's *Sterling in the Sixties* (Chatham House Essays, Oxford University Press, 1964). On the proliferation of plans to resolve the world's liquidity problems, *World Monetary Reform*, edited by Herbert G. Grubel (Stanford University Press, 1964) is a most useful collection of excerpts from articles and books by the main authors of the plans.

Finally the Bank of England's *Quarterly Bulletin* has contained a detailed series of articles covering different sections of the City—the gold market, Euro-dollar market, how the money market works, the foreign banks, overseas banks, export finance.

INDEX

223